Boost Your
Metabolism
Cookbook

FIRE UP YOUR DIET FOR A FIT AND FIRM YOU

CHEF SUSAN IRBY, *the Bikini Chef,*
WITH RACHEL LAFERRIERE, MS, RD

Aadamsmedia
AVON, MASSACHUSETTS

ACKNOWLEDGMENTS

To Paula, Matt, and Katie at Adams Media for pushing me to make this book the best it could possibly be, and to my agent, Uwe Stender, for putting the pieces of the puzzle together.

Published by
Adams Media, a division of F+W Media, Inc.
57 Littlefield Street, Avon, MA 02322. U.S.A.
www.adamsmedia.com

ISBN 10: 1-4405-0400-8
ISBN 13: 978-1-4405-0400-6
eISBN 10: 1-4405-0854-2
eISBN 13: 978-1-4405-0854-7

Printed in the United States of America.

10   9   8   7   6   5   4   3   2   1

**Library of Congress
Cataloging-in-Publication Data**

Irby, Susan.
Boost your metabolism cookbook / Chef Susan Irby, the Bikini Chef, with Rachel Laferriere.
p. cm.
Includes bibliographical references and index.
ISBN 978-1-4405-0400-6 (alk. paper)
1. Reducing diets—Recipes. 2. Metabolism—Popular works. I. Laferriere, Rachel. II. Title.
RM222.2.I63 2010
641.5′635—dc22
2010019353

This publication is designed to provide accurate and authoritative information with regard to the subject matter covered. It is sold with the understanding that the publisher is not engaged in rendering legal, accounting, or other professional advice. If legal advice or other expert assistance is required, the services of a competent professional person should be sought.

—From a *Declaration of Principles* jointly adopted by a Committee of the American Bar Association and a Committee of Publishers and Associations

Many of the designations used by manufacturers and sellers to distinguish their product are claimed as trademarks. Where those designations appear in this book and Adams Media was aware of a trademark claim, the designations have been printed with initial capital letters.

This book is available at quantity discounts for bulk purchases. For information, please call 1-800-289-0963.

Contains material adapted and abridged from: *365 Ways to Boost Your Metabolism*, by Rachel Laferriere, copyright © 2010 by F+W Media, Inc., ISBN 10: 1-4405-0213-7, ISBN 13: 978-1-4405-0213-2; *The Everything® Flat Belly Cookbook*, by Fitz Koehler, MSESS with Mabelissa Acevedo, LDN, copyright © 2009 by F+W Media, Inc., ISBN 10: 1-60550-676-1, ISBN 13: 978-1-60550-676-0; *The Everything® Gluten-Free Cookbook*, by Rick Marx and Nancy T. Maar, copyright © 2006 by F+W Media, Inc., ISBN 10: 1-59337-394-5, ISBN 13: 978-1-59337-394-8; *The Everything® Glycemic Index Cookbook*, by Nancy T. Maar, with technical review by Barb Pearl, MS, RN, LD, copyright © 2006 by F+W Media, Inc., ISBN 10: 1-59337-581-6, ISBN 13: 978-1-59337-581-2; *The Everything® Calorie Counting Cookbook*, by Paula Conway, technical review by Brierley E. Wright, RD, copyright © 2008 by F+W Media, Inc., ISBN 10: 1-59869-416-2, ISBN 13: 978-1-59869-416-1; *The Everything® Low-Cholesterol Cookbook*, by Linda Larsen, copyright © 2008 by F+W Media, Inc., ISBN 10: 1-59869-401-4, ISBN 13: 978-1-59869-401-7; *The Everything® Mediterranean Cookbook*, by Dawn Altomari-Rathjen, LPN, BPS, and Jennifer M. Bendelius, MS, RD, copyright © 2003 by F+W Media, Inc., ISBN 10: 1-58062-869-9, ISBN 13: 978-1-58062-869-3; *The Everything® No Trans Fat Cookbook*, by Linda Larsen, copyright © 2007 by F+W Media, Inc., ISBN 10: 1-59869-533-9, ISBN 13: 978-1-59869-533-5; *The Everything® Sugar-Free Cookbook*, by Nancy T. Maar, Technical review by Julie Negrin, MS, copyright © 2008 by F+W Media, Inc., ISBN 10: 1-59869-408-1, ISBN 13: 978-1-59869-408-6; *The Everything® Whole-Grain, High-Fiber Cookbook*, by Lynette Rohrer Shirk, technical review by Julie Negrin, MS, copyright © 2008 by F+W Media, Inc., ISBN 10: 1-59869-507-X, ISBN 13: 978-1-59869-507-6; *The Everything® Soup, Stew, and Chili Cookbook*, by Belinda Hulin, copyright © 2009 by F+W Media, Inc., ISBN 10: 1-60550-044-5, ISBN 13: 978-1-60550-044-7.

Contents

INTRODUCTION

Metabolism is a concept that most people just don't understand, and for that reason, talking about metabolic rates and increases or decreases in a person's metabolism can sound confusing and intimidating. Luckily it doesn't have to be that way, since boosting your metabolism is as simple as paying closer attention to what you eat and drink. But where should you begin? How about right here, with the *Boost Your Metabolism Cookbook*? The following recipes and tips for healthy living will help you figure out how you can immediately increase your metabolism. More than 300 recipes are included to help you on your journey toward a healthy, balanced lifestyle.

Just say to yourself, "It's time for a change and that change should begin now!" Increasing your metabolism is so simple to do. With a few simple changes, you can lose weight, feel better, have more energy, and become more productive, just by cooking with fresh foods, increasing fiber in your diet, consuming more—and the right—proteins, adding spice to your foods, and making other easy adjustments! So get your metabolic furnace firing on all cylinders and, before you know it, you'll be on your way to feeling better, processing information more efficiently, and filling your days with increased energy!

CHAPTER 1

Sure-Fire Metabolism Boosters

Think of your body as a machine that needs oiling; each part of your body functions best when "oiled" with the proper vitamins, minerals, and other nutrients that it needs. Achieving the right metabolic balance for your body, or using the right oil, means you will feel better, have more energy, think more effectively, and function more efficiently in your daily life. Understanding your metabolism and giving it the boost it needs may seem like an impossible process at first, but it's not as difficult as you might think. In this cookbook, we've laid out a few simple guidelines that you can use when choosing foods that will increase your metabolism, help you achieve your weight loss goals, and improve your overall health.

A Simple Understanding of Your Metabolism

So what exactly is metabolism? And how can eating certain foods help your metabolism skyrocket? Well, your metabolism is comprised of three major elements:

- Basal metabolic rate (B)
- Physical activity level (PAL)
- Thermic effect of food (TEF)

Each one of these elements affects the way your body processes—and burns through—the food that you eat. How? Read on!

Basal Metabolic Rate (BMR)

The basal metabolic rate is a measurement of how many calories your body burns when it is resting. This represents approximately 75 percent of your total energy expenditure and is determined by your body size, gender, and age. Taller or heavier individuals naturally have

higher metabolic rates, as well as those with a greater percentage of lean body mass (or a smaller percentage of fat). Because aging is related to the loss of lean body mass and therefore affects your BMR, females tend to have more fat in proportion to muscle than males. While these two factors, age and gender, cannot be changed, there are ways to increase your metabolic rate and turn body fat into lean, fat-free mass which will in turn help you burn more calories.

Physical Activity Level (PAL)

As you're probably aware, physical activity is key to burning calories and is the only way to increase muscle mass. The amount of calories burned depends upon the intensity and duration of the activity. If you are not currently following an exercise regimen, start slowly by walking 20–30 minutes at least three times per week, participating in sports, joining a gym and taking classes, or anything else that will get your body moving. Remember: the fewer calories you eat each day, the fewer you'll need to burn. However, consult a physician or nutritionist for the recommended daily calorie consumption that is best for you.

Thermic Effect of Food (TEF)

The thermic effect of food is a measurement of the energy our bodies expend to eat and digest, metabolize, and store food. It basically measures the number of calories expended by the processing of foods you eat, and is influenced by portion size, the quantity of carbohydrates, protein, fat, fiber, caffeine, and even spices in the foods. Essentially, the more energy your body expends to digest the foods you consume, the higher your metabolic rate is going to be.

By making key adjustments in all or some of these areas, you will begin to see changes in how you feel, how you think, and how you look. But for now, let's talk about how the food you eat affects the way your metabolism works.

How Does Food Affect Metabolism?

The term *metabolism* refers to the rate at which your body converts food into energy. To achieve maximum efficiency, or maximum calorie burn, you need to consume nutrient-rich foods—foods that are high in vitamins and minerals, filled with good oils, and are naturally low in fat. Clearly, the amount of calories consumed vs. the amount of calories burned is also important, so the calories consumed must be equal to or less than the amount of calories expended to maintain a steady weight or to lose weight. In other words, if you eat more calories than you burn on a regular basis, you will most likely gain weight. So, it's important to eat the right foods, in the right

quantities, to increase your body's efficiency and boost your metabolism.

How Much Is Too Much?

So you know that you need to watch your food intake to lose weight and maintain a healthy lifestyle, but how much should you eat? How much is too much? Here are some guidelines to help you on your path to a hard working metabolism:

- Total fat calories should represent between 25–35 percent of total calories consumed daily.
- Saturated fat intake should account for less than 7 percent of total calories consumed daily.
- Carbohydrate consumption should account for between 45–65 percent of total calories consumed daily, and should focus on complex carbohydrates such as whole grains, beans, vegetables, and high-fiber fruits such as apples.
- Total percentage of daily protein should be between 10–35 percent of your daily total calories.
- Daily sodium content should be limited to no more than 2,300 milligrams.
- Be aware of the amount of alcohol you consume, if any. Alcohol is high in what we call "empty calories," and at seven calories per gram they add up pretty quickly!

What to Do

Below we'll discuss some of the main metabolism-boosting foods you'll be using in the recipes throughout the book, but we wanted to give you some general tips to help maximize your metabolic potential first. Use these guidelines to get the most out of your body.

Stay Hydrated

Water is essential to a healthy body: it regulates body temperature, flushes out toxins, and helps maintain efficient body function. However, it's not logical to drink nothing but water all of the time. Pay attention to other beverages you consume by limiting high-calorie drinks such as fruit juices, sodas, and alcoholic beverages that can slow your metabolism down. Instead, focus on low-calorie beverages such as green or herbal tea, and enjoy moderate amounts of caffeinated drinks—including coffee—as caffeine helps to stimulate the metabolism. You should still keep total daily coffee consumption to one to three cups daily, but no one is saying you have to give up your morning rituals. Consume alcohol in moderation, but feel free to relax with a glass of red wine every once in a while. Red wine is said to contain elements that may block the formation of fat cells, and it is rich in antioxidants. However, don't rely on red wine for your nutrition! It still contains alcohol and sugar, both of which are counterproductive to boosting your metabolism.

Work Your Body

Physical activity is essential in promoting optimal body function, maintaining toned muscles and strong bones, and increasing flexibility and overall physical and mental health. Even just thirty minutes of activity three times per week can have a positive impact on your metabolism. Beginners should start slowly and work up to more frequent, more intense exercise. If you already exercise regularly, keep up the good work. You may want to consult a licensed physical trainer or doctor to see if you are maximizing the metabolism-boosting potential of your workouts.

Pay Attention to Portion Size

Too much of even a healthy food can sabotage your metabolism-boosting progress, so make sure you don't eat too much of a good thing. For example, stick to ¼ or ½ of an avocado or a small number of nuts, around seven or eight, when eating these nutrient-rich but high-calorie snacks. Also, be sure to limit the portion size of your entrees and side dishes to ½ cup or 4 ounces.

Use these visual comparisons to help estimate your portion sizes:

- A 3-ounce portion of cooked meat, poultry, or fish is about the size of a deck of playing cards.
- A medium potato is about the size of a computer mouse.
- A cup of rice or pasta is about the size of a fist or a tennis ball.
- A cup of fruit or a medium apple or orange is the size of a baseball.
- A ½ cup of chopped vegetables is about the size of three regular ice cubes.
- A 1-ounce piece of cheese is the size of four dice.
- A teaspoon of peanut butter equals one die; 2 tablespoons is about the size of a golf ball.
- An ounce of snack foods—pretzels, etc.—equals a large handful.
- A thumb tip equals 1 teaspoon; 3 thumb tips equal 1 tablespoon; and a whole thumb equals 1 ounce.

Eat Early

It's often said that eating breakfast is essential to a healthy diet, and this is actually true. After resting for eight hours or more, your body needs to know that additional nutrients are coming or it will "think" it needs to store calories and fat, in case the next meal is a long time in coming.

You can also boost your energy by consuming your highest-calorie meal early in the day. You are up and awake during the day and, by default, you burn energy, consume carbs, and break down proteins—all natural occurrences that translate to burning calories and fat. It's logical that you would want to eat foods high in carbs, protein, and fat during the earlier parts of your day so your body can use them to keep you going, process them to keep you thinking, and burn them off to keep you fit and trim.

Eat Often

It is a proven fact your body functions more efficiently when you feed it nutrients every three to four hours. Still, every person is different, which means you'll need to find the best daily eating pattern for you. Regardless of your unique chemistry, your body needs to be triggered to function. By eating on a regular basis, you remind your body that it needs to go to work processing and digesting the carbs, proteins, and fats that you just consumed. If you skip vital meals, your body will send a processing message to your brain to slow down and conserve energy because it's not sure when or where it's next batch of nutrients is going to come from.

What to Look For

This book is filled with more than 300 recipes, each of which includes ingredients that will help rev your metabolic engine and burn those unwanted calories. The types of metabolism-boosting foods and ingredients that you'll find in each recipe are detailed below. Look for the icons next to the ingredients—and next to

the recipes throughout the book—to see how making healthy food choices will help you push your metabolic rate through the roof.

Spice It Up

Certain spices and foods contain a metabolism-increasing molecule called capsaicin that has been shown to decrease cholesterol absorption and increase the enzymes that metabolize fat. Capsaicin is found in spicy foods such as peppers, cayenne, chili powder, paprika, and spicy sauces and salsas like Tabasco. In fact, the "heat" found in cayenne peppers stimulates the metabolism in a short period of time. The hotter the pepper or spice, the more capsaicin the ingredient has. Capsaicin also has a protective activity against some chemical carcinogens (cancer-causing agents). Look for this icon SPICY in the recipe section.

Give Me More Protein

Protein helps build muscle tissue and strengthen the cells in the body, working within the body as the primary building blocks for all tissues and cells, including your muscles. It also provides fuel once the energy released from carbohydrates is used. Protein is found in meat, fish, eggs, dairy, and legumes (beans and peas), and one gram of it equals about four calories. While legumes are low in fat and high in fiber, animal sources of protein (which can be higher in unwanted fats) can deliver all of the necessary amino acids, so it's important to have a balance of the two to lose weight effectively.

Basically, you must feed your body protein to help it function properly. Look for this icon PROTEIN in the recipe section.

Fill Up with Fiber

Believe it or not, fiber helps boost your metabolism by increasing the efficiency with which your body processes foods. It acts as a sort of "brush" for your digestive system, scrubbing out your system quickly and taking other foods away with it. As fiber travels through your digestive tract, it pulls along excess calories before they can turn into fat, helps get rid of cancer-causing toxins, and stimulates healthy digestion. Fiber also gives you that full feeling, which typically causes you to eat less. Examples of high-fiber foods include oats and oat bran, fruits such as apples, nuts, leafy vegetables, and dried beans. Look for this icon HIGH FIBER in the recipe section.

Eat Foods with Antioxidants

Certain foods contain antioxidants that help prevent health problems such as heart disease, cancer, and even diabetes. But what are antioxidants exactly? They are nutrients that attack by-products in your body resulting from the use of oxygen. Those by-products are known as free radicals, and they can cause damage to cells throughout your body, thereby slowing down your metabolism. Consuming foods high in antioxidants is a natural way to prevent disease while at the same time promoting optimum metabolic health. Examples of antioxidant-rich foods include carrots, squash, sweet potatoes, kale, tomatoes, cantaloupe, citrus fruits like oranges and limes, richly colored vegetables like broccoli, and green or red leafy vegetables like spinach and Swiss chard. Pomegranates, cranberries, fish and shellfish, chicken, grains, and garlic also include antioxidants. Look for this icon ANTIOXIDANTS in the recipe section.

Fall in Love with Superfoods

As the name implies, superfoods are foods that are super good for you. They are filled with nutrients, are low in or free of cholesterol, help reduce your risk for certain health problems such as heart disease and cancer, improve the way your body functions, and increase your metabolic rate. To add these healthy options to your diet, learn to enjoy nutrient-rich vegetables like broccoli, asparagus, spinach, cabbage, bok choy, tomatoes, yams, sweet potatoes, and other richly colored vegetables such as beets and avocados. Herbs like fresh Italian flat-leaf parsley, cilantro, and chives are also super healthy. Superfood proteins include salmon, trout, mackerel, walnuts, and pinto beans, while blueberries, blackberries, and olives are all superfood fruits packed with healthy fats, antioxidants, and other vitamins and minerals that are essential to body function and maximum metabolic-rate levels. Look for this icon SUPERFOOD in the recipe section.

Be Calcium Rich

Calcium strengthens bones and may aid in weight loss, so it's a bit of a no-brainer that it helps improve your metabolism. Calcium-rich foods include kale, spinach, sesame seeds, yogurt, cheese, and fortified foods such as soymilk and some cereals. As most are aware, milk is naturally rich in calcium and also contains large doses of vitamins A, D, and K. If you are lactose intolerant, don't fear; instead enjoy lactose-free milk or fortified milks made from rice, almonds, and soy. To find calcium-rich foods, look for this icon CALCIUM in the recipe section.

Get Going!

Now that you're armed with this knowledge and an outline of key foods and important ingredients, it's time for you to get cooking and put your metabolism boosting plan into action. Good luck!

CHAPTER 2

Appetizers and Dips

You need to make every bite count for maximum metabolizing power, and this includes appetizers, too! Just because they're small doesn't mean they can't pack a fat-burning punch. Liven up your starters with spices, add in nutrient-rich herbs, squeeze in some citrus, or add superfoods. Any way you look at it, appetizers can give you the extra energy you need to burn more calories, be more alert, and feel better.

Citrus Ceviche

SPICY PROTEIN

SERVES 4

½ pound fresh raw shrimp, peeled and deveined
½ pound fresh raw bay scallops
2 green onions, minced
1 green chili pepper, seeded and minced
1 teaspoon fresh lime zest, finely grated
Juice of 1 lime
1 teaspoon fresh orange zest, finely grated
2 tablespoons fresh orange juice
1 tablespoon chili sauce
2 tablespoons fresh cilantro leaves, chopped
Sea salt and pepper to taste
2 tablespoons extra-virgin olive oil

You can use almost any type of fish for ceviche, however, shrimp, scallops, octopus, and snapper are among the most popular. Tuna is not recommended because it turns opaque in color when marinated and is therefore not as visually appealing. **Note: consuming raw fish may present a health risk. Consult your physician before consumption and only buy from reputable markets.**

1. Rinse seafood and pat dry. In a medium mixing bowl, combine onions, chili pepper, lime zest and juice, orange zest and juice, chili sauce, and cilantro. Mix well. Season lightly with salt and pepper and whisk in olive oil. Toss with shrimp and scallops.
2. Cover bowl and refrigerate for 8 hours or overnight. When ready to serve, divide into martini or other cocktail glass.

CALORIES 159
FAT 11G
CARBOHYDRATES 4G
PROTEIN 18G

Spicy Boneless Chicken Wings

SPICY PROTEIN SUPERFOOD

SERVES 10

2 pounds chicken tenders
⅓ cup low-sodium soy sauce
¼ cup apple cider vinegar
2 tablespoons Dijon mustard
¼ cup honey
¼ cup brown sugar
1 teaspoon sea salt
1 teaspoon hot sauce
4 cloves garlic, minced
½ cup white or yellow onion, minced
1 cup low or nonfat sour cream
2 cups celery sticks

Marinating naturally skinless chicken tenders will keep this protein-packed chicken moist. The reserved marinade is safe for baking since it is heated for a period of 15 minutes or more. However, discard any remaining marinade and the used freezer bag to prevent contamination from salmonella.

1. Slice chicken tenders in half crosswise. In a large, heavy-duty freezer storage bag, combine all ingredients except the chicken, sour cream, and celery. Mix together well. Add chicken tenders and seal bag. Place bag in small baking dish and refrigerate for 8 hours or overnight.
2. When ready to cook, preheat oven to 400°F. Coat baking dish with nonstick cooking spray and arrange chicken tenders in single layer in the small baking dish. Drizzle with ½ cup of the reserved marinade. Bake for 20–25 minutes, or until chicken is cooked through.

3. While chicken is baking, place remaining marinade in a small quart boiler over medium-high heat. Bring to a simmer, then reduce heat to low and cook for 10–15 minutes, stirring frequently, until mixture is syrupy. Combine with sour cream and serve as a dipping sauce for chicken with the celery alongside.

CALORIES 199
FAT 4G
CARBOHYDRATES 17G
PROTEIN 21G

Cheese-Stuffed Cucumbers

SUPERFOOD

SERVES 4

> 2 large cucumbers
> 3 ounces low-fat cream cheese
> 1 tablespoon low-fat blue cheese
> 1 teaspoon fresh dill, chopped
> 1 teaspoon fresh Italian flat-leaf parsley leaves, chopped
> 1 teaspoon red onion, minced

If you like this recipe, but want to mix it up, pipe this cheese mixture into hollowed-out, lycopene-filled and nutrient-rich cherry tomatoes. Serve them with these metabolism-boosting Cheese-Stuffed Cucumbers for a colorful, nutritious appetizer.

1. Using a vegetable peeler, create stripes down the length of the cucumber by peeling off strips about ¼ inch apart. Slice off the ends of each cucumber. Slice cucumber in half, lengthwise. Using a melon baller, scoop out seeds.
2. In a medium mixing bowl, combine cream cheese, blue cheese, dill, parsley, and onion. Mix well to combine.
3. Place mixture into hollowed-out cucumbers using a pastry bag with star tip.
4. Cover cucumbers with plastic wrap and refrigerate for at least 1 hour. When ready to serve, slice cucumbers into 1-inch slices and serve.

CALORIES 75
FAT 5G
CARBOHYDRATES 5G
PROTEIN 4G

Jalapeño Bean Dip

SUPERFOOD SPICY

MAKES 2 CUPS; SERVING SIZE: 2 TABLESPOONS

> 1 16-ounce can kidney beans, drained and rinsed
> 2 jalapeño peppers, seeded and finely chopped
> 1 tablespoon red wine vinegar
> 1 teaspoon chili powder
> ¼ teaspoon ground cumin
> 1 tablespoon white or yellow onion, minced
> 1 tablespoon fresh Italian flat-leaf parsley leaves, chopped

Put your own metabolism-boosting twist on this dish by creating a unique combination of chili peppers, seasoning, and beans. The more spice you use, the more you'll enhance your metabolism.

1. Place the beans, jalapeños, vinegar, chili powder, and cumin in a food processor.

Process until smooth. Transfer mixture to a medium mixing bowl and stir in onion.

2. To serve, garnish with parsley and serve with pita crisps, baked tortilla chips, or the snack cracker of your choice.

CALORIES 44
FAT <1G
CARBOHYDRATES 8G
PROTEIN 3G

Steamed Artichoke with Lemon Aioli

SUPERFOOD ANTIOXIDANTS

SERVES 4, SERVING SIZE: 1 ARTICHOKE WITH 3 TABLESPOONS AIOLI

4 whole artichokes
1 lemon, cut in half
1½ cups water
½ cup dry white wine
1 clove garlic, minced
1 tablespoon olive oil
1 teaspoon fresh lemon juice
¾ cup low-fat mayonnaise, or soynnaise

Fresh artichokes are superfoods that are low in calories, high in fiber, and contain lots of antioxidants and vitamins, including the B vitamins that play a role in carbohydrate, amino acid, and fatty acid metabolism.

1. Prepare the artichokes by cutting the stems off the bottoms first. Next, cut the top inch off each artichoke with a serrated knife. Snip the thorny tips off the remaining leaves with kitchen scissors. Rub the lemon on all the places you have cut to prevent browning.

2. Pull out the center leaves to expose the fuzzy choke in the center. Scoop out the choke with a melon baller. Squeeze the juice from the lemon halves into the center of each artichoke.

3. Pour the water and white wine into the bottom of a large pot. Place a steamer rack in the bottom of the pot and put the artichokes upside-down on the rack. Cover the pot with a tight-fitting lid and simmer for 50 minutes, or until a leaf can be pulled easily from an artichoke. Remove the artichokes and let them drain and cool upside down. Turn them over and chill them in the refrigerator.

4. Combine the garlic, olive oil, lemon juice, and mayonnaise in a food processor while the artichokes chill. Chill until ready to serve.

5. Put each chilled artichoke on an appetizer plate, spoon the aioli into the middle of each artichoke, and serve.

CALORIES 412
FAT 36G
CARBOHYDRATES 17G
PROTEIN 5G

Herb-Crusted Grilled Baby Lamb Chops

SUPERFOOD PROTEIN

4 garlic cloves, coarsely chopped
4 tablespoons coarsely chopped fresh
  Italian flat-leaf parsley leaves
3 tablespoons coarsely chopped fresh
  rosemary leaves
Fine zest of ½ lemon
3 tablespoons Dijon mustard
2 tablespoons olive oil
Sea salt and black pepper to taste
14 baby lamb chops, fat trimmed
  from bones

Not only is lamb naturally carb free and high in protein, but it also has many elements of a superfood. In addition to being low in calories, lamb contains high percentages of iron, zinc, potassium, and riboflavin.

1. Combine all ingredients, except lamb chops, in a food processor or blender and process until smooth. Coat lamb chops on each side with pureed mixture.
2. Warm up grill or grill pan to medium heat. Place lamb chops on grill for about 3 minutes per side, or until desired doneness. Serve hot.

CALORIES 261
FAT 13G
CARBOHYDRATES 0G
PROTEIN 34G

BURN IT UP

Products like milk, cheese, cream, beef, and lamb have small amounts of naturally occurring trans fat. This type of unsaturated fat is produced when bacteria in a cow's or sheep's stomach transforms some of the fats found in plant material. In your body, trans fats are converted into conjugated linoleic acid, which helps protect against free-radical damage to cells and boosts your metabolism.

Baked Spinach and Cheese Mushrooms

`SUPERFOOD` `SPICY`

SERVES 6

> 1 tablespoon butter
> 24 medium-sized white mushrooms, quartered
> Nonstick cooking spray
> 1½ cups drained, lightly cooked fresh or frozen spinach
> ½ cup Low-Fat White Sauce (see recipe below)
> ¼ cup shredded low-fat Cheddar cheese
> ¼ cup shredded low-fat mozzarella cheese
> Sea salt and black pepper to taste

Use metabolism-boosting ingredients to enhance the flavors in this recipe by adding capsaicin-filled nutmeg and superfood Italian flat-leaf parsley leaves to this delicious low-fat white sauce.

1. Preheat oven to 350°F. In a heavy skillet, melt the butter over medium heat until it foams. Add the mushrooms and sauté until tender and lightly browned, about 4–6 minutes. Set aside.
2. Spray a small baking dish with nonstick cooking spray. Line bottom of dish with spinach. Arrange mushrooms evenly on top. Pour the white sauce over the mushrooms, then sprinkle with the Cheddar and mozzarella cheeses. Season lightly with salt and pepper.
3. Bake until the cheeses are hot and bubbly, or about 25 minutes. Serve hot with crackers or chips.

`CALORIES` 74
`FAT` 2G
`CARBOHYDRATES` 8G
`PROTEIN` 7G

Low-Fat White Sauce

`CALCIUM`

MAKES 1 CUP

> 2 tablespoons plain flour
> 1 tablespoon cornstarch
> 1 teaspoon lemon pepper
> 1 cup nonfat milk

This calcium-rich white sauce is also lower in calories than its full-fat counterparts. Use this on fresh or baked vegetables and pasta, or as a base for cheese sauces or gravy.

1. Place the cornstarch and flour in a small saucepan over medium-low heat. Cook until lightly toasted but not browned, stirring constantly.
2. Add the cornstarch, lemon pepper, and milk, stirring constantly.
3. Continue cooking and stirring until thickened, or about 10 minutes.

`CALORIES` 43
`FAT` <1G
`CARBOHYDRATES` 8G
`PROTEIN` 3G

Petite Italian-Style Meatballs with Toasted Pine Nuts

SUPERFOOD PROTEIN

1 pound lean ground sirloin
3 cloves garlic, minced
½ cup Italian-style bread crumbs
1 egg, beaten
Pinch sugar substitute such as
  Splenda
½ teaspoon ground cinnamon
1 teaspoon sea salt
1 teaspoon fresh oregano leaves
⅓ cup pine nuts, toasted and crushed

Meatballs are a tasty way to get the protein you need, and adding nutrient-rich flavors such as garlic, cinnamon, and oregano is just a bonus. For even more metabolic power, add ½ cup raisins for their iron, calcium, and vitamin C.

1. Preheat oven to 375°F. Line two baking sheets with parchment paper. In large mixing bowl, combine all ingredients and mix together by hand or using a wooden spoon.
2. Roll into marble-sized meatballs, about ¾ inch round. Bake for 8–10 minutes, turning the baking sheets midway through for even heat.
3. Serve with toothpicks or use to make petite sandwiches.

CALORIES 66
FAT 3G
CARBOHYDRATES 5G
PROTEIN 5G

BURN IT UP

The water-soluble nutrient known as biotin, or B7, plays a key part in the formation of fatty acids and glucose (which are later broken down into energy) as well as in the metabolism of carbohydrates, fats, and proteins. It also helps transfer carbon dioxide and generate energy during aerobic exercise when the body is engaged in the citric acid cycle. Biotin can be found in healthy foods like milk, liver, and egg yolks—such as those found in this recipe.

Crab Cake Medallions

PROTEIN | SPICY | CALCIUM

SERVES 8, SERVING SIZE: 2 CAKES

8 ounces crabmeat
¼ cup low-fat mayonnaise
Fine zest of ½ lemon
Juice of ½ lemon, seeds removed
1 egg
1 tablespoon chili sauce
2 tablespoons white onion, minced
1 tablespoon fresh dill, leaves chopped
1 teaspoon dry mustard blended with 2 teaspoons water
½ cup panko bread crumbs

Crab cakes are a party favorite and are rich in vital vitamins and minerals.

1. Preheat oven to 450°F. Line baking sheet with parchment paper or spray with non-stick cooking spray.
2. Mix the first 9 ingredients together in a medium mixing bowl. Spread the panko bread crumbs on a piece of wax paper.
3. Form crab mixture into half-dollar-sized medallions. Coat with panko bread crumbs on both sides. Place on prepared baking sheets and bake for 5 minutes. Turn over and bake an additional 5 minutes or until crisp. Serve as is or with a side of your favorite aioli, remoulade, or other dipping sauce.

CALORIES 117
FAT 7G
CARBOHYDRATES 6G
PROTEIN 7G

Crostini with Eggplant and Pecorino Romano

HIGH FIBER | ANTIOXIDANTS | PROTEIN

SERVES 4, SERVING SIZE: 4 SLICES

1 sourdough baguette, sliced
½ cup extra-virgin olive oil, divided
6 cloves garlic, peeled
2 Japanese eggplants
1 teaspoon sea salt
½ cup grated Pecorino Romano cheese
¼ cup diced roasted red bell peppers

Eggplant is a great metabolism booster as it is naturally low in calories, saturated fat, and cholesterol; is high in fiber; and is loaded with vitamins and minerals such as potassium, phosphorus, and vitamins B6, C, and K.

1. Preheat oven to 350°F. Slice baguette into ¼-inch thick rounds and lay them out on a parchment paper–lined baking sheet. Brush each side with olive oil. Toast them in oven for about 5 minutes. Turn and toast an additional 5 minutes.
2. Remove from oven, rub one side of each toast with fresh garlic clove; set aside.
3. Slice the eggplant into ¼-inch-thick slices, brush with olive oil, and sprinkle with salt. Grill eggplant on heated grill or grill pan about 5 minutes on each side.
4. Top each crostini (toast) with grilled eggplant slice, sprinkle with cheese, and top with about 1 tablespoon roasted red bell peppers.

CALORIES 406
FAT 33G
CARBOHYDRATES 23G
PROTEIN 7G

Cannellini Bean Dip

PROTEIN **HIGH FIBER**

2 cloves garlic, peeled
½ teaspoon sea salt
1½ cups cooked white beans such as
   cannellini or northern beans
⅓ cup tahini
2 tablespoons fresh lemon juice
2 tablespoons olive oil
1 teaspoon fresh thyme leaves,
   chopped

Beans are naturally high in fiber and a good source of protein. Cannellini beans in particular are lower in fat than garbanzo beans, which are traditionally used in hummus.

1. Puree the garlic and salt in a food processor. Add the beans and puree to form a paste. Add the remaining ingredients and process until smooth, scraping down sides of bowl when needed.
2. Transfer puree mixture to a decorative serving dish and serve with freshly chopped vegetables, crackers, or pita crisps.

CALORIES 281
FAT 18G
CARBOHYDRATES 23G
PROTEIN 10G

BURN IT UP

To make sure your metabolism is firing on all cylinders, plan to eat high-fiber foods such as fruits, vegetables, legumes, or whole-grain starches at every meal.

Asian Chicken Drummettes

PROTEIN

3 tablespoons sesame seed oil
1 tablespoon fresh lime juice
4 tablespoons low-sodium soy sauce
1 teaspoon cayenne pepper
2 tablespoons apple cider vinegar
1 teaspoon sugar substitute such as
   Splenda
1 clove garlic, minced
1 tablespoon fresh gingerroot, peeled
   and minced
24 small chicken drumsticks

Chicken drummettes are high in protein and naturally low in carbs. Combined with flavorful, energy-boosting ingredients, they are the perfect snack to eat at home or bring to a party. For even leaner drummettes, remove the skin before eating.

1. Whisk the first 8 ingredients together in a large mixing bowl. Add the chicken drummettes and toss to coat. Marinate in the refrigerator for about 1 hour.
2. Preheat grill or broiler to high heat. Drain the chicken and discard the marinade. Place chicken on grill or, if using broiler pan, spray pan with nonstick cooking spray and place chicken on pan.
3. Grill chicken about 4 minutes per side, turning once or twice, until browned and cooked through. Serve with chutney or other sauce.

CALORIES 308
FAT 17G
CARBOHYDRATES 4G
PROTEIN 32G

BURN IT UP

Your body has to work twice as hard to digest protein as carbohydrates or fats, which means your metabolism has to work harder, too. Also, a study published in the *American Journal of Clinical Nutrition* found that people reduced their calorie intake by 441 calories a day when they ate more protein and cut down on fat. In fact, experts think that eating protein actually enhances the effect of leptin, a hormone that helps the body feel full.

Tomato Basil Bruschetta

SUPERFOOD ANTIOXIDANTS

SERVES 4, SERVING SIZE: 4 CROSTINI

1 14½-ounce can diced tomatoes
2 scallions, chopped
2 tablespoons extra-virgin olive oil plus ½ cup
Ground pepper and sea salt to taste
1 teaspoon fresh basil leaves, finely chopped
1 loaf Italian bread such as ciabatta, sliced into
    ½-inch thick slices

Tomatoes are a superfood. In addition to working to boost your metabolism in a multitude of ways, they are loaded with vitamins and minerals and are naturally low caloric and fat free.

1. Preheat oven to 350°F. Mix together tomatoes, onions, oil, salt, pepper, and basil. Set aside.
2. Brush bread slices with olive oil. Place on parchment paper–lined baking sheet and bake until crisp, or about 10 minutes. Remove from oven and top with tomato mixture and serve.

CALORIES 163
FAT 8G
CARBOHYDRATES 20G
PROTEIN 4G

Focaccia of Grilled Vegetables

HIGH FIBER ANTIOXIDANTS SUPERFOOD

SERVES 4

4 pieces sourdough focaccia bread
1¼ pound marinated kalamata olives
½ cup marinated Sicilian cracked green olives
½ cup roasted red bell peppers
3 Roma tomatoes, seeded and diced
2 tablespoons extra-virgin olive oil
Sea salt and pepper to taste
½ teaspoon Italian seasoning

Focaccia is an Italian flat bread that can be enjoyed simply with a little olive oil or with various toppings such as meats and vegetables. For maximum health benefits, look for whole wheat focaccia, which is higher in fiber and harder to digest than those made with white flour.

1. Preheat broiler. Place focaccia slices under broiler for 1 minute.
2. Mix all ingredients, except bread, in a large mixing bowl. Divide equally among focaccia slices and serve.

CALORIES 425
FAT 24G
CARBOHYDRATES 44G
PROTEIN 8G

Fresh Figs Stuffed with Honey and Cheese

HIGH FIBER ANTIOXIDANTS CALCIUM

8 medium ripe figs
⅓ cup crumbled Gorgonzola cheese
1 teaspoon olive oil
¼ cup honey

A delicious metabolism-boosting food, figs are naturally low in fat, high in fiber, and filled with minerals such as potassium, calcium, and vitamins A and C.

1. Preheat oven to 300°F. Slit each fig in half, beginning from top to bottom, but leaving fig intact with a "hinge." Stuff each fig with cheese. Roll each fig in the olive oil.
2. Transfer figs to a parchment paper–lined baking sheet and bake figs about 30 minutes. Drizzle honey on baked fig.

CALORIES 183
FAT 4G
CARBOHYDRATES 37G
PROTEIN 3G

BURN IT UP

A diet low in fat and cholesterol and rich in foods containing potassium, magnesium, and calcium—such as fruits, vegetables, legumes, and dairy foods—is known to reduce blood pressure. Potassium-rich foods include fresh meat, poultry, fish, figs, prunes, lentils, kidney beans, black beans, baked potatoes, avocados, orange juice, cantaloupes, bananas, and cooked spinach.

Oven-Baked Empanadas with Firm Tofu

SPICY | ANTIOXIDANTS | PROTEIN

SERVES 10, SERVING SIZE: 4 EMPANADAS

½ tablespoon olive oil
½ yellow onion, finely chopped
1 teaspoon curry powder
8 ounces firm tofu, diced
1 small can kernel corn, drained
1 red bell pepper, seeded and finely chopped
½ teaspoon cayenne pepper
Sea salt to taste
Black pepper to taste
1 package square wonton wrappers
1 egg beaten with 1 tablespoon of water

Wonton wrappers are a great way to conserve on both fat and calories. As an added bonus, these easy empanadas are baked, not fried. Serve them with Asian Ginger Sauce (see following recipe).

1. Preheat oven to 400°F. In heavy saucepan, heat oil over medium heat. Add onion and curry powder. Sauté until onion is tender, about 3 minutes. Add tofu, corn, bell pepper, and cayenne. Sauté until moisture cooks out and all vegetables are tender, or about 7 minutes. Season with salt and pepper as desired.
2. Line a baking sheet with parchment paper. Pour about ¼ cup of water into a small bowl. Place 1 wonton wrapper onto baking sheet. Spoon approximately ½ to 1 tablespoon of tofu mixture into center of wonton. Using fingertip, lightly coat all four edges of wonton wrapper with water. Fold wonton diagonally over tofu mixture to form a triangle and gently press the edges together to seal. Place on prepared baking sheet. Repeat with remaining wontons until all wontons and tofu mixture are used.
3. Brush each prepared empanada with egg mixture, top side only. Place in oven and bake for 8–12 minutes, or until wonton is crisp and lightly golden brown. Serve warm.

CALORIES 140
FAT 1G
CARBOHYDRATES 16G
PROTEIN 6G

Asian Ginger Sauce

SPICY | ANTIOXIDANTS | SUPERFOOD

MAKES 1 CUP, SERVING SIZE: 1 TABLESPOON

½ cup tamari
1 teaspoon fresh gingerroot, peeled and minced
1 clove garlic, minced
1 teaspoon sesame oil
2 tablespoons fresh lemon juice
½ teaspoon sugar
½ teaspoon cayenne pepper

Fresh ginger root is high in antioxidants and is also known to be rich in metabolism-boosting minerals such as potassium and magnesium, and vitamin B6.

Blend all ingredients in a food processor or blender until smooth. Pour in airtight container or bottle. Use as desired.

CALORIES 10
FAT <1G
CARBOHYDRATES 1G
PROTEIN 1G

Jalapeño Salsa with Apricots

SPICY ANTIOXIDANTS

MAKES 2 CUPS, SERVING SIZE: 2 TABLESPOONS

1 16-ounce can apricots in syrup, drained, rinsed
    and cut into chunks
2 tablespoons red onion, chopped
1½ teaspoons extra-virgin olive oil
1 tablespoon fresh cilantro leaves, chopped
½ teaspoon fresh lime zest, fine grate
1½ teaspoons fresh lime juice
½ teaspoon white vinegar
½ teaspoon jalapeño pepper, minced
¼ teaspoon ground cumin
Sea salt and black pepper to taste
Baked pita crisps

Fresh and dried apricots are rich in vitamin A, beta carotene, and calcium, and are perfect for chutneys and salsas like this one.

Combine all ingredients in a medium mixing bowl and mix well. Cover and refrigerate until ready to serve with pita crisps.

CALORIES 45
FAT <1G
CARBOHYDRATES 10G
PROTEIN <1G

Vegetable Skewers of Olives, Tomatoes, and Monterey Jack Cheese

ANTIOXIDANTS SUPERFOOD

SERVES 6

Nonstick cooking spray
6 4- to 5-inch bamboo skewers soaked in water
    for 30 minutes
6 cherry tomatoes
½ pound Monterey jack cheese, cut into 1-inch
    cubes
6 large green marinated olives

Olives and tomatoes are a metabolism-friendly combination, as you gain iron, protein, and other essential vitamins and minerals. Plus they are high in the fiber that helps your body process foods.

1. Spray each skewer with nonstick spray. Arrange 1 tomato, 1 olive, and 1 cube of cheese on each skewer.
2. Grill on grill pan for 1 minute or less, just until cheese begins to melt. Turn and grill other side very briefly. Serve warm.

CALORIES 232
FAT 19G
CARBOHYDRATES 2G
PROTEIN 14G

Grilled Chicken Skewers

PROTEIN

SERVES 8 AS AN APPETIZER, SERVING SIZE:
2 SKEWERS

4 boneless, skinless chicken breasts
Sea salt as needed
Black pepper as needed
16 6-inch wooden skewers soaked in water for
    about 30 minutes
1 tablespoon olive oil

Boneless, skinless chicken breasts are one of the best foods for boosting your metabolism. They are naturally free of carbohydrates and are low in fat, and they give your body the energy-boosting, muscle building protein you need. Serve these chicken skewers warm with Asian Pear Sauce with Apples (see recipe below).

1. Slice chicken breasts into ½–1-inch-thick strips and thread onto soaked skewers. Season lightly with salt and pepper.
2. Heat oil on grill pan or in heavy skillet over medium heat until hot but not smoking. Add chicken and cook thoroughly, turning once, about 10–15 minutes.

CALORIES 98
FAT 2G
CARBOHYDRATES 0G
PROTEIN 18G

Asian Pear Sauce with Apples

HIGH FIBER ANTIOXIDANTS

MAKES ABOUT 5 CUPS, SERVING SIZE:
2 TABLESPOONS

1 cup sugar
2 cups water
1 cinnamon stick
3 Asian pears, peeled, cored, and cut into 2-inch
    chunks
3 apples (such as Gala), peeled, cored, and cut
    into 2-inch chunks
Fine zest of 1 lemon
Fine zest of 1 orange

Pears contain vitamins A and C, potassium, and several other essential minerals and may help lower blood pressure. This sauce is delicious as a healthy "butter" for pancakes and waffles and can also be used as a sauce for chicken, pork, and turkey.

1. In a large, heavy saucepan over medium heat, combine the sugar, water, and cinnamon stick. Cook about 30 minutes, until sugar is dissolved, stirring often. Add the pears and apples and cook an additional 35 minutes, until apples have softened.
2. Remove from heat and discard the cinnamon stick. Puree in food processor or using an immersion blender.
3. Serve warm, at room temperature, or chilled. Refrigerate any leftover sauce in an airtight container for up to 1 week.

CALORIES 57
FAT <1G
CARBOHYDRATES 15G
PROTEIN <1G

Cranberry Orange Chutney

SUPERFOOD ANTIOXIDANTS

1½ cups walnut pieces, lightly toasted
2 cups dried cranberries
1 cup golden raisins
1 red onion, thinly sliced
½ cup orange marmalade
½ cup orange juice
2 tablespoons orange zest
⅓ cup white wine vinegar
1 cup granulated sugar
½ cup firmly packed brown sugar
½ teaspoon sea salt
¼ teaspoon cayenne pepper
½ teaspoon ground ginger
1 cinnamon stick
1 bay leaf
3 whole endives, stems trimmed,
   leaves separated

Cranberries are rich in the vitamins and minerals essential to the cardiovascular system and immune system, and they help make this chutney a superfood on its own.

1. In a pressure cooker, combine all ingredients. Stir well. Secure the lid and bring to medium pressure over high heat. Maintain pressure and cook for 5 minutes. Release the pressure according to manufacturer's directions. Remove the lid when safe to do so.

2. Remove and discard the cinnamon stick and bay leaf. Stir the chutney well, then ladle into sterilized canning jars. Cover tightly and store in the refrigerator for up to 4 weeks.

3. To serve, spoon approximately ½–1 tablespoon of chutney onto endive leaves, arrange on platter, and serve. You can also serve the chutney on melba rounds, pita crisps, or fresh cucumber slices.

CALORIES 28
FAT <1G
CARBOHYDRATES 5G
PROTEIN <1G

Basil Pasta Sauce with Mushrooms

MAKES 1 QUART, SERVING SIZE: ¼ CUP

ANTIOXIDANTS SUPERFOOD

1 white or yellow onion, chopped

3 cloves garlic, minced

½ pound cremini mushrooms, cleaned and sliced

1 green bell pepper, cut into 1-inch chunks, seeds reserved

1 celery stalk, chopped

1 28-ounce can diced tomatoes, undrained

1 6-ounce can tomato paste

1 8-ounce can tomato sauce

½ cup red wine such as cabernet sauvignon

1 teaspoon brown sugar

2 teaspoons fresh oregano leaves, chopped

4 tablespoons fresh basil leaves, chopped

2 teaspoons fresh Italian flat-leaf parsley leaves, chopped

⅛ teaspoon red pepper flakes

Sea salt and black pepper to taste

You won't believe that such an instant metabolic boost can come from something as flavorful as this sauce! Antioxidants, fiber, and spice are just a few of the enhancers you'll enjoy here.

1. In a nonstick skillet, over low heat, combine the onion and garlic with 4 tablespoons water and cook until tender, about 4 minutes. Add the mushrooms and continue cooking over low heat for about 3 minutes. Add the bell pepper, pepper seeds, and celery, and cook until just tender, about 4 minutes. Add the tomatoes with their juice.

2. In small bowl, whisk together the tomato paste, sauce, and wine. Add to the mushroom mixture along with the sugar, oregano, basil, parsley, and red pepper flakes. Season with salt and pepper. Cook for about 15 minutes to blend flavors.

3. Serve over cooked chicken breasts or with whole wheat pasta such as spaghetti, fettuccini, or penne.

CALORIES 41

FAT <1G

CARBOHYDRATES 8G

PROTEIN 2G

CHAPTER 3
Breakfasts

If breakfast is the most important meal of the day, why do you often feel sluggish and tired after you eat it? This most likely happens when you are not eating the right foods or the right combinations of foods. This chapter gives you some great lean-protein combinations and high-fiber breakfast alternatives that will help supercharge your metabolism and get your day going.

Oatmeal Buttermilk Pancakes

`HIGH FIBER` `CALCIUM` `PROTEIN`

SERVES 6

1 cup quick-cooking oats
½ cup plain flour
¼ cup sugar
1 teaspoon baking powder
1 teaspoon baking soda
⅛ teaspoon sea salt
2 cups low-fat buttermilk
¼ cup egg beaters
Butter flavored nonstick spray

Buttermilk is a super replacement for regular milk. It's lower in fat than whole milk and high in potassium, vitamin B12, and calcium. Plus, it adds a tremendous amount of flavor!

1. Combine oats, flour, sugar, baking powder, baking soda, and salt in a medium mixing bowl and mix well. Separately, whisk together buttermilk and egg beaters. Pour buttermilk mixture into oat mixture and stir until just blended.
2. Spray hot griddle with butter flavored spray. Pour ¼ cup pancake batter onto griddle. Cook until bubbles appear and edges are brown. Flip and cook until done, about 1–2 minutes.

`CALORIES` 158
`FAT` 2G
`CARBOHYDRATES` 29G
`PROTEIN` 7G

Waffles with Fresh Fruit Cream

`ANTIOXIDANTS`

SERVES 2

½ cup quick cooking oats
½ cup nonfat cottage cheese
3 egg whites
1 tablespoon Splenda
1 teaspoon cinnamon
1 teaspoon vanilla extract
1 banana, chopped
½ cup strawberries, chopped
2 tablespoons heavy cream

Using egg whites keeps these waffles cholesterol free. For an even leaner breakfast, substitute nonfat sour cream for the heavy cream. This simple switch will give you more calcium and fewer calories and fat.

1. Combine oats, cottage cheese, egg whites, Splenda, cinnamon, and vanilla in a food processor or blender and blend until smooth.
2. Separately, combine chopped banana and strawberries with heavy cream. Reserve for later.
3. Heat waffle maker. Pour about ¼ cup batter onto heated waffle iron. Cook until done. When serving, top with fruit mixture.

`CALORIES` 281
`FAT` 8G
`CARBOHYDRATES` 38G
`PROTEIN` 16G

Cream Cheese French Toast

CALCIUM

Butter-flavored nonstick cooking
  spray
4 slices French bread
4 teaspoons reduced-fat cream
  cheese
4 teaspoons of your favorite preserves, such as antioxidant-rich
  strawberry or raspberry
1 cup low-fat milk
1 cup skim milk divided into 4
  servings
1 teaspoon vanilla extract
1 teaspoon cinnamon
½ teaspoon nutmeg

A lighter way to enjoy French toast, this calcium-rich food gives you energy and keeps your bones strong.

1. Prepare a skillet or grill pan by spraying lightly with nonstick spray. Slice French bread into 1-inch-thick slices. Cut a pocket through the top of each slice, ¾ the way through the bread. Insert the cream cheese and preserves.
2. In medium mixing bowl, combine milk, vanilla, cinnamon, and nutmeg. Mix well to make batter.
3. Heat griddle or grill pan. Dip prepared bread slices into milk mixture, coating both sides. Place on heated griddle and cook until one side is lightly browned; flip and cook other side. Enjoy.

CALORIES 319
FAT 4G
CARBOHYDRATES 58G
PROTEIN 11G

BURN IT UP

As carbohydrates are easily metabolized into fat, eat the bulk of your carbohydrates early in the day so your body will have plenty of time to metabolize them. For example, rather than eating a light breakfast and a heavy dinner, eat your heaviest meal for breakfast and your lightest meal at dinnertime. Doing so will not only get your engine going in the morning, but will help you metabolize the bulk of your daily calories when you're most active.

Breakfast Pizza of Egg and Feta

PROTEIN CALCIUM

SERVES 8

1 tablespoon all purpose flour
16-ounces fresh or frozen pizza dough
Nonstick cooking spray
6 eggs
½ cup non fat milk
½ cup Feta cheese, crumbled

Feta cheese is loaded with essential vitamins such as vitamins A and B and minerals like calcium and zinc, making it one of the best cheeses to add to your diet.

1. Preheat oven to 375°F. Sprinkle flour on flat work surface and roll out pizza dough to 12-inch circle, building up the edges so they are thick and high. Place dough on nonstick baking sheet or pizza stone, then prick dough thoroughly with a fork.
2. Bake until light brown, or about 15 minutes. While crust is baking, coat skillet with nonstick spray. In large mixing bowl, whisk together eggs and milk. Heat skillet over medium heat and pour mixture into skillet. Cook eggs, stirring to scramble, until just cooked. Place cooked eggs on baked crust and sprinkle with cheese.
3. Return prepared pizza to oven and bake until cheese starts to melt, or about 7 minutes. Slice and serve.

CALORIES 229
FAT 3G
CARBOHYDRATES 30G
PROTEIN 10G

Low-Fat Egg, Spinach, and Cheese Breakfast Cakes

HIGH FIBER SUPERFOOD ANTIOXIDANTS

SERVES 5

Cupcake liners
10 ounces chopped frozen spinach
2 eggs
1 cup skim ricotta cheese
1 cup low-fat shredded mozzarella cheese
Sea salt and black pepper to taste

Spinach is a superfood that provides your body with tons of antioxidants and fiber to help fight cancer. Give this recipe a boost by adding a few freshly diced tomatoes, diced red onion, and a pinch of cayenne pepper.

1. Preheat oven to 350°F. Place cupcake liners in cupcake tin. In medium skillet over medium-low heat, add spinach and cook until warmed.
2. Separately, whisk eggs and add the spinach to them. Blend well. Add the ricotta and mozzarella. Season with salt and pepper. Fill each cup with egg mixture ¾ the way. Bake for 30–35 minutes. Serve warm.

CALORIES 175
FAT 10G
CARBOHYDRATES 5G
PROTEIN 16G

Eggs Florentine over English Muffins

SERVES 2

2 whole wheat English muffins, halved
4 eggs
8 ounces chopped frozen spinach
2 tablespoons low-fat mayonnaise
Sea salt and black pepper to taste
4 teaspoons shredded low-fat Monterey jack cheese

Whole grain English muffins are a metabolism-boosting option as they are high-fiber and will help regulate your digestive tract.

1. Preheat oven to 350°F. Place muffin halves on a parchment paper–lined baking sheet. Crack one egg on each of four muffin halves. Bake for 10 minutes.
2. In medium skillet over medium heat, add spinach and cook until warmed. Stir in mayonnaise, salt, and pepper and blend. Remove muffins from oven and top with spinach mixture. Add cheese and serve.

CALORIES 260
FAT 10G
CARBOHYDRATES 31G
PROTEIN 15G

Omelet of Fresh Chives, Cheese, and Tomatoes

SERVES 2

4 egg whites
1 egg
Pinch sea salt
1 tablespoon olive oil
2 Roma tomatoes, diced
¼ cup reduced-fat Cheddar cheese, grated
2 tablespoons freshly chopped chives

Using fewer eggs and more egg whites helps lower calories and cholesterol.

1. In large mixing bowl, whisk together egg whites and egg. Add salt.
2. Heat olive oil in small skillet over medium-low heat. Pour egg mixture into skillet. Cook until edges begin to firm. Sprinkle the tomatoes and cheese evenly into the egg mixture. Top with chives. Fold one side over the other, then flip to cook both sides evenly.

CALORIES 156
FAT 11G
CARBOHYDRATES 1.5G
PROTEIN 14G

Omelet of Sausage, Mushrooms, and Onions

SERVES 2

4 egg whites
1 egg
¼ teaspoon sea salt
1 tablespoon olive oil
½ cup turkey sausage, chopped
½ cup cremini mushrooms, chopped
2 tablespoons white or yellow onion, chopped

Turkey sausage is a metabolism-friendly food as it is high in protein and leaner in fat than regular bacon and yet is still packed with flavor.

1. In medium mixing bowl, beat egg whites and egg using wire whisk or fork until combined.
2. In medium skillet over medium heat, add sausage, mushrooms, and onions. Sauté for 4–5 minutes, until sausage is cooked through. Remove from heat and set aside.
3. Return skillet to heat and add oil. Add egg mixture and cook until edges become slightly firm. Spread sausage mixture evenly over eggs. Fold one half over top of the other. Flip to cook both sides evenly.

CALORIES 266
FAT 20G
CARBOHYDRATES 2.5G
PROTEIN 20G

Breakfast Panini with Smoked Bacon

SERVES 2

4 slices smoked turkey bacon
4 slices whole wheat bread
2 teaspoons low-fat mayonnaise
Dijon mustard to taste, about 1 tablespoon
2 medium tomatoes, sliced
8 fresh basil leaves, coarsely chopped
2 ounces sharp Cheddar cheese, grated
Freshly ground black pepper to taste
2 tablespoons butter

This low-carb, high-protein breakfast gives you enough energy to see you through until lunch.

1. In heavy skillet over medium heat, cook bacon until crisp. Drain on paper towels and crumble.
2. Spread half the bread slices with mayonnaise and mustard. Add the bacon, tomato, basil, cheese. Sprinkle with pepper. Top with remaining bread slices.
3. Return skillet to heat and add butter. Add the sandwiches and grill on each side until browned and cheese is melting. Slice in half and serve.

CALORIES 457
FAT 31G
CARBOHYDRATES 32G
PROTEIN 15G

Polenta Pancakes with Blueberries

SERVES 4

HIGH FIBER | SUPERFOOD

1 cup plain flour
½ cup yellow cornmeal
3 tablespoons sugar
1½ teaspoons baking powder
½ teaspoon baking soda
½ teaspoon sea salt
2 eggs
3 tablespoons melted butter
1½ cups buttermilk
1 cup blueberries

High in potassium, cornmeal also contains other valuable minerals and fiber that make it great for both your digestion and overall health.

1. In a large mixing bowl, whisk together flour, cornmeal, sugar, baking powder, baking soda, and salt. Separately, whisk together eggs, butter, and buttermilk. Gradually stir egg mixture into flour mixture until combined. Be careful not to over mix, acknowledging that there will be some lumps.

2. Heat griddle or heavy skillet over medium heat. Pour about ⅓ cup batter for each pancake onto heated griddle. Scatter a few blueberries over batter. When bubbles have formed in the center and edges are slightly firm, flip pancakes. Cook other side for about 1 minute. Serve with hot maple syrup or fruit sauce.

CALORIES 374
FAT 12G
CARBOHYDRATES 56G
PROTEIN 11G

BURN IT UP

Blueberries, a superfood filled with antioxidants, vitamin C, and fiber, give these metabolism-friendly cornmeal pancakes an extra boost.

Frittata of Onions, Potatoes, and Turkey Sausage

HIGH FIBER | PROTEIN

SERVES 8

2 turkey sausage patties, chopped, or ½ cup ground turkey sausage
½ white or yellow onion, diced
4 red new potatoes, parboiled and thinly sliced
8 eggs, beaten
½ cup nonfat milk
1 tablespoon fresh thyme leaves, chopped
Sea salt and black pepper as needed
2 tablespoons olive oil

Thyme leaves, like many herbs, are high in fiber, calcium, iron, and vitamins like A and C. Remember, herbs aren't just for garnish anymore!

1. In large oven-proof skillet, add sausage and cook over medium heat until just browned, breaking up large pieces as you cook, for about 3 minutes. Add in onion and potatoes and cook until tender, for about 8 minutes. Turn off heat and carefully drain any excess grease, removing sausage mixture from the pan and setting aside.

2. In mixing bowl, whisk together eggs, milk, fresh thyme, and lightly season with salt and pepper. Preheat broiler to high heat. Return skillet to medium heat and add 1 tablespoon of the olive oil. Pour in egg mixture, do not stir. Evenly distribute sausage mixture amongst skillet. Let cook about 5 minutes, or until eggs are setting.

3. When mixture is cooked but still runny on center top, transfer skillet to broiler and broil until top has finished cooking and appears lightly browned. Remove from broiler, slice into 8 servings. When serving, drizzle with remaining olive oil, if desired, for added flavor.

CALORIES 131
FAT 9G
CARBOHYDRATES 7G
PROTEIN 6G

Breakfast Egg and Cheese Wraps

PROTEIN | SPICY

SERVES 4

4 6-inch flour or corn tortillas
4 eggs
Sea salt and black pepper to taste
1 tablespoon butter
4 tablespoons spicy hot salsa
4 tablespoons grated Monterey jack or pepper jack cheese

Tortillas contain the fiber, carbs, protein, and minerals that will give you the energy you need to start your day off right.

1. Preheat broiler to high. Place the tortillas on a parchment paper–lined baking sheet and place under broiler until toasted on one side. Remove from broiler and set aside. Turn broiler off.

2. In small mixing bowl, whisk together eggs and season lightly with salt and pepper. Heat butter in a nonstick skillet over medium heat. Add eggs and stir using a wooden spoon or spatula until just cooked. Place 1 tablespoon salsa on one side of each tortilla, covering roughly ⅓ of each half. Top

the salsa with eggs and then with cheese. Rolling from "filled" edge first, roll tortilla into a wrap. Serve 1 wrap per person.

CALORIES 242
FAT 13G
CARBOHYDRATES 21G
PROTEIN 11G

Scones of Oatmeal and Raisins

SUPERFOOD PROTEIN

SERVES 6

1½ cups rolled oats
½ cup plain flour
2 tablespoons wheat germ
3 tablespoons sugar plus 2 tablespoons
½ teaspoon sea salt
1⅛ teaspoons baking powder
6 tablespoons cold unsalted butter, cut into pieces
2 eggs
⅔ cup buttermilk
½ teaspoon vanilla extract
1 cup raisins
1 egg white

Wheat germ is a superfood. It's filled with fiber and protein, and loaded with vitamins and minerals such as zinc, selenium, and iron.

1. Preheat oven to 400°F. Line a baking sheet with parchment paper or spray with nonstick spray. In a food processor, grind half the oats with the flour. Combine the remaining oats, oat flour mixture, plain flour, wheat germ, 3 tablespoons of sugar, salt, baking powder, and butter in a food processor using a metal blade. Process until mixture resembles cornmeal.

2. In a large mixing bowl, whisk together eggs, buttermilk, and vanilla. Stir in raisins. Add dry ingredients gradually, folding in with a spatula. Drop scones in rounded spoonfuls onto prepared baking sheet.

3. Brush scones with egg white, sprinkle with remaining sugar. Bake for 15 minutes or until done.

CALORIES 373
FAT 15G
CARBOHYDRATES 54G
PROTEIN 9G

Citrus Omelet with Fresh Wild Berries

SERVES 2

¼ cup fresh blackberries
¼ cup fresh raspberries
¼ cup fresh blueberries
1 tablespoon sugar
Fine zest of ½ orange
Juice of ½ orange
1 tablespoon butter
4 eggs
¼ cup nonfat milk
Sea salt and black pepper to taste

Wild berries like those in this recipe are super-rich in antioxidants and metabolism-boosting fiber, vitamins like B and C, and minerals such as manganese.

1. Toss the berries, sugar, orange zest, and orange juice in a small to medium mixing bowl. Let stand for 30 minutes.
2. Heat the butter in a nonstick skillet over medium heat. Quickly whisk together the eggs and milk, seasoning lightly with salt and pepper. Pour egg mixture into heated skillet and cook until it just starts to set. Spoon berry mixture onto middle of egg mixture and flip one side of eggs over the other. Let cook until set.
3. Divide the omelet into 2 portions and serve, drizzling with any remaining berry juice.

CALORIES 186
FAT 12G
CARBOHYDRATES 9G
PROTEIN 12G

BURN IT UP

Try eating different fruits every day to get different types of dietary fiber. Fruits with edible seeds, such as strawberries, are sources of lignin, while apples and citrus fruits are excellent sources of pectin. In addition to nutrient-rich wild berries, these fiber-filled fruits will also help boost your metabolism: bananas, cantaloupes, grapefruits, mangos, papayas, peaches, pineapples, tangerines, and watermelons.

Swiss Muesli

HIGH FIBER ANTIOXIDANTS

SERVES 4

½ cup rolled oats
¾ cup warm water
¼ cup coarsely chopped pistachio nuts, roasted
2 apples, such as Fuji or Gala, peeled and grated or finely chopped
2 tablespoons brown sugar
¾ cup nonfat vanilla yogurt
Juice of 2 lemons

Pistachio nuts pack a whopping number of vitamins and minerals and are high in antioxidants. Because of their nutritional content and high fiber content, they are a great pick-me-up snack food.

Combine oats and warm water in a small mixing bowl and soak for about 15 minutes. Add the nuts, apple, brown sugar, yogurt, and lemon juice and mix well. Chill in the refrigerator for 20–30 minutes. Or serve warm by heating in a small quart boiler over low heat for about 3 minutes, stirring occasionally.

CALORIES 153
FAT 3G
CARBOHYDRATES 32G
PROTEIN 4G

Jalapeño French Toast with Crispy Bacon

PROTEIN SPICY

SERVES 2

4 eggs, beaten
½ cup nonfat milk
1 jalapeño, seeded and minced
2 slices whole wheat bread
Nonstick cooking spray
¼ cup chili sauce
2 slices bacon, cooked crisp and crumbled

Both eggs and bacon provide maximum protein in this recipe, but for a leaner, more low-fat version, substitute lean turkey bacon without sacrificing flavor.

1. In medium mixing bowl, whisk together eggs and milk. Add the jalapeños and stir to combine. Place bread slices in egg mixture and coat both sides.
2. Spray heavy skillet or griddle with non-stick spray and heat over medium heat. Add coated bread slices and cook until browned on each side, about 4 minutes per side. Serve topped with chili sauce and crumbled bacon.

CALORIES 237
FAT 13G
CARBOHYDRATES 24G
PROTEIN 20G

Creamy Oatmeal with Honey-Glazed Fresh Fruit

SERVES 4

1 fresh whole peach, seed removed, chopped
½ cup raisins
1 Granny Smith apple, cored and chopped
½ cup water
3 tablespoons honey
½ teaspoon sea salt
2 cups traditional oatmeal (non-quick-cooking)
1½ cups nonfat milk
1½ cups nonfat plain or vanilla yogurt
1 cup toasted walnuts, coarsely chopped

If you love to workout in the morning, this breakfast is perfect for you. Oats provide slow-releasing carbs that combine with the quick energy of natural fruit sugars to keep you going all day long.

1. In a saucepan, combine the peach, raisins, apple, water, honey, and salt and stir to coat. Bring to a boil and remove from heat. Allow to stand.
2. Separately, in a medium quart boiler over medium heat, combine the oatmeal, milk, and yogurt. Mix well and cook according to oatmeal package directions. When oatmeal is tender, add the fruit mixture and cook another 2–3 minutes. Top with walnuts when serving.

CALORIES   350
FAT   24G
CARBOHYDRATES   61G
PROTEIN   32G

Scrambled Egg Whites with Fresh Herbs and Tomatoes

SERVES 4

Nonstick cooking spray
6 green onions, chopped
1½ cups fresh zucchini, julienned
1 pint cherry tomatoes, halved
1 dozen egg whites or 1½ cups egg beaters, beaten
2 tablespoons fresh basil leaves, chopped
1 tablespoons fresh thyme leaves, chopped
Sea salt and black pepper to taste

Many people may think that egg whites have little nutritional value, but the truth is quite to the contrary. They contain potassium and several B vitamins, but none of the cholesterol found in the yolks. Plus, the yolks contain most of the calories!

1. Spray skillet with nonstick spray and heat over medium heat. Add the onions, zucchini, and tomatoes. Sauté until just tender, about 5 minutes.
2. Add the egg whites and herbs and stir to scramble, about 1 minute. Season with salt and pepper as desired and serve.

CALORIES   23
FAT   0G
CARBOHYDRATES   2G
PROTEIN   4G

Chestnut-Filled Pancakes

`PROTEIN`

SERVES 6

½ cup canned chestnuts
1½ cups plain flour
½ teaspoon sea salt
2 teaspoons baking powder
½ teaspoon baking soda
2 eggs, beaten
1 cup nonfat milk
2 tablespoons honey
2 tablespoons butter, melted

Chestnuts are a nutritious alternative to the usual favorites because they are lower in fat than walnuts and almonds and have no cholesterol.

1. Boil the chestnuts in a small quart boiler for about 2 minutes. Drain and peel the thin membrane off the nut. Puree in a food processor until smooth. Set aside.
2. In a large mixing bowl, mix together flour, salt, baking powder, and baking soda. Stir in eggs, milk, chestnut puree, honey, and butter until just blended.
3. Spray griddle or heavy skillet with nonstick spray and heat over medium heat. Pour ¼ cup of batter onto heated griddle. When bubbles rise, flip pancake and cook until done, about 30 seconds. Serve with maple syrup or fruit topping.

CALORIES 184
FAT 8G
CARBOHYDRATES 5G
PROTEIN 14G

English Muffin Panini of Roasted Peppers and Canadian Bacon

`PROTEIN`

SERVES 2

1 red bell pepper
2 whole wheat English Muffins
4 eggs
Sea salt and black pepper to taste
2 Roma tomatoes, seeded and diced
½ white or yellow onion, diced
1 tablespoon olive oil
2 slices cooked Canadian bacon
2 slices reduced-fat feta cheese

Not only does Canadian bacon pack in the protein, it's leaner than traditional bacon. Other metabolism-friendly protein alternatives are turkey bacon or lean turkey sausage.

1. Preheat broiler to high. Split red bell pepper in half and lay, skin side up, onto broiler pan or baking sheet. Place under broiler until charred black. Remove from baking sheet and place in plastic bag and seal tightly. Let stand for 15 minutes.
2. Meanwhile, toast muffin halves lightly. Then, in medium mixing bowl, combine eggs, salt, and pepper. Whisk together until well combined.
3. Remove charred peppers from bag and rub off skin. Do NOT rinse. Dice peppers. Add peppers to egg mixture along with tomatoes and onions.
4. Heat 1 tablespoon of olive oil in heavy skillet over medium heat. Add Canadian bacon and heat until hot or very warm, about 2 minutes. Add egg and pepper mixture and cook until egg is slightly firm.

5. Lay 2 muffin halves on serving plate. Stir egg mixture and then divide between each of 2 muffin halves. Top with cheese, bacon, and finish with remaining muffin half. Serve.

CALORIES 236
FAT 3G
CARBOHYDRATES 30G
PROTEIN 28G

Egg and Parmesan Corn Crepes

HIGH FIBER SPICY

SERVES 6

2 eggs, whole (for batter)
1 cup nonfat milk
Pinch sea salt
1 cup corn flour
2 tablespoons butter, unsalted
Canola oil for frying
¼ cup hot salsa
12 ½-ounce slices pepper jack cheese
12 eggs, poached or fried sunny-side up
¼ cup grated Parmesan cheese

Crepes are lighter than pancakes and, when made with fiber-rich corn flour, are great metabolism boosters.

1. Prepare batter: Combine eggs, milk, and salt in a food processor and blend until smooth. On low speed or pulsing, gradually add flour and butter, scraping sides of bowl if needed.
2. Heat 2 teaspoons of oil in a nonstick skillet over medium heat. Pour in ¼ cup of batter. Tilt pan to spread batter evenly. Cook until set and lightly browned. Transfer crepes to parchment paper dusted with a little corn flour to prevent sticking.
3. Preheat broiler to high heat. Place crepes on baking sheet lined with parchment paper. Place slice of jack cheese on each crepe. Place one egg on each piece of cheese. Spoon a little salsa on top of each egg. Sprinkle crepes with parmesan cheese and broil until cheese is hot and beginning to melt, about 2 minutes.

CALORIES 302
FAT 17G
CARBOHYDRATES 8G
PROTEIN 20G

Chocolate Pecan Pancakes with Sliced Bananas

HIGH FIBER ANTIOXIDANTS SUPERFOOD

2 1-ounce squares semi-sweet baking chocolate
1 cup pecans
1 cup whole wheat flour
2 teaspoons baking powder
½ teaspoon sea salt
3 eggs, beaten
¾ cup low-fat milk
6 tablespoons honey
1 teaspoon vanilla extract
Nonstick cooking spray
2 bananas, peeled and sliced ¼-inch thick

Bananas are most commonly known for their potassium, but are also high in vitamins B6 and C.

1. Melt chocolate with 2 tablespoons of water in small quart boiler over low heat. Set aside.
2. In heavy skillet, add pecans and cook over medium heat until lightly toasted. Remove from heat and finely chop.
3. In a large mixing bowl, combine flour, baking powder, and salt. Stir. Then beat in eggs, milk, honey, and vanilla, blending well. Stir in chocolate.
4. Spray griddle or heavy skillet with nonstick spray. Heat over medium-high heat and pour in about ¼ cup of the batter. Top with a few banana slices and cook until bubbles begin to form in the center and top of pancake. Flip and finish cooking, about 30 seconds. Serve with hot butter, marmalade, or other topping.

CALORIES 200
FAT 7G
CARBOHYDRATES 24G
PROTEIN 10G

BURN IT UP

Fruit's sweet flavor comes from fructose, a naturally occurring sugar that serves as a good source of energy. Fruit is full of healthy substances such as vitamins A and C, potassium, folic acid, antioxidants, phytochemicals, and fiber, just to name a few. Almost all fruits and vegetables are good for you, but some are better than others. When it comes to fruit, apples, bananas, berries, citrus fruit, and melons are your best bets because of their high fiber and nutrient content.

Simply Delicious Waffles

PROTEIN

MAKES 6 WAFFLES

2 cups plain flour
4 teaspoons baking powder
¼ teaspoon sea salt
2 eggs
1¾ cups low-fat or nonfat milk
½ cup canola oil

Eggs sometimes get a bad rap because they do have a fairly high level of cholesterol. However, enjoyed in moderation, eggs also contain cell-protecting vitamins A and E. They are one of the few foods that have vitamin D which, among other things, is essential for bone growth.

1. Preheat waffle iron following manufacturer's instructions. Stir together the flour, baking powder, and salt, and make a well in the middle of the mixture. Lightly beat the eggs in a separate bowl, then beat in the milk and oil until well combined. Add all at once to the dry ingredients and combine until just moistened. Batter will have a few lumps.
2. Use the manufacturer's directions to determine how much batter to use per waffle; use about 1 cup for a standard 7-inch circular waffle. Do not open the iron while the waffle is cooking. Remove with a fork to avoid burning your fingers.

CALORIES 350
FAT 20G
CARBOHYDRATES 38G
PROTEIN 6G

Oat Bran Pancakes with Dried Cranberries

HIGH FIBER ANTIOXIDANTS

SERVES 2

½ cup oat bran
1 cup low-fat buttermilk
½ cup dried cranberries
2 eggs, lightly beaten
2 teaspoons honey
½ teaspoon sea salt
½ cup all-purpose (plain) flour
1 teaspoon baking powder
½ teaspoon baking soda
Nonstick cooking spray

Dried cranberries contain natural, energy-boosting sugars, which are best consumed early in the day or before a workout.

1. In a large mixing bowl, combine oat bran, buttermilk, and cranberries. Stir to combine and let stand for 10 minutes.
2. In a blender or food processor, combine eggs, honey, and salt. Pulse once or twice to combine, then gradually add the salt, flour, baking powder, and baking soda. Pulse once or twice to combine. Add cranberry mixture and pulse again 2 to 3 times to combine all.
3. Spray griddle or heavy skillet with nonstick spray and heat over medium heat. Pour ¼ cup of batter onto heated griddle and cook until bubbles form on top, about 1 minute. Turn and cook until just browned. Serve.

CALORIES 338
FAT 8G
CARBOHYDRATES 61G
PROTEIN 11G

CHAPTER 4
Sandwiches, Wraps, and Pizza

Picture a sandwich . . . it's usually made up of two pieces of carbohydrate-rich bread with some mayo slapped on each slice, then maybe some deli roast beef or ham, a leaf of lettuce, and maybe a slice of tomato. That doesn't sound too appetizing. What if your sandwich could be exciting, filled with fiber-rich and flavorful vegetables, lean roasted proteins, and nutrient-rich fresh herbs? The great news is that it can! There can be much more to your sandwich than just carbs. Keep reading to find out how.

Pan-Grilled Crab Cake Wrap with Avocado

SERVES 6

CALCIUM SUPERFOOD

1 pound canned, pasteurized lump
   crabmeat
4 tablespoons nonfat mayonnaise
Fine zest of 1 lemon
Juice of ½ lemon
1 teaspoon Dijon mustard
1 egg
Sea salt to taste
Black pepper to taste
4 large cabbage leaves
Canola oil for frying
1 ripe avocado, pitted, peeled, and
   sliced

Surprisingly, crab meat is rich in calcium and has other essential minerals, such as selenium, copper, and zinc, which assist with the immune system and brain function.

1. Lightly mix crabmeat, mayonnaise, lemon zest, half the lemon juice, mustard, egg, salt, and pepper. Form into 2½-inch diameter crab cakes.
2. Fill medium quart boiler ¾ full with water. Bring to a boil over high heat and add cabbage leaves. Boil cabbage for 30 seconds, then remove and place in cold water filled with ice (ice bath). Drain well and pat dry with paper towels.
3. In heavy skillet over medium heat, pour oil ⅛-inch deep, or about ½ cup. When oil is hot but not burning, add crab cakes and cook until golden on each side, about 2 minutes.
4. Lay cabbage leaves onto work surface. Using a fork, mash the avocado. Place crab cakes onto cabbage leaves, spread each cake with avocado. Drizzle avocado with remaining lemon juice. Roll cabbage leaf into log (or wrap). Serve.

CALORIES   245
FAT   17G
CARBOHYDRATES   7G
PROTEIN   18G

BURN IT UP

Good fats from avocado are an important part of this recipe. Research has also shown that these tasty fruits help the body absorb nutrients from other foods eaten with them. Just keep in mind that an avocado is high in calories—each fruit contains approximately 300 calories and 35 grams of fat—as you figure out new ways to incorporate it into your lunch, dinner, appetizers, or snacks.

Roasted Vegetable Focaccia

SERVES 4

1 large red bell pepper
1 small eggplant, sliced into ½-inch slices
1 yellow summer squash, sliced into ½-inch slices
½ red onion, sliced into ½-inch slices
1 fennel bulb, sliced into ½-inch slices
1 tablespoon olive oil
1 teaspoon sea salt
1 teaspoon black pepper
2 tablespoons low-fat mayonnaise
2 tablespoons basil pesto
4 4-inch-square focaccia bread, sliced in half
   horizontally
1 cup alfalfa sprouts
1–2 carrots, peeled and cut into 8 sticks

A member of the pea family, alfalfa sprouts contain a vast array of vitamins, including A, B, C, E, and K, and minerals such as calcium, folic acid, magnesium, manganese, phosphorus, potassium, sodium, and zinc. They are a also top source of antioxidants, and consuming them may help prevent heart disease, osteoporosis, and cancer.

1. Preheat broiler to high. Slice red bell pepper in half and place skin side up under broiler. Broil until blackened and charred. Remove peppers from broiler and place in plastic bag to sweat for 10 minutes.

2. Preheat oven to 375°F. Brush eggplant, summer squash, red onion, and fennel with olive oil and sprinkle with the salt and pepper. Place them on a parchment paper lined baking sheet and roast them in the oven for about 35 minutes. Remove and set aside.

3. In a small mixing bowl, whisk together the mayonnaise and pesto. Separately, slice the roasted red bell peppers, do not rinse them.

4. Spread the mayonnaise mixture lightly onto focaccia slices. Top the focaccia with layers of the roasted vegetables, including the roasted bell peppers. Top with the remaining slice of focaccia. Slice the sandwich on the diagonal and serve with fresh carrot sticks.

CALORIES 343
FAT 19G
CARBOHYDRATES 40G
PROTEIN 7G

Pita Pockets with Hummus and Cucumber

SERVES 4

1 cup plain low-fat yogurt
1 teaspoon dry ranch dressing mix
3 garlic cloves, chopped
Pinch sea salt
Pinch black pepper
1 cup canned garbanzo beans, drained
3 tablespoons tahini
Fine zest of ½ lemon
1 tablespoon fresh lemon juice
1 tablespoon olive oil
Small pinch ground cumin
4 whole wheat pita pockets
1 cup shredded carrots
1 cup diced Roma tomatoes
1 cucumber, peeled in "stripes," sliced into
   ½-inch-thick slices
1 cup alfalfa sprouts

Also known as chickpeas, garbanzo beans are a terrific source of zinc, folate, fiber, and protein. They are naturally low in fat and are rich in vitamins and minerals.

1. In small mixing bowl, combine the yogurt and ranch dressing mix. Whisk well and place in the refrigerator.
2. To prepare the hummus, puree the garlic, salt, and pepper in a food processor. Add the garbanzo beans and puree to a paste. Add the tahini, lemon juice, olive oil, and cumin. Process until smooth, scraping down the sides of the bowl.
3. Slice the pita pocket in half. Open the pocket and spread the hummus on one side of the pita pocket. Add carrots, tomatoes, cucumbers, and sprouts. Drizzle with the yogurt sauce and serve 2 pockets per person.

CALORIES 452
FAT 18G
CARBOHYDRATES 63G
PROTEIN 15G

Smoked Turkey Salad on Whole Wheat Croissants with Dried Cranberries

HIGH FIBER PROTEIN

SERVES 2

1 cup diced smoked turkey breast
4 tablespoons low-fat mayonnaise
2 tablespoon diced celery
4 tablespoons dried cranberries
Sea salt to taste
Black pepper to taste
2 whole wheat croissants
2 lettuce leaves such as red or green leaf lettuce

Croissants are traditionally high in fat and heavy in white flour carbs. Luckily, using whole wheat croissants provides fiber, which helps rid the body of fat and toxins. So, if you're going to eat a croissant, make it whole wheat.

1. In a large mixing bowl, mix together the turkey, mayonnaise, celery, and cranberries. Season with salt and pepper as desired.
2. Slice croissants in half horizontally, place lettuce on bottom of each half. Divide turkey salad equally between the two croissants and top with the lettuce. Top with other croissant half and enjoy.

CALORIES 455
FAT 23G
CARBOHYDRATES 39G
PROTEIN 22G

Halibut Soft Tacos with Shredded Cabbage and Jalapeño

SERVES 2

4 small corn tortillas
½ pound firm white fish such as halibut
2 teaspoons olive oil
Pinch sea salt
Pinch black pepper
2 lemon wedges
½ cup cooked corn kernels, canned (okay if drained)
1 small jalapeño, seeded and diced
½ cup shredded purple cabbage
2 teaspoons prepared tartar sauce

Halibut is not only deliciously low in fat, it's also a great source of vitamins B6 and B12, magnesium, phosphorus, and potassium, as well as protein, niacin, and selenium.

1. Wrap tortillas in a paper towel and warm in the microwave for 25 seconds. Remove and wrap in foil to keep warm. Or warm over gas stove using tongs to turn, then wrap in foil to keep warm.
2. Brush the fish with olive oil and sprinkle with salt and pepper. Grill on outdoor grill or grill pan for 4 minutes on each side. Break cooked fish into smaller pieces. Stack two tortillas one on the other. Lay fish down the middle of tortilla. Squeeze lemon over fish. Top with corn, jalapeño, cabbage, and tartar sauce.
3. Fold the tortillas in half, creating a taco, and serve.

CALORIES 341
FAT 11G
CARBOHYDRATES 36G
PROTEIN 28G

BURN IT UP

Halibut contains the amino acid tryptophan, which assists the metabolism by potentially improving stress levels and contributing to the production of niacin, a B vitamin that lowers "bad" and raises "good" cholesterol levels in the blood. Other sources of tryptophan include egg whites, cod, Parmesan cheese, chicken breast, beef tenderloin, and, of course, turkey.

Open-Face English Muffin Turkey Ham Salad

SERVES 4

4 large slices deli turkey ham, diced
¼ cup shredded white Cheddar cheese
1 tablespoon minced red onion
¼ cup diced celery
1 tablespoon chopped fresh Italian flat-leaf
    parsley leaves
Pinch celery seed
1 tablespoon whole-grain spicy mustard
3 tablespoons olive oil
1 egg
4 whole wheat English muffins, split in half

Protein-filled turkey ham is leaner than traditional ham and helps build calorie-burning muscle.

1. Preheat broiler to high heat. Place turkey ham in a food processor with the cheese, onion, celery, parsley, celery seed, mustard, olive oil, and egg. Pulse to combine to a thick spreadable paste.
2. Spread mixture onto muffin halves and place them on aluminum foil–lined broiler pan. Broil until browned and bubbly, about 4 minutes. Serve hot.

CALORIES 332
FAT 18G
CARBOHYDRATES 29G
PROTEIN 16G

Egg Salad with Cayenne on Toasted Bagel

SERVES 4

6 hard-boiled eggs
½ cup nonfat mayonnaise
¼ cup chopped celery
1 teaspoon cayenne pepper
2 tablespoons finely chopped Italian flat-leaf
    parsley
1 tablespoon finely chopped red onion
Sea salt to taste
Black pepper to taste
4 whole wheat bagels, sliced in half crosswise and
    toasted

Even though eggs are high in cholesterol, they still have protein, vitamins, and minerals essential for overall body function. Consume in moderation, but consume for certain!

1. Finely chop the hard-boiled egg whites and yolks and place in a medium mixing bowl. Add mayonnaise, celery, cayenne, parsley, and onion. Mix until well combined. Season with salt and pepper to taste. Chill for one hour.
2. Divide egg salad into 4 equal portions and place on bottom half of toasted bagel. Top with top half of bagel. Serve.

CALORIES 383
FAT 13G
CARBOHYDRATES 44G
PROTEIN 17G

Grilled Chicken on Sourdough with Tarragon Mayonnaise

SERVES 6

SUPERFOOD PROTEIN

3 boneless, skinless chicken breasts
Sea salt to taste
Black pepper to taste
2 tablespoons red wine vinegar
2 tablespoons minced fresh tarragon leaves
3 tablespoons butter
4 teaspoons minced shallots
1 cup nonfat mayonnaise
½ teaspoon white pepper
6 small sourdough rolls, split in half
6 red lettuce leaves, rinsed and dried
6 slices large tomato

Shallots are part of the onion family and are equally nutritious. They contain calcium, phosphorus, potassium, and vitamin A.

1. Pound chicken breasts using meat pounder until they are ½-inch thick. Slice into 1-inch strips. Season with salt and pepper and hold in refrigerator until ready to use.

2. In small saucepan, combine vinegar and tarragon. Bring to a boil. Boil until reduced by half. Set aside. Separately, in a medium skillet or saucepan, melt 2 tablespoons of the butter over medium heat and add shallots. Sauté until shallots are tender, about 3 minutes. Remove from heat and stir in mayonnaise, tarragon mixture, and white pepper. Whisk together well. Using rubber spatula, scrape out mayonnaise mixture into a small mixing bowl. Set aside.

3. Heat remaining tablespoon of butter in nonstick skillet over medium heat. Add chicken strips. Spread 2 tablespoons of mayonnaise mixture over chicken and cook until done, about 8 minutes, turning once.

4. When chicken is done, spread remaining mayonnaise mixture onto each side of roll. Top one side of roll with chicken and the with lettuce and tomato. Finish by combining halves of the roll. Serve.

CALORIES 370
FAT 12G
CARBOHYDRATES 35G
PROTEIN 30G

BURN IT UP

Tomatoes are full of vitamin C, which may lower the risk of heart disease by barring free radicals from building up on artery walls and causing atherosclerosis.

Thai Chicken Wrap with Fresh Gingerroot

SERVES 4

¼ cup olive oil
1 cup chopped boneless, skinless chicken breasts
¼ cup chopped green onions
¼ cup diced peanuts
1 14-ounce package frozen oriental mixed vegetables
⅔ cup nonfat mayonnaise
2 tablespoons low-sodium soy sauce
1 teaspoon crushed red pepper flakes
1 heaping teaspoon freshly minced gingerroot
4 6-inch corn tortillas

A great source of protein, peanuts also contain niacin, which helps convert food into energy and improves in the digestive system, skin, and nerves.

1. In large sauté pan over medium heat, heat olive oil. Add chicken and sauté about 3 minutes. Add onion and sauté until chicken is cooked, about 3 to 5 more minutes. Add peanuts and vegetables and cook until vegetables are heated and tender, about 5–6 minutes.
2. Transfer all to a large mixing bowl, add mayonnaise, soy sauce, red pepper flakes and gingerroot. Mix well.
3. Heat tortillas over open flame on stove top or wrap tortillas in aluminum foil and place in 300°F oven for 30 minutes. Spoon chicken mixture into warm tortilla and roll into a wrap. Serve.

CALORIES 310
FAT 16G
CARBOHYDRATES 24G
PROTEIN 16G

BURN IT UP

The gingerroot found in this recipe is a great metabolism booster! An Australian study found that ginger may increase metabolic rates by as much as 20 percent for a short time after it is eaten. Ginger may also lower cholesterol and has as many antioxidants as a cup of spinach.

Grilled Chicken Breasts with Crisp Bacon and Gouda Cheese

PROTEIN CALCIUM

SERVES 8

4 slices turkey bacon
2 boneless, skinless chicken breasts
¼ cup raspberry jam
8 slices whole wheat bread
8 thin slices gouda cheese
4 1-ounce slices turkey ham
2 tablespoons butter, softened

The turkey bacon, chicken breast, and turkey ham make this recipe a great way to ensure you're getting a maximum lean protein boost that'will see you through the day!

1. In medium skillet over medium heat, cook bacon until crisp. Drain on paper towels and lightly wipe out skillet, leaving a little grease but not too much. Add chicken and cook over medium heat until done, about 5 minutes on each side. Remove chicken and set aside.

2. Spread jam on one side of each slice of bread. Layer half the slices with cheese, then turkey ham. Thinly slice the chicken breasts and place on top of ham. Cover with remaining cheese slices, sprinkle with bacon, and top sandwiches with remaining bread slices.

3. Spread outsides of sandwiches with a little softened butter. Preheat griddle or grill pan over medium heat. Grill sandwiches about 4 minutes per side (or use a Panini maker), turning once, until bread is golden brown and cheese is melted. Serve immediately.

CALORIES 373
FAT 19G
CARBOHYDRATES 27G
PROTEIN 22G

BLT with Mache Greens on Whole Wheat Kaiser Roll

SUPERFOOD

SERVES 4

6 slices lean turkey bacon
4 tablespoons nonfat mayonnaise
4 whole wheat Kaiser rolls
2 large tomatoes, thinly sliced
2 cups mache greens (or substitute mixed greens)
Sea salt to taste
Black pepper to taste

Mache greens, or corn salad, have three times the amount of vitamin C as lettuce. They are also full of beta-carotene, B vitamins, vitamin E, and omega-3 fatty acids, making them the superfood of greens.

In large skillet over medium heat, cook bacon until crisp. Drain on paper towels and coarsely chop. Spread a thin layer of mayonnaise on each side of roll. Place 2 tomato slices on bottom half of roll, top with mache greens and bacon. Place top of roll on top. Serve.

CALORIES 245
FAT 8G
CARBOHYDRATES 35G
PROTEIN 12G

Baked Whole Wheat Pita with Buffalo Mozzarella, Greek Olive, and Roasted Red Bell Peppers

SERVES 6

HIGH FIBER CALCIUM SUPERFOOD

½ cup pitted, chopped Greek olives
½ cup chopped marinated roasted red bell peppers
2 tablespoons red wine vinegar
4 ounces buffalo mozzarella, thinly sliced
3 large whole wheat pita pockets, cut in half
Sea salt to taste
Black pepper to taste

Originating in Italy, buffalo mozzarella is made from the milk of domestic water buffalos and is higher in protein, fat, and minerals than its cow's milk counterpart.

1. Preheat oven to 350°F. In medium bowl, mix together the olives, peppers, and vinegar. Toss to combine. Place the mozzarella into each pita pocket half, add 2–3 heaping tablespoons of olive mixture to pita pocket. Season with salt and pepper, if desired.

2. Line a baking sheet with parchment paper and place filled pita pockets on baking sheet. Bake in oven for about 15 minutes, or until lightly golden. Remove from oven and serve.

CALORIES 58
FAT 1G
CARBOHYDRATES 11G
PROTEIN 4G

BURN IT UP

You may be surprised to learn that olives actually contain iron—a mineral that is crucial to metabolic health. Iron brings oxygen to cells, strengthens the immune system, and is involved in the processes of energy (ATP) generation.

Tuna Melt

SERVES 4

1 6-ounce can tuna in water, drained
1 small Vidalia onion, finely chopped
Fine zest of ½ lemon
Fine zest of ½ orange
¼ cup chopped black olives
½ large tomato, seeded and diced
2 tablespoons chopped Italian flat-leaf parsley
½ cup olive oil
2 tablespoons apple cider vinegar
Sea salt to taste
Black pepper to taste
4 whole wheat pita pockets, cut in half
½ cup crumbled feta cheese

Tuna is high in protein and is a good source of omega-3 fatty acids, which may aid in depression relief, handling anxiety, and improving cardiovascular health.

1. Preheat broiler. In medium mixing bowl, combine tuna, onion, lemon and orange zest, olives, tomato, and parsley. Mix well. Separately, whisk together oil and vinegar until well combined. Pour over tuna mixture and stir to combine. Season with salt and pepper, if desired.
2. Stuff mixture into pita pocket halves and top with feta cheese. Place under broiler and cook until pita is browned and cheese is melting. Serve warm.

CALORIES 535
FAT 35G
CARBOHYDRATES 40G
PROTEIN 20G

Spicy Chicken Ranch Wrap

SERVES 4

4 6-inch corn tortillas
2 cups diced boneless, skinless chicken breasts
1 teaspoon minced garlic
¼ teaspoon ground red hot pepper
⅛ teaspoon ground cumin
½ cup plain, all-purpose flour
¾ cup chicken broth
½ cup nonfat milk
2 tablespoons low-fat sour cream
Sea salt to taste
Black pepper to taste
½ cup light ranch dressing

Ranch dressing doesn't have to be a metabolism killer. This light version still provides flavor without containing heavy fat.

1. Preheat oven to 300°F. Wrap tortillas in aluminum foil and place in oven to warm.
2. In large mixing bowl, combine chicken, garlic, hot pepper, and cumin. Stir to combine and add to a medium saucepan over medium heat. Cook for 15 minutes or until chicken is cooked through. Stir in flour, chicken broth, milk, and sour cream. Season with salt and pepper and cook until thickened, about 5 minutes, stirring frequently.
3. Place chicken mixture in warmed tortillas, drizzle with ranch dressing, and roll into a wrap. Serve.

CALORIES 325
FAT 11G
CARBOHYDRATES 29G
PROTEIN 26G

Three-Cheese Panini with Grilled Vegetables

SERVES 2

¼ cup light Italian dressing
2 baby eggplants, thinly sliced
½ yellow squash, cut in ¼ inch slices
1 red bell pepper, seeded and sliced into ½-inch slices
2 teaspoons grated Parmesan cheese
4 slices ciabatta-style mini loaf, halved crosswise
2 slices Muenster cheese, thinly sliced
2 teaspoons crumbled Gorgonzola cheese
2 tablespoons olive oil

This three-cheese combination provides much-needed calcium for strong bones as well as protein, vitamin A, and phosphorus.

1. Brush eggplant with half the Italian dressing. Heat grill pan over medium heat and grill eggplant, squash and red bell pepper until tender and lightly charred with grill marks. Remove from heat and toss with Parmesan cheese and set aside.
2. Spread both sides of bread with remaining Italian dressing. Top the two bottom halves with the grilled vegetables, top with both Muenster and Gorgonzola cheeses. Top with top half of bread slices.
3. Heat oil in heavy skillet over medium heat. Place sandwiches in skillet and heat until bread is lightly browned, turning once. Serve hot.

CALORIES 459
FAT 24G
CARBOHYDRATES 48G
PROTEIN 23G

Chicken Curry in Pita Pockets

SERVES 4

1 cup nonfat plain yogurt
½ teaspoon curry powder
¼ teaspoon ground mace
1½ cups cooked diced boneless, skinless chicken breasts
½ cup low-fat Italian dressing
1 Granny Smith apple, cored and diced
¼ cup diced celery
¼ cup coarsely chopped almonds, toasted
4 tablespoons golden raisins
1 small ripe avocado, pitted, peeled, and diced
4 whole wheat pita breads, cut in half
8 red or green lettuce leaves, rinsed and dried

Almonds are good for you! They are nearly carbohydrate free and are rich in vitamin E and the monounsaturated fat responsible for lowering LDL (or 'bad') cholesterol.

1. In a small bowl, stir the yogurt until smooth and creamy. Add the curry powder and mace and mix well. Cover and refrigerate for 4 hours or up to 24 hours.
2. Meanwhile, in a medium mixing bowl, combine the chicken and Italian dressing. Cover and marinate in the refrigerator for 4 hours or up to 24 hours.
3. Add the apple, celery, almonds, and raisins to the chicken. Stir the curry yogurt dressing into the chicken mixture. Add the avocado and gently fold into chicken mixture.

4. Prepare pita pockets by lining pita with 1 lettuce leaf, spoon in chicken mixture, dividing evenly between pita pockets. Serve.

CALORIES 507
FAT 14G
CARBOHYDRATES 58G
PROTEIN 24G

Grilled Chicken Breasts with Caramelized Onions on Whole Wheat Bun

PROTEIN HIGH FIBER

SERVES 4

¼ cup olive oil, plus 1 tablespoon if needed
2 cloves fresh garlic, chopped
2 red onions, thinly sliced
Sea salt to taste
Black pepper to taste
¼ cup chopped fresh Italian flat-leaf parsley leaves
Pinch cayenne pepper
Pinch sugar
4 boneless, skinless chicken breasts
4 whole wheat hamburger buns

Believe it or not, onions are one of the best sources for minerals such as potassium and manganese, are high in fiber, and are packed with vitamins B6 and C. They are also cholesterol free and naturally low in fat and calories. Overall, onions are one of the best foods you can consume!

1. In heavy skillet, heat 1 tablespoon oil over medium heat. Add garlic and sauté about 1 minute. Add onions and season with salt and pepper. Sauté until tender, about 5 minutes, and add parsley, cayenne, and sugar. Reduce heat to low and sauté an additional 10 minutes, or until onion is turning slightly brown.

2. While onions are sautéing, lightly coat each chicken breast with olive oil, then season with salt and pepper. Heat grill pan or grill to medium heat. Add 1 tablespoon of oil. When hot but not smoking, add chicken and grill about 10 minutes on each side or until cooked through.

3. To serve, place chicken breasts on bun and top with caramelized onion. If desired, spread each bun half with low-fat mayonnaise for added flavor.

CALORIES 436
FAT 11G
CARBOHYDRATES 49G
PROTEIN 36G

Seared Ahi on Whole Wheat with Wasabi Mayonnaise

SERVES 2

SPICY PROTEIN SUPERFOOD

8 ounces fresh ahi tuna steak
Sea salt to taste
Black pepper to taste
10 long Asian green beans
¼ cup nonfat mayonnaise
1 teaspoon wasabi powder
4 slices tomato, thinly sliced
2 mini whole wheat bread loaves, split
    in half and then sliced crosswise

Green beans are high in vitamins A and C and also provide fiber. Metabolism-boosting spices pepper and wasabi top off this high-protein, low-fat ahi tuna delight.

1. Lightly season the tuna with salt and pepper. Heat grill pan or heavy skillet over medium heat. Add tuna and sear about 2–3 minutes on each side. Remove from heat and set aside.
2. Fill medium quart boiler ¾ full with water and bring to a boil over high heat. Add a pinch of salt. Add beans and boil for 30 seconds. Remove beans from water, drain, and chop into ½-inch pieces. Separately, whisk together mayonnaise and wasabi.
3. Slice tuna thinly against grain. Place on bottom half of bread slices. Top with tomato and beans. Spoon ½ of mayonnaise mixture on each sandwich. Top with remaining bread slice. Serve.

CALORIES 571
FAT 30G
CARBOHYDRATES 41G
PROTEIN 35G

BURN IT UP

Wasabi, also known as Japanese horseradish, helps boost the metabolism by stimulating digestion, especially that of fatty foods. The spice comes from the glucosinolates in the root, which has an extremely strong flavor and may increase the liver's ability to process toxins and suppress the growth of cancer cells.

Grilled Pork on Corn Muffin with Mango Salsa

SERVES 4

1 package corn muffin mix
1 pound pork tenderloin, trimmed
2 tablespoons soy sauce
Sea salt to taste
Black pepper to taste
2 tablespoons peanut oil
½ cup prepared mango salsa

Pork is leaner than most beef products and is a healthy alternative to chicken and turkey. It is also rich in minerals such as iron, magnesium, and phosphorus, which are essential to body function.

1. Follow directions on corn muffin mix package. Once baked, cut into 8 2-inch squares.
2. Sprinkle the pork tenderloins with soy sauce, salt, and pepper. Separately, heat heavy skillet with peanut oil. Sauté the pork for 8 minutes per side or until cooked through, turning frequently. When done, let pork rest for 10 minutes, then slice thinly on the diagonal.
3. Place two pieces of corn bread on serving plates. Stack 3 slices of pork on each corn bread slice. Top with mango salsa. Serve.

CALORIES 371
FAT 17G
CARBOHYDRATES 16G
PROTEIN 39G

Pizza of Black Olives, Roasted Peppers, and Mozzarella

SERVES 6

2 pounds prepared pizza dough
1 tablespoon cornmeal
½ cup pizza sauce
½ cup shredded mozzarella cheese
¼ cup sliced black olives
½ cup diced marinated roasted red bell peppers

Pizza sauce is made from tomatoes—one of the best foods you can enjoy! They are filled with vitamins and minerals, and contain lycopene, which is known to aid in the prevention of cancer.

Preheat oven to 375°F. Roll pizza dough into a 12-inch round pizza. Transfer to cornmeal-dusted baking sheet or pizza stone. Spoon pizza sauce over dough. Sprinkle with mozzarella cheese. Top with black olives and roasted peppers. Bake in oven for 15–20 minutes. Serve hot.

CALORIES 489
FAT 22G
CARBOHYDRATES 63G
PROTEIN 16G

Grilled Radicchio Pizza with Arugula Greens

SERVES 4

½ package yeast
3 tablespoons warm water
½ teaspoon sugar
1¼ cups whole wheat flour, plus more for kneading
1 tablespoon olive oil
¼ cup cool water
¼ teaspoon sea salt
3 tablespoons butter
½ white or yellow onion, thinly sliced
1 head radicchio lettuce
1 cup arugula

Richly colored radicchio and arugula are high in fiber and loaded with vitamins like A, C, and K, and minerals like riboflavin and potassium.

1. In a medium mixing bowl, combine yeast with warm water, sugar, and ¼ cup of flour. Stir gently to combine and let rest 10 minutes. Add olive oil, cool water, salt, and ½ cup flour. Stir using wooden spoon. Add remaining flour and mix to form dough.

2. Knead dough on a floured board for 5 minutes. Adding flour as needed to prevent sticking. Coat inside of medium to large mixing bowl with oil. Place kneaded dough in the oiled bowl, cover, and let dough rise for 1 hour in a warm place. Punch down dough and roll into a tight ball. Cover again, and let rise again for 1 hour.

3. While the dough is rising, melt the butter in a large skillet over medium low heat. Add onion and sauté until tender, about 10 minutes. Season with salt and pepper. Separately, quarter the radicchio and brush with olive oil. Add to skillet with onion and grill about 3 minutes. Remove from pan and coarsely chop.

4. Preheat oven to 450°F. Roll and stretch dough into a 12-inch round on a lightly floured surface. Place the dough onto a cornmeal-dusted baking sheet or pizza stone. Spread the cooked onions and radicchio onto the pizza dough. Bake for 15 minutes or until crisp. Top with arugula and slice into wedges. Serve warm.

CALORIES 265
FAT 13G
CARBOHYDRATES 33G
PROTEIN 5G

BURN IT UP

Selenium—found in the onion used in this recipe—is a very powerful antioxidant that benefits the body by preventing oxidation of fat. It also works with glutathione peroxidase to keep metabolism-busting free radicals under control. In Japan, where people traditionally consume about 500 micrograms of selenium a day, the cancer rate is nearly five times lower than in countries where daily selenium intake is less.

CHAPTER 5
Salads

You may not believe it, but there's more to salad than just greens. Sure, mixed greens or red leaf lettuce are nutritious, but think of the other possibilities. There's no hard-and-fast rule to salads, so mix it up. Have fun. Add some lean protein, or kick it up with interesting spices and fresh herbs. You'll be surprised at how your ordinary salad can taste great and send your metabolism through the roof!

Grilled Chicken Salad with Honey Dijon Vinaigrette

SERVES 2

½ tablespoon olive oil
4 ounces boneless, skinless chicken breasts, cubed
4 cups romaine lettuce
2 ounces chopped deli ham
2 large plum tomatoes, seeded and chopped
½ cup coarsely chopped shiitake mushrooms
2 tablespoons low-fat shredded Swiss cheese
2 tablespoons fat-free honey Dijon vinaigrette

Naturally low in calories, shiitake mushrooms are one of the most nutritious mushrooms you can eat. They are rich in iron and contain lentinan, which may exhibit antitumor effects.

1. In small skillet or on grill pan, heat oil over medium heat and add chicken. Cook until done, about 4–5 minutes. Remove from heat.
2. In large mixing bowl, toss together cooked chicken, romaine, ham, tomatoes, mushrooms, cheese, and dressing. Divide into 2 portions and serve.

CALORIES 381
FAT 5G
CARBOHYDRATES 56G
PROTEIN 35G

Mixed Greens with Grilled Chicken, Mango, and Pine Nuts

SERVES 2

¼ cup extra-virgin olive oil
Fine zest of ½ orange
Fine zest of ½ lemon
1 teaspoon fresh orange juice
1 teaspoon fresh lemon juice
2 tablespoons balsamic vinegar
4 cups mixed greens
6 ounces cooked boneless, skinless chicken breasts, cubed
2 large plum tomatoes, seeded and chopped
1 mango, diced
1 tablespoon toasted pine nuts
2 tablespoons crumbled low-fat feta cheese

Pine nuts are high in thiamine, niacin, and protein. They are one of the primary ingredients in pesto sauce.

In a large mixing bowl, whisk together the oil, orange and lemon zest, orange and lemon juice, and vinegar. Whisk well. Add in the lettuce, chicken, tomatoes, mangos, pine nuts, and cheese. Toss to coat. Divide into 2 equal portions and serve.

CALORIES 181
FAT 6G
CARBOHYDRATES 9G
PROTEIN 24G

Fresh Spinach Salad with Broiled Salmon

SUPERFOOD PROTEIN

SERVES 2

1 tablespoon olive oil
8 ounces salmon fillet
4 cups fresh spinach leaves, stems trimmed
1 cup red seedless grapes, sliced in half
1 tablespoon whole roasted almonds
2 tablespoons dried cranberries
3 tablespoons fat-free Italian dressing

Salmon is not only healthy, but it is also a versatile fish that tastes delicious whether it's grilled, poached, broiled, baked, and smoked.

1. Preheat broiler to high heat. Coat salmon with olive oil. Place on aluminum foil and place under broiler for 4 minutes. Turn over and cook an additional 4 minutes, or until done. Remove and set aside.
2. Toss together spinach, grapes, almonds, cranberries, and dressing. Divide into 2 equal portions and top with 4 ounces each of salmon. Serve.

CALORIES 211
FAT 7G
CARBOHYDRATES 5G
PROTEIN 30G

Grilled Chicken on Asian Greens with Sesame Ginger Dressing

HIGH FIBER SUPERFOOD

SERVES 2

2 cups Napa (Chinese) cabbage, shredded
4 cups mixed greens
6 ounces grilled boneless, skinless chicken
   breasts, cubed
2 large or 3 small Roma tomatoes, seeded and
   diced
2 cups alfalfa sprouts
½ cup shredded carrots
2 teaspoons sesame seeds
¼ cup mandarin oranges
¼ cup fat free sesame ginger dressing

Chinese cabbage, also called Napa cabbage, is high in vitamin C, folate, and calcium.

1. In a large mixing bowl, combine cabbage, greens, chicken, tomato, sprouts, carrots, sesame seeds, and oranges. Toss well to combine.
2. Pour dressing over salad mixture and toss well to coat.

CALORIES 187
FAT 3G
CARBOHYDRATES 16G
PROTEIN 23G

Marinated Soy Steak over Mixed Greens with Dijon Vinaigrette

SERVES 4

½ cup low-sodium soy sauce

1 tablespoon minced fresh gingerroot

2 tablespoons honey

12 ounces lean steak, sliced into ½-inch strips

¼ cup extra-virgin olive oil

¼ cup apple cider vinegar

2 tablespoons lemon juice

2 cloves garlic, minced

1 tablespoon Dijon mustard

¼ cup Parmesan cheese, grated

Sea salt and black pepper to taste

10 to 12 ounces mixed greens, washed and dried

Steak is high in protein and contains essential amino acids, zinc, B vitamins, selenium, and iron, making it the ideal food for those looking to develop and tone their muscles.

1. In medium mixing bowl, whisk together soy sauce, ginger, and honey. Whisk well. Place steak in bowl or dish. Pour soy sauce mixture over. Cover and refrigerate for 1–2 hours. Remove from refrigerator. Heat heavy skillet over medium heat. Add marinated steak and cook until done, about 7 minutes. Remove from heat and set aside.

2. In separate large mixing bowl, whisk together oil, vinegar, lemon juice, garlic, and mustard. Whisk well to combine. Add greens and toss to coat.

3. Divide salad among 4 serving plates. Top with steak, parmesan cheese, and serve.

CALORIES 216

FAT 14G

CARBOHYDRATES 2G

PROTEIN 12G

BURN IT UP

A high metabolism requires a diet with a good balance of protein, fat, carbs, vitamins, minerals, and fiber. And you can always add spice to your meals to gain a metabolic bonus. So let yourself enjoy everything this recipe has to offer, including the protein-filled steak, vitamin C–filled citrus, spicy pepper, calcium-rich cheese, and high-fiber mixed greens.

Caesar Salad with Grilled Steak

SERVES 2

4 cups romaine lettuce, washed and dried
4 tablespoons nonfat Caesar salad dressing
4 ounces grilled lean steak such as sirloin
1 tablespoon reduced-fat grated Parmesan
   cheese

Caesar salad dressing can often be high in fat due to the oil and the traditional use of raw eggs. Try several low and nonfat versions to find the flavor you like best.

In large mixing bowl, toss together lettuce and dressing. Divide between two serving plates. Top with steak and sprinkle with cheese.

CALORIES 282
FAT 10G
CARBOHYDRATES 24G
PROTEIN 14G

Taco Salad with Beef, Black Beans, and Jalapeño

SERVES 2

6 ounces 95% lean ground beef
½ white onion, diced
1 ear of white or yellow corn, kernels removed
Fine zest of one lime
Pinch sea salt and black pepper
4 cups chopped romaine lettuce leaves
2 Roma tomatoes, seeded and diced
½ can black beans, rinsed
2 tablespoons freshly chopped cilantro leaves
¼ cup low-fat or nonfat shredded Cheddar
   cheese
1–2 jalapeño peppers, sliced

Taco salads are an easy way to get all the metabolism boosting nutrients you need. Even better, you can customize them with your favorite lettuce, beans, cheese, and peppers.

1. In heavy skillet over medium heat, add beef and onion and cook until beef is browned, about 5 minutes. Drain off any excess grease, return to pan over low heat, and add corn and lime zest. Season to taste with salt and pepper. Stir to combine.
2. Layer lettuce on serving plate in 2 equal portions. Top with beef mixture, then add tomatoes, black beans, and cilantro. Finish with cheese and top with sliced jalapeños. Serve.

CALORIES 233
FAT 2G
CARBOHYDRATES 34G
PROTEIN 29G

Garden Salad with Mixed Greens, Red Bell Peppers, and Dried Cranberries

SERVES 4

4 cups romaine lettuce

4 cups fresh spinach leaves

½ cup diced red bell pepper, about 1 pepper

1 red onion, diced

4 Roma tomatoes, seeded and chopped

1 cucumber, seeded and chopped

¼ cup dried cranberries

1½ cups fresh broccoli florets

¼ cup fresh or frozen English peas

¼ cup plus 2 tablespoons shredded fresh carrots

½ cup shredded nonfat Cheddar cheese

¼ cup balsamic vinegar

Fine zest of ½ lemon

1 teaspoon fresh lemon juice

Pinch sea salt

Pinch black pepper

Dark, leafy vegetables such as spinach are high in vitamins A and E, which may help prevent cancer and protect your body's cells. When making your garden salad, avoid using the traditional iceberg lettuce, as it is low in nutritional value.

1. In large mixing bowl, toss together the romaine, spinach, red bell pepper, red onion, tomatoes, cucumber, cranberries, broccoli, peas, carrots, and cheese. Toss well to combine.

2. In a small mixing bowl, whisk together vinegar, lemon zest, juice, salt, and pepper. Whisk well, then pour over prepared salad. Toss to coat. Serve immediately.

CALORIES 87

FAT 1G

CARBOHYDRATES 16G

PROTEIN 6G

BURN IT UP

Romaine lettuce, spinach, tomatoes, and cucumbers have a high water content that flushes toxins out of your body. The metabolism-boosting fiber found in the spinach, red bell pepper, onion, broccoli, and peas helps move things along as well.

Mandarin Oranges with Candied Pecans on Red and Green Leaf Lettuce

`HIGH FIBER` `SUPERFOOD`

SERVES 4

4 cups red leaf lettuce, washed and dried
4 cups green leaf lettuce, washed and dried
¼ cup diced red onions
¼ cup plus 2 tablespoons mandarin oranges
¼ cup candied pecans, whole
½ cup crumbled reduced-fat feta cheese
¼ cup fat-free raspberry vinaigrette

Pecans are a good source of protein and healthy, unsaturated fats.

In large mixing bowl, toss together red and green leaf lettuce leaves with onion, oranges, pecans, and cheese. Pour vinaigrette over and toss to coat. Serve in 4 equal portions for lunch or dinner.

`CALORIES` 59
`FAT` 4G
`CARBOHYDRATES` 13G
`PROTEIN` 2G

Chinese Chicken Salad

`PROTEIN`

SERVES 4

¼ cup sugar
6 tablespoons rice vinegar
Pinch sea salt and black pepper
½ cup plus 1 tablespoon peanut oil
¼ cup sliced almonds
¼ cup sesame seeds
6 green onions, chopped
1 head cabbage, grated or minced
1½ cups cooked chicken breast, chopped
1 package ramen noodles, broken

Peanut oil is naturally low in saturated fat and high in polyunsaturated and monoun-saturated fats that help lower cholesterol levels. Its high smoke point also makes it a good oil to cook with.

1. In a small mixing bowl, combine sugar, vinegar, salt, pepper, and ½ cup peanut oil. Whisk together and set aside.
2. Heat remaining tablespoon of oil on large skillet over medium heat. Add almonds and sesame seeds. Sauté until lightly browned, about 2 minutes. Add the onions and cabbage. Sauté for 5 minutes, or until tender. Add the chicken, sauté for 1 minute. Add the noodles and stir to combine. Add vinegar mixture, tossing well to coat. Serve.

`CALORIES` 535
`FAT` 40G
`CARBOHYDRATES` 23G
`PROTEIN` 21G

Chopped Grilled Vegetable Salad

SERVES 4

1 cup chopped red bell peppers
1 red onion, chopped
1 cup chopped fresh asparagus
1 cup chopped yellow squash
1 cup sliced cremini or porcini mushrooms
1 head romaine lettuce, washed, dried, and
    roughly chopped
¼ cup crumbled nonfat feta cheese
¼ cup toasted pine nuts
¼ cup olive oil
¼ cup balsamic vinegar
Sea salt to taste
Black pepper to taste

Grilling gives ingredients a robust flavor you can't get with other methods of cooking. Plus, the vegetables retain their nutrients, something that doesn't happen if they are boiled or fried.

1. Heat grill or grill pan to medium heat. Add bell peppers, onion, asparagus, squash, and mushrooms. Grill until lightly charred and just tender. Remove from heat.
2. In large mixing bowl, toss together grilled vegetables, lettuce, feta, and pine nuts. Toss to combine.
3. Separately, in small mixing bowl, whisk together oil, vinegar, pinch of salt, and pinch of pepper. Whisk well and pour over salad mixture. Toss to coat. Serve in 4 equal portions.

CALORIES 75
FAT 2G
CARBOHYDRATES 12G
PROTEIN 5G

Mixed Greens with Balsamic Vinaigrette and Fresh Pears

SERVES 4

¼ cup balsamic vinegar
¼ cup extra-virgin olive oil
Sea salt and black pepper to taste
6 cups mixed greens
1 red bell pepper, seeded and diced
1 medium red onion, diced
1 large tomato, diced
1 cucumber, diced
1 Bartlett pear, cored and diced

Pears go well with many foods, including pork, chicken, and citrus fruits like oranges. They are packed full of vitamins and minerals and are low in calories.

In large mixing bowl, whisk together vinegar, oil, salt, and pepper. Add in remaining ingredients and toss well to coat.

CALORIES 143
FAT 10G
CARBOHYDRATES 12G
PROTEIN 1G

BBQ Chicken Salad

HIGH FIBER

4 cups chopped romaine lettuce

2 Roma tomatoes, seeded and diced

1 cucumber, peeled, seeded, and diced

1 red bell pepper, seeded and diced

¼ cup shredded nonfat Cheddar cheese

¼ cup garbanzo beans

¼ cup fresh or frozen English peas

¼ cup fresh or canned corn kernels

6 ounces chopped cooked boneless, skinless chicken breasts

¼ cup barbeque sauce

BBQ sauce can often be laden with sugar and preservatives. Try to look for all-natural BBQ sauces that use natural sugars such as honey and natural fruit juice such as orange and lemon.

1. In large mixing bowl, toss together lettuce, tomatoes, cucumber, bell pepper, cheese, garbanzo beans, peas, and corn.
2. Separately, in medium mixing bowl, toss together chicken and barbeque sauce. Add chicken mixture to lettuce mixture and toss to combine. Serve in two equal portions.

CALORIES 198

FAT 3G

CARBOHYDRATES 17G

PROTEIN 26G

BURN IT UP

Fiber-filled lettuce, tomatoes, and cucumbers have a high water content that helps you stay hydrated and feeling full. Water makes up 55–75 percent of your body, and drinking just a pint can cause your metabolism to rev up and burn around 25 calories

Mixed Greens with Grapefruit, Pomegranate, and Parmesan

SERVES 4

> 7 cups mixed greens
> 2 ruby red grapefruits, supreme (pith removed)
> 1 fresh pomegranate, cut in quarters, berries removed
> 2 tablespoons balsamic vinegar
> 4 ounces grated Parmesan cheese

Grapefruit may help lower cholesterol and is a natural source of vitamin C and the antioxidant lycopene.

In mixing bowl, toss together greens, grapefruits, pomegranate, and vinegar, tossing well to coat. Divide onto 4 serving plates, sprinkle with Parmesan cheese and serve.

CALORIES 175
FAT 19G
CARBOHYDRATES 1G
PROTEIN 2G

Hearts of Romaine with Balsamic Vinegar and Shallots

SERVES 4

> ¼ cup cooked chickpeas
> 2 cloves garlic, minced
> 1 shallot, minced
> ¼ bunch fresh Italian flat-leaf parsley, chopped
> ¼ cup extra-virgin olive oil
> ½ cup balsamic vinegar
> Sea salt and black pepper to taste
> 6 cups coarsely chopped romaine hearts

Extra-virgin olive oil is a flavorful oil used frequently in cooking and salad dressings. It is high in monounsaturated fats that have been linked to a reduction in coronary heart disease.

1. In a food processor, puree the chickpeas. Add the garlic, shallot, and parsley; pulse until well blended. While processing, drizzle in olive oil and vinegar. Process until mixture thickens. Season to taste with salt and pepper.
2. In mixing bowl, place greens and toss with chickpea puree. Toss well to coat and serve.

CALORIES 101
FAT 11G
CARBOHYDRATES 5G
PROTEIN 1G

Roasted Beet Salad with Arugula, Toasted Pine Nuts, and Black Currants

ANTIOXIDANTS SUPERFOOD

SERVES 6

3 large beets, cleaned but unpeeled
2 tablespoons olive oil
1 teaspoon sea salt
¼ cup balsamic vinegar
3 cups arugula greens
¼ cup black currants
1 teaspoon toasted pine nuts
Sea salt to taste
Black pepper to taste

Beets are a tasty, healthy ingredient. Enjoy them roasted or grilled for maximum flavor and nutritional value.

1. Preheat oven to 350°F. Toss the beets in the oil. Sprinkle the teaspoon of salt on the beets and toss. Place on parchment paper–lined baking sheet and roast in oven for about 1½ hours, until beets are fork tender.
2. While the beets are roasting, heat the balsamic in a large sauté pan over medium heat. Add the greens and currants. Heat until greens are just wilted and currants are slightly plump.
3. Remove beets from oven, peel, and slice thinly. Toss together the beets, greens mixture, and pine nuts. Season with salt and pepper and serve.

CALORIES 137
FAT 7G
CARBOHYDRATES 6G
PROTEIN 2G

Orzo Salad with Red Bell Pepper and Fresh Herbs

HIGH FIBER

SERVES 4

¼ cup extra-virgin olive oil
2 cups fresh basil leaves, finely chopped
½ cup fresh Italian flat-leaf parsley, finely chopped
4 cloves garlic, finely chopped
Sea salt to taste
1 pound orzo pasta, cooked al dente and drained thoroughly
1 red bell pepper, seeded and diced
½ red onion, finely chopped

Orzo is a healthy grain made from wheat semolina flour and is actually categorized as a pasta. Rich in fiber, this nontraditional pasta helps with digestion.

1. In mixing bowl, whisk together oil, basil, parsley, garlic, and salt. Add the orzo, red pepper, and red onion.
2. Toss well to combine and serve.

CALORIES 188
FAT 10G
CARBOHYDRATES 20G
PROTEIN 3G

Salad of Green Beans, Bacon, and Warm Gorgonzola Dressing

HIGH FIBER PROTEIN CALCIUM

SERVES 4

1 large head romaine lettuce, chopped
1 pound fresh green beans, trimmed, rinsed, and blanched
2 slices bacon, cooked crisp and chopped
4 ounces Gorgonzola cheese, crumbled
2 tablespoons red wine vinegar
2 tablespoons honey

Gorgonzola cheese is a good source of calcium, protein, and vitamin A and adds a distinct flavor to this recipe that your taste buds will love.

1. Divide lettuce equally among 4 salad plates. Arrange beans on top. Sprinkle bacon over each.
2. In separate small mixing bowl, whisk together Gorgonzola, vinegar, and honey. Mix well. Transfer to small quart boiler and heat over low heat until cheese is melted, stirring occasionally. If you are short on time, you can heat in microwave oven.
3. Pour cheese equally over prepared salads. Serve immediately.

CALORIES 231
FAT 13G
CARBOHYDRATES 10G
PROTEIN 9G

Salad of Tomatillos and Tomatoes with Salsa Aioli

ANTIOXIDANTS SUPERFOOD

SERVES 4

2 cups mixed greens
4 tomatillos, peeled and chopped
2 large tomatoes, seeded and diced
½ red onion, thinly sliced
½ cup fresh mild tomato salsa
¼ cup nonfat mayonnaise
Fine zest of ½ lemon
Black pepper to taste

Tomatillos are related to the tomato family and therefore contain vitamins A and C. Among their other benefits, these vitamins are good for your vision, immune system, and skin.

1. Divide greens equally among 4 serving plates. In medium mixing bowl, combine tomatillos, tomatoes, and onion. Toss to combine and divide equally among the four salads.
2. In medium mixing bowl, whisk together the salsa, mayonnaise, lemon zest, and pepper. Whisk well to combine. Spoon over the salads and serve.

CALORIES 153
FAT 12G
CARBOHYDRATES 12G
PROTEIN 2G

Salad of Apples, Pine Nuts, and Brown Rice with Curry

SERVES 4

¼ cup nonfat mayonnaise
1 teaspoon curry powder
1 tablespoon fresh lemon juice
2 Granny Smith apples, peeled, cored, and diced
½ red onion, diced
2 cups cooked brown rice, chilled and fluffed with fork
½ cup toasted pine nuts

There is evidence that apples reduce the risk of colon cancer, prostate cancer, and lung cancer. Brown rice is a good source of B vitamins and is high in fiber and protein, giving your body the metabolic balance it needs in this well-rounded meal.

1. Whisk together the mayonnaise, curry powder, and lemon juice in a medium mixing bowl. Add in apples, onion, rice, and nuts. Toss well to combine.
2. Serve at room temperature or chilled.

CALORIES 354
FAT 27G
CARBOHYDRATES 26G
PROTEIN 5G

Lobster Salad of Arugula and Roasted Peanuts

PROTEIN SPICY ANTIOXIDANTS

SERVES 4

1 cup nonfat mayonnaise
Juice of ½ lime
1 teaspoon curry powder
1 teaspoon prepared Dijon mustard
Sea salt to taste
Black pepper to taste
1½ tablespoons unsweetened pineapple juice
1 pound cooked lobster meat, removed from the shell, coarsely chopped
2 cups arugula greens

Pineapples are rich in a special enzyme called bromelain that breaks down proteins making their juice perfect for marinades, tenderizing meats, and helping digest rich proteins such as lobster, steak, and chicken.

1. In a large mixing bowl, combine mayo, lime juice, curry, Dijon, pinch salt, pinch pepper, pineapple juice, and lobster.
2. Toss with arugula and serve.

CALORIES 640
FAT 56G
CARBOHYDRATES 10G
PROTEIN 28G

Romaine Lettuce with Coriander and Steamed Mussels

SERVES 6

2 pounds fresh mussels, drained and trimmed
Zest of 1 lemon
Juice of 1 lemon
¼ cup extra-virgin olive oil
1 teaspoon chopped fresh oregano leaves
2 cloves garlic, minced
1 teaspoon coriander seeds
Sea salt taste
Black pepper to taste
1 egg
2 large tomatoes, seeded and diced
½ bunch green onions (about 5), chopped
2 cups fresh romaine lettuce, chopped
2 tablespoons capers, drained
4 large sprigs Italian flat-leaf parsley, for garnish

Mussels are easy to steam, but make sure they are live before cooking, as they can become toxic soon after dying. Check for live mussels by tapping on the shell; if the mussel closes right away, it is still alive. Discard if it does not close,.

1. To steam mussels: place water in bottom of double boiler about 1½ inches deep. Place mussels in steamer basket and place in double boiler. Cover with lid and place on stove on high heat. Steam until mussels open, about 5–10 minutes. Discard any unopened mussels.
2. In a food processor or blender, puree the lemon zest, lemon juice, olive oil, oregano, garlic, coriander, salt, pepper, and egg. Pour into a large bowl. Add in steamed mussels, tomatoes, and green onions.
3. Chill or serve at room temperature over the greens with capers sprinkled on top. Finish with a sprig of parsley.

CALORIES 383
FAT 47G
CARBOHYDRATES 22G
PROTEIN 44G

BURN IT UP

Mussels are a definitive metabolism booster. They are very high in protein and contain high levels of selenium, vitamin B12, zinc, and folate. The digestion of these mineral-rich mussels is aided by the fiber found in the romaine lettuce, tomatoes, and capers.

Cucumber Salad with Shrimp and Fresh Dill

PROTEIN

SERVES 4

1 tablespoon chopped fresh dill leaves
½ cup nonfat mayonnaise
¼ cup nonfat vanilla yogurt
Juice of 1 lemon
Sea salt to taste
Black pepper to taste
Red pepper flakes to taste
1 teaspoon sweet Hungarian paprika
1 teaspoon Worcestershire sauce
1 English cucumber, diced
1 pound cooked bay shrimp

Shrimp has high levels of calcium, iodine, and protein. It's naturally low in carbs, but unfortunately is a significant source of cholesterol. Enjoy shrimp in moderation.

1. In a large mixing bowl, combine the dill, mayonnaise, yogurt, lemon juice, salt, black pepper, red pepper, paprika, and Worcestershire sauce. Mix until well combined. Add the cucumber and shrimp and stir to coat.
2. Chill mixture for 1 hour or overnight. Serve chilled with crackers or your favorite mixed greens.

CALORIES 329
FAT 24G
CARBOHYDRATES 4G
PROTEIN 25G

Whole Wheat Pasta Salad with Chipotle Peppers

SUPERFOOD

SERVES 4

¼ cup extra-virgin olive oil
4 cloves garlic, minced
1 red onion, finely chopped
4 jalapeño peppers, seeded and minced
2 chipotle peppers, minced
½ cup red wine vinegar
¼ cup nonfat mayonnaise
Sea salt to taste
Black pepper to taste
½ pound whole wheat pasta, cooked as directed
4 cups mixed greens

Jalapeño peppers are low in calories and fat, but rich in vitamins A, B6, C, and K, as well as minerals such as riboflavin, iron, magnesium, potassium, and copper.

1. In medium saucepan over medium heat, heat olive oil and add in garlic, onion, and peppers. Sauté until softened, about 5 minutes. Stir in vinegar, mayonnaise, salt, and pepper until just combined and heated through. Add the pasta and mix well.
2. Divide greens equally among serving plates. Divide pasta mixture equally between plates and place on top of greens. Serve.

CALORIES 316
FAT 16G
CARBOHYDRATES 30G
PROTEIN 8G

Radicchio Salad with Cucumber, Gorgonzola, and Toasted Walnuts

CALCIUM

1 cup apple cider vinegar
½ cup nonfat mayonnaise
1 pinch sugar
Sea salt to taste
Black pepper to taste
1 large cucumber, thinly sliced
2 heads radicchio, shredded
½ cup crumbled Gorgonzola cheese
1 tablespoon chopped fresh cilantro
    leaves
½ cup toasted walnuts

Gorgonzola is not only naturally rich in calcium, but it is also a great source of protein and vitamin A.

1. In medium mixing bowl, whisk together vinegar, mayonnaise, sugar, salt, and pepper. Whisk well to combine. Add in cucumbers and toss to coat. Refrigerate for 2 hours.
2. When ready to serve, place radicchio onto 4 separate serving plates. Spoon cucumber mixture over radicchio. Top with Gorgonzola cheese, cilantro, and walnuts. Serve.

CALORIES 358
FAT 36G
CARBOHYDRATES 7G
PROTEIN 6G

BURN IT UP

Walnuts are filled with good fats, protein, and essential vitamins and minerals just waiting to boost your metabolism. The walnut is the only nut that provides significant amounts of alpha-linolenic acid, one of the three omega-3 fatty acids. Because your body cannot produce this acid, it needs to be provided daily from other sources. Seven walnuts can fulfill your daily need for these essential fatty acids.

CHAPTER 6
Soups

Soups are often treated like an afterthought; people tend to think of them when they're not that hungry or if they're not sure what else to have. However, soup can be a super delicious metabolism-boosting meal all on its own! The recipes in this chapter are all packed with essential vitamins, minerals, and other metabolism-boosting ingredients that will help you get the most out of your meal. Enjoy!

Egg Drop Soup

SERVES 6

1 tablespoon olive oil
1 yellow onion, diced
1 shallot, diced
6 cloves garlic, minced
2 quarts low-sodium chicken broth
1 bay leaf
½ bunch fresh Italian flat-leaf parsley, leaves
  chopped, stems discarded
3 sprigs thyme, leaves chopped, stems discarded
1 pound fresh spinach leaves, chopped
2 whole eggs
4 egg whites
Black pepper to taste
Sea salt to taste
2 ounces grated Parmesan cheese

Egg drop soup is not hard to make and, more importantly, is good for you! Eggs provide much-needed protein, riboflavin, and selenium and make any dish delicious.

1. Heat oil in large stockpot or quart boiler over medium heat. Add onion, shallot, and garlic. Sauté until flavorful and slightly tender, about 5 minutes. Add the broth, bay leaf, parsley, and thyme. Simmer for 40 minutes.
2. Remove the bay leaf. Add spinach and stir until wilted, about 3 minutes.
3. In a separate bowl, whisk together the eggs and egg whites. Stir the eggs into the soup until eggs are cooked, about 1–2 minutes. Season with pepper and salt to taste. Serve with grated Parmesan.

CALORIES 188
FAT 7G
CARBOHYDRATES 9G
PROTEIN 8G

Roasted Potato Soup with Fresh Herbs

SERVES 6

1 tablespoon olive oil
2 parsnips, peeled and coarsely chopped
3 carrots, peeled and coarsely chopped
2 large baking potatoes, peeled and coarsely
  chopped
3 stalks celery, coarsely chopped
3 yellow onions, peeled and coarsely chopped
1 fresh rosemary sprig
4 cups low-sodium vegetable broth
3 sprigs fresh thyme, leaves chopped, stems
  discarded
¼ bunch fresh Italian flat-leaf parsley, leaves
  chopped
2 bay leaves
Sea salt to taste
Black pepper to taste

Parsnips are naturally fat free and are also high in fiber, vitamin C, and potassium.

1. Preheat oven to 375°F. Place oil in a large roasting pan and add parsnips, carrots, potatoes, celery, onions, and rosemary. Toss to coat. Roast about 40 minutes or until tender. Remove from oven, let cool, and discard rosemary.

2. In a blender or food processor, puree vegetables in batches with broth. Pour puree into large stockpot (quart boiler) and simmer over medium heat.

3. Add in thyme, parsley, bay leaves, and season to taste with salt and pepper. Let simmer for 45 minutes, adding broth if needed and stirring occasionally. Remove bay leaves and serve.

CALORIES 120

FAT 3G

CARBOHYDRATES 22G

PROTEIN 2G

Fish Chowder

PROTEIN ANTIOXIDANTS

SERVES 6

1 tablespoon olive oil
3 partially baked potatoes, skin on, cut into 1-inch cubes
3 ears of fresh corn, kernels cut off cob, cobs discarded
6 roma tomatoes, diced
1 leek, cleaned and chopped
1 pound skinless, boneless fillet whitefish
1 teaspoon curry powder
Back pepper to taste
½ cup dry white wine such as sauvignon blanc
2 quarts low-sodium vegetable broth
1 head fresh kale, rinsed and chopped
½ teaspoon capers

Fish is typically high in good oils and protein while staying low in calories. This combination of fish and kale provides protein and antioxidants and is perfect for lunch or dinner.

1. In a large stockpot or quart boiler, heat oil over medium heat and add potatoes, corn, tomatoes, leeks, and fish. Sauté until the leeks begin to wilt. Add the curry powder and season with black pepper. Then add the wine, stirring to combine. Simmer until wine is reduced by half. Pour in the broth and simmer for 45 minutes.

2. Add the kale and simmer an additional 10 minutes. Remove from heat and serve with capers on top.

CALORIES 285

FAT 4G

CARBOHYDRATES 29G

PROTEIN 32G

Minestrone with Fresh Oregano and Basil

SERVES 6

1 tablespoon olive oil
2 yellow onions, chopped
3 cloves garlic, minced
2 carrots, peeled and chopped
2 stalks celery, chopped
8 cups low-sodium chicken broth
1 16-ounce can chopped tomatoes, undrained
½ tablespoon fresh oregano, leaves chopped
½ bunch fresh basil, leaves chopped, stems discarded
½ cup fresh green beans, trimmed and chopped
Sea salt and pepper to taste
2 cups cooked pasta, such as shells, rotini
⅓ cup grated Parmesan cheese

Pasta provides instant energy, so it's best to consume carbohydrates earlier in the day when your body needs that extra boost. Make your own pasta or buy it fresh or dried.

1. Heat oil in large stockpot (boiler) over medium heat. Add onion, garlic, carrots, and celery, and sauté for 5 minutes. Stir in broth, tomatoes, oregano, basil, and beans and simmer for 25 minutes, uncovered.
2. Season with salt and pepper. Add pasta and simmer for 5 minutes, until heated through. Serve and sprinkle with cheese.

CALORIES 156
FAT 2G
CARBOHYDRATES 24G
PROTEIN 3G

Barley Soup with Turkey and Mushrooms

SERVES 6

1 tablespoon butter
1 white or yellow onion, diced
1 cup sliced cremini mushrooms
2 garlic cloves, minced
8 cups low-sodium chicken broth
1 stalk celery, chopped
1 carrot, peeled and sliced
½ cup pearl barley
1½ cups diced or shredded cooked turkey breast
Sea salt to taste
Black pepper to taste
¼ cup minced fresh Italian flat-leaf parsley leaves

Barley is a complex carbohydrate that contains eight essential amino acids. It is known to aid in the regulation of blood sugar for up to 10 hours after consumption. Barley is also rich in B vitamins and minerals.

1. In a large stockpot or quart boiler, heat butter over medium heat. Add onion, mushrooms, and garlic. Sauté until tender, about 4 minutes.
2. Pour in broth and add celery and carrots. Bring to a boil and stir in barley. Reduce heat to medium, cover, and simmer 40 minutes. Stir occasionally. Add turkey and simmer about 7 minutes. Season with salt, pepper, and parsley. Stir and let stand about 5 minutes. Serve.

CALORIES 235
FAT 14G
CARBOHYDRATES 12G
PROTEIN 16G

Spicy Gumbo with Chicken and Turkey Sausage

SUPERFOOD

8 cups low-sodium chicken broth
2 tablespoons olive oil
¼ cup plain flour
1 yellow onion, diced
1 pound lean turkey sausage
2 cups diced chicken
1 green bell pepper, seeded and
    diced
1 stalk celery, diced
3 cloves garlic, minced
1 14½-ounce can Italian stewed toma-
    toes, undrained
2 baking potatoes, peeled and cut
    into 1 to 2-inch cubes
1 10-ounce package frozen mixed
    vegetables
1 bay leaf
2 teaspoons Tabasco
1 teaspoon freshly chopped thyme
    leaves
1 teaspoon freshly chopped sage
    leaves
1 teaspoon cayenne pepper
Sea salt and black pepper to taste
3 green onions, diced
⅓ cup minced fresh Italian flat leaf
    parsley leaves

Spice is nice, especially in this recipe where fiery Tabasco, cayenne, and black pepper provide maximum energy boosting nutrients.

1. In large quart boiler, bring broth to a boil.
2. In heavy saucepan over medium heat, add oil and flour. Stir to form a paste. Cook, stirring constantly, until paste becomes brown in color. Remove from heat and add onions. Mix to combine and carefully stir into boiling broth. Stir until flour mixture dissolves into broth. Reduce heat and simmer for 30 minutes. Add additional broth or water if needed.
3. While broth is simmering, in large sauté pan, heat turkey sausage and chicken and sauté until browned and chicken in cooked through, about 5 minutes. Add turkey sausage mixture to broth. Add bell pepper, celery, garlic, tomatoes, potatoes, mixed vegetables, bay leaf, Tabasco, thyme, sage, and cayenne. Season with salt and pepper. Let simmer about 20 minutes. Stir and simmer an additional 15–20 minutes.
4. Remove from heat and serve topped with green onions and parsley.

CALORIES 388
FAT 6G
CARBOHYDRATES 37G
PROTEIN 34G

BURN IT UP

This recipe is full of high fiber foods like bell peppers, tomatoes, mixed vegetables, celery, onions, and parsley. The typical American takes in an average of only 11 grams of fiber each day. According to the National Cancer Institute, consuming double that would be far more beneficial.

Tortilla Soup with Chicken

PROTEIN SPICY

3 tablespoons olive oil
1 yellow onion, chopped
3 cloves garlic, chopped
½ head broccoli, chopped
1 red bell pepper, seeded and
  chopped
2 jalapeño peppers, seeded and
  diced
2 16-ounce cans fire-roasted tomatoes
6 cups low-sodium chicken broth
1½ tablespoons chili powder
1 teaspoon ground cumin
1 16-ounce can black beans
2 cups fresh cut kernel corn
2 cups cooked chicken, diced
Sea salt to taste
¼ cup minced fresh cilantro leaves
¼ cup green onion
2 tablespoons Italian parsley,
  chopped
1½ cups shredded Cheddar or Monterey jack cheese
2 cups tortilla strips
6 fresh lime wedges

Tortilla soup is a nice twist on traditional soups that provides a flavorful lunch or dinner. What's great about this soup is that the black beans give you extra protein and fiber while being low in fat.

1. Heat oil in a large quart boiler over medium heat. Add the onions and garlic and cook until soft, about 5 minutes. Add broccoli, red bell pepper, and jalapeño. Stir to coat and sauté until just tender, about 4 minutes. Add tomatoes, broth, chili powder, and cumin. Bring to a boil; reduce heat to medium low and simmer. Continue by adding beans, corn, and chicken. Simmer about 20 minutes.
2. Season with salt and add cilantro, green onion, and parsley. Simmer about 5 minutes. Stirring occasionally. Remove from heat and serve with tortilla strips, cheese, and a lime wedge.

CALORIES 135
FAT 2G
CARBOHYDRATES 5G
PROTEIN 23G

Cauliflower Soup with Carrots and Caraway

SERVES 4

1 pound cauliflower florets
1 pound carrots, peeled and sliced
4 cups low-sodium chicken broth
1 teaspoon caraway seeds
Juice of ½ lemon
1 tablespoon fine grated orange zest
Sea salt to taste
Black pepper to taste
1 cup nonfat sour cream
½ cup nonfat milk
½ cup chopped fresh Italian flat-leaf parsley
   leaves
½ cup chopped fresh chives

This very lean soup is packed full of fiber and vitamins A and B, both good for improving your skin and sight.

1. In large quart boiler or stockpot, combine cauliflower, carrots, broth, and caraway seeds with lemon juice, orange zest, salt, and pepper. Bring to a boil and let boil for 15–20 minutes until tender.
2. Working in batches, puree everything in a food processor or blender until smooth. Add sour cream and milk and puree again to combine. Season if needed with salt and pepper. Serve with parsley and chives.

CALORIES 195
FAT 6G
CARBOHYDRATES 24G
PROTEIN 10G

Tuscan Tomato Soup with Fresh Basil

SERVES 4

2 tablespoons butter
½ yellow onion, chopped
2 cups grape or cherry tomatoes
2 cups low-sodium vegetable broth
2 cups fresh basil leaves, chopped
2 tablespoons fresh oregano leaves, chopped
1½ cups nonfat milk
1 cup nonfat sour cream
¼ cup cornstarch mixed with 3 tablespoons water,
   stirred to blend
Sea salt and pepper to taste

Fresh basil leaves are rich in antioxidants, which will help boost your metabolism. Basil also has been known to have positive antibacterial and anti-inflammatory effects.

1. Heat butter in large quart boiler or stockpot over medium heat and add onions. Sauté until tender, about 4 minutes. Add the tomatoes, broth, basil, and oregano. Reduce heat to low and simmer for 20 minutes. Stir in milk, sour cream, and cornstarch. Season with salt and pepper. Simmer over low heat an additional 5 minutes. Do not boil.
2. Working in batches, puree the soup in a food processor or blender until smooth. Serve hot.

CALORIES 126
FAT 2G
CARBOHYDRATES 13G
PROTEIN 4G

Cream of Broccoli Soup

SUPERFOOD CALCIUM

SERVES 5

1 head broccoli, stems and florets chopped
1 medium onion, chopped
2 cloves garlic, chopped
1½ cups vegetable broth
Fine zest of 1 lemon
Juice of 1 lemon
2 large baking potatoes, peeled and diced
2 teaspoons fresh thyme, leaves chopped
Pinch nutmeg
Sea salt to taste
Black pepper to taste
1 cup nonfat sour cream
½ cup low-fat milk
¼ cup minced prosciutto or other smoked ham

Superfood broccoli easily boosts your metabolism! It is high in vitamins A, C, and K, and is also high in fiber. Additionally, according to the American Cancer Society, broccoli is believed to have cancer fighting qualities particularly for colon cancer.

1. In a large quart boiler, combine broccoli stems and florets, onion, garlic, broth, lemon zest and juice, potatoes, thyme, and nutmeg. Bring to a boil. Reduce the heat, cover, and simmer for 15–20 minutes or until potatoes are tender. Season with salt and pepper to taste.
2. Working in batches, purée soup in a food processor or blender until smooth. Return to the saucepan. Whisk in the sour cream and milk. Heat through on medium heat without boiling, about 5 minutes. Serve topped with a little prosciutto.

CALORIES 126
FAT 3G
CARBOHYDRATES 24G
PROTEIN 4G

Chilled Vegetable Gazpacho

HIGH FIBER

SERVES 6

8 tomatoes, seeded and finely diced
2 cucumbers, peeled and finely diced
2 green bell peppers, seeded and finely diced
1 clove garlic, finely diced
2 tablespoons extra-virgin olive oil
1½ teaspoons red wine vinegar
2 teaspoons Worcestershire sauce
1 teaspoon sea salt
2 cups tomato juice
Dash hot sauce or more as desired

Key ingredients tomatoes and green bell peppers fill this recipe with vitamin A, fiber, and immune-boosting antioxidants.

Combine all ingredients and mix well using a wooden spoon, adding additional hot sauce as your taste allows. Cover and refrigerate for 1 hour or overnight. Note: for a smoother gazpacho, work in batches and purée in a blender or food processor.

CALORIES 112
FAT 4G
CARBOHYDRATES 5G
PROTEIN 2G

Corn Chowder with Potatoes, Red Bell Peppers, and Crumbled Bacon

SERVES 6

½ pound lean turkey bacon
1 large onion, chopped
1 red bell pepper, seeded and
   chopped
2 stalks celery, chopped
6 red potatoes, cut into 1-inch chunks
4 ears sweet corn, shucked, kernels
   cut, cobs reserved
3 sprigs fresh thyme, leaves chopped
1 bay leaf
3 teaspoons sea salt
1 teaspoon chili powder
4 ounces (1 stick) unsalted butter
8 cups vegetable broth or water
4 teaspoons cornstarch mixed in ¼
   cup water
8 cups nonfat milk
White pepper to taste

This starchy soup is the perfect energy booster for a midday meal! It is stocked full of vitamins like A and C, and is high in fiber and calcium.

1. Heat heavy skillet over medium heat and add bacon. Cook until done and crispy. Drain on paper towels and crumble. Set aside, leaving grease in pan.
2. Return pan to heat and add onion, bell pepper, celery, and potatoes. Mix to combine and cook until just tender, about 8 minutes.
3. Transfer onion mixture to large quart boiler or stockpot and add corn, corn cob, thyme, bay leaf, salt, and chili powder. Cook for 5 minutes. Add butter and cook gently, allowing vegetables to stew in the butter, about 5 minutes.
4. Add the vegetable stock. Increase heat to high and bring to a full boil Allow to boil for 1 minute, reduce heat to simmer, and cook for 10 minutes. Remove the corn cobs, add cornstarch mixture, and simmer 5 minutes more. Stir in the milk, and adjust seasoning with salt and white pepper to taste. Serve sprinkled with crumbled bacon.

CALORIES 370
FAT 9G
CARBOHYDRATES 32G
PROTEIN 15G

BURN IT UP

An 8-ounce serving of milk, especially cow's milk, helps build strong bones by supplying the body with nearly 30 percent of its daily calcium needs and 20 percent of its phosphorous needs. It also contains plenty of vitamins A and D, and several of the B vitamins that are needed for heart health and energy production.

Shrimp and Scallop Bisque

`CALCIUM`

SERVES 6

2 tablespoons butter

2 shallots, minced

2 tablespoons cornstarch, mixed with 2 table-
    spoons water

1 tablespoon tomato paste

4 cups vegetable broth

2 16-ounce cans clam juice

½ pound shrimp, peeled and deveined

½ pound bay scallops

1 cup nonfat sour cream

½ cup nonfat milk

Sea salt to taste

Black pepper to taste

6 tablespoons dry sherry wine, 1 for each serving

¼ cup chopped fresh Italian flat leaf parsley
    leaves

*Sour cream, milk, shrimp, and scallops
all have high natural amounts of calcium,
making them great for bone development
and strength.*

1. In a large saucepan over medium heat, melt butter and add shallots. Sauté until shallots are just tender, about 3 minutes. Add cornstarch mixture and tomato paste. Stir to combine. Add broth and clam juice, and bring to a boil. Simmer for 10 minutes.
2. Add shrimp and scallops and cook until just opaque, about 1–2 minutes. Remove from heat and let cool. Working in batches, puree in a food processor or blender until smooth.
3. Return mixture to deep sauté pan or stockpot and add sour cream and milk, stirring to combine. Season to taste with salt and pepper. When serving, add a tablespoon of sherry and a few sprinkles of parsley.

CALORIES 210

FAT 5G

CARBOHYDRATES 18G

PROTEIN 20G

Tuscan Bean Soup with Italian Sausage

`HIGH FIBER` `ANTIOXIDANTS`

SERVES 4

1 tablespoon olive oil

1 red onion, chopped

2 cloves garlic, minced

1 pound hot or mild Italian sausage, removed
    from casing

1 28-ounce can crushed tomatoes, with juice

1 tablespoon fresh thyme, leaves chopped

2 large cans cannellini or white beans, with juice

4 cups beef or chicken broth

Sea salt and black pepper to taste

½ cup grated Parmesan cheese

*Tuscan bean soup is an Italian favorite
during the winter months due to its hearty
flavor. The protein from the Italian sausage
is enhanced by adding seasoning like fresh
thyme. You can also add in freshly chopped
rosemary leaves or fresh Italian flat-leaf
parsley leaves, both of which add fiber and
antioxidant qualities to the recipe.*

1. In large quart boiler over medium heat, heat oil and add onion and garlic. Sauté for 5 minutes, until tender. Add sausage and brown about 5 minutes.

2. Add tomatoes, thyme, beans, and broth. Reduce heat to low, cover, and simmer for 30 minutes, allowing flavors to blend. Season with salt and pepper to taste. Serve with a sprinkle of Parmesan cheese.

CALORIES 548
FAT 29G
CARBOHYDRATES 67G
PROTEIN 33G

Spiced Beef and Black Bean Soup

PROTEIN | HIGH FIBER | SPICY

SERVES 12

2 tablespoons olive oil
1 white or yellow onion, chopped
3 cloves garlic, chopped
1 red bell pepper, seeded and chopped
1 green bell pepper, seeded and chopped
2 jalapeño peppers, seeded and chopped
½ pound lean ground sirloin
½ pound lean ground pork
4 cups low-sodium beef broth
2 tablespoons chili powder
¼ teaspoon ground cloves
¼ teaspoon ground cinnamon
1 teaspoon cocoa powder
1 28-ounce can crushed Italian tomatoes, with juice
3 13-ounce cans black beans, drained
Juice of 1 lime
Sea salt to taste
Black pepper to taste

This soup is loaded with metabolism-boosting ingredients such as chili powder, protein-rich beef, pork, chicken, and beans, as well as tomatoes, which are themselves filled with essential vitamins and minerals. Put this soup at the top of your list for a quick, easy, metabolism-friendly meal. A must-have soup, enjoy this for lunch or dinner as an entrée or side dish.

1. Heat oil in a large quart boiler over medium heat. Add the onions, garlic, red and green bell peppers, and jalapeño. Cook until soft, about 5 minutes.
2. Add sirloin and pork and sauté until browned, about 5 minutes. Add broth, chili powder, cloves, cinnamon, cocoa, tomatoes, beans, and lime. Add salt and pepper to taste. Stir well to combine. Cover and reduce heat to simmer. Let cook for 1–2 hours, adding water or broth if needed. Do not allow to boil. Serve.

CALORIES 196
FAT 8G
CARBOHYDRATES 22G
PROTEIN 14G

Creamy Potato Leek Soup

SERVES 6

HIGH FIBER   CALCIUM   PROTEIN

2 tablespoons butter
4 leeks, white part only, thinly sliced
1 large sweet onion such as Vidalia, chopped
2 tablespoons plain flour
2 large Idaho or Yukon gold potatoes, peeled and diced
3 cups chicken broth
1 teaspoon sea salt
Fresh ground black pepper to taste
1 teaspoon curry powder
1 cup nonfat milk
1 cup nonfat sour cream
½ cup chopped fresh Italian flat-leaf parsley leaves
2 slices turkey bacon, cooked crisp, drained, and crumbled

This soup is great for lunch because the carbs will give you energy and you'll have the rest of the day to burn them off. The leeks add vitamin A and fiber, which are required for good vision and skin maintenance and digestion.

1. Melt the butter in a large heavy-bottomed stockpot or quart boiler. Add the leeks and onion. Cook until tender, about 4 minutes.
2. Stir in the flour and blend. Add the potatoes, broth, and salt. Stir to combine, cover, and reduce heat to low. Simmer until potatoes are tender, about 15 minutes. Add additional broth, if needed, to maintain level.
3. Stir in the pepper, curry, milk, and sour cream, mixing well. Keep warm over low heat until ready to serve. Serve with sprinkle of parsley and bacon.

CALORIES   263
FAT   12G
CARBOHYDRATES   29G
PROTEIN   8G

BURN IT UP

Milk is a major metabolism booster due to its high protein and calcium levels. If you're lactose intolerant or are opposed to drinking cow's milk but still want the milk you drink to have a positive impact on your metabolism, make sure your rice, soy, or almond milk is fortified with vitamins and minerals.

Miso Soup

SERVES 4

¼ cup miso paste
3½ cups chicken broth
8 ounces medium to firm tofu, cubed
4 sprigs Italian parsley, chopped
4 cremini or button mushrooms, brushed and
   sliced
2 shiitake mushrooms, sliced
Sea salt and black pepper to taste

Tofu is a great meat substitute. It's super healthy and contains the good carbs, calcium, and natural proteins your body needs.

1. In large quart boiler, whisk the miso into 2 tablespoons of slightly warmed broth and blend well. Gradually add the miso liquid into the remaining broth. Bring the soup to a simmer.
2. Add the tofu cubes, parsley, and mushrooms. Maintain a simmer until the mushrooms and tofu are heated. Do not boil or the soup will become bitter and cloudy. Serve soup in bowls and serve immediately.

CALORIES 61
FAT 2G
CARBOHYDRATES 8G
PROTEIN 3G

Hearty Beef Stew

SERVES 6

3 tablespoons olive oil
3 garlic cloves, minced
1 large white or yellow onion, chopped
1 16-ounce package cooked roast beef, chopped
1 large can brown gravy
2 carrots, peeled and sliced
1 cup broccoli florets
1 red bell pepper, seeded and chopped
1 green bell pepper, seeded and chopped
2 medium baking potatoes, peeled and cut into
   1-inch cubes
1 10-ounce can cream of mushroom soup
2½ cups water
½ tablespoon fresh thyme leaves, chopped
Sea salt to taste
Black pepper to taste

Beef is a good source of protein and is great for building muscle tissue.

1. In heavy large saucepan, heat olive oil over medium heat. Add garlic and onion; cook and stir until tender, about 4 minutes. Add beef, gravy, carrots, broccoli, bell peppers, potatoes, soup, water, and thyme leaves. Bring to a boil and cook until vegetables start becoming tender, about 10 minutes.
2. Taste for seasoning, adding salt and pepper as desired. Cover and reduce heat to low and simmer for an additional 10 minutes, or until potatoes are fork tender. Serve.

CALORIES 162
FAT 7G
CARBOHYDRATES 5G
PROTEIN 17G

Tuscan White Bean Soup with Tomatoes and Shredded Chicken

SERVES 12

PROTEIN **HIGH FIBER**

2 tablespoons extra-virgin olive oil

1 large sweet Vidalia onion, chopped

3 cloves garlic, finely chopped

1½ cups fresh basil leaves, torn into small pieces

½ cup chopped fresh Italian flat-leaf parsley leaves

1 28-ounce can crushed Italian tomatoes

1½ cups diced or shredded cooked chicken breasts

4 cups beef broth

Juice of 1 lemon

1 32-ounce can white northern beans with juice

Sea salt to taste

Black pepper to taste

Basil is filled with flavonoids that provide antioxidants, vitamins A, C, E, and K, and minerals such as calcium, iron, zinc, and fiber.

1. In large quart boiler over medium heat, heat olive oil until fragrant, about 30 seconds. Add onion and garlic and sauté about 3 minutes. Add basil, parsley, tomatoes, chicken, broth, lemon, and beans. Bring to a boil, reduce heat, and cover.

2. Simmer for 10 minutes. Taste and season with salt and pepper. Stir to combine. Simmer, covered, for an additional 10 minutes. Serve.

CALORIES	276
FAT	5G
CARBOHYDRATES	45G
PROTEIN	14G

BURN IT UP

Beans are so jam-packed with nutrients that they qualify as both a vegetable and a protein. A cup of beans provides a whopping 13 grams of fiber (half of our daily requirement), about 15 grams of protein, and dozens of key nutrients, including calcium, potassium, and magnesium. Eating more bean-based meals every week is recommended.

Chicken and Wild Rice Soup with Vegetables

SERVES 8

1 tablespoon olive oil
½ cup yellow onions, diced
1 clove fresh garlic, minced
1 16-ounce package frozen California-blend
   vegetables
2 14- to 16-ounce cans vegetable broth
1 celery stalk, chopped
2 cups water
1 teaspoon fresh oregano, leaves chopped
¼ cup fresh Italian flat-leaf parsley, leaves
   chopped
1½ cups diced cooked chicken breasts
2 cups quick cooking wild rice
Sea salt to taste
Black pepper to taste

Although it is an herb, the oregano in this recipe has essential vitamin A, calcium, and iron.

1. Heat oil in large boiler over medium heat. Add in onions and garlic and sauté until fragrant, about 3 minutes. Add vegetables, broth, celery, water, oregano, parsley, and chicken. Stir to combine and bring to a boil. Stir in rice.
2. Reduce heat and simmer for 25 minutes, or until rice is tender. Add more water or broth, if needed, to thin soup.

CALORIES 141
FAT 0.5G
CARBOHYDRATES 28G
PROTEIN 5G

Beef Stew with Green Chilies and Cayenne

SERVES 6

2 tablespoons olive oil
1 yellow onion, chopped
1 pound lean ground beef
1 package taco seasoning
2 15-ounce cans chili beans, undrained
1½ cups fresh corn kernels
1 14-ounce can tomatoes with green chilies,
   undrained
2 cups water
1 tablespoon chili powder
½ teaspoon cumin
1 teaspoon cayenne pepper

Spices such as cumin and cayenne are a source of iron, which gives your body the strength needed for workouts. These spices will also help rev your metabolic engine.

1. In large saucepan over medium heat, heat olive oil. Add in onions and sauté until tender, about 5 minutes.
2. Add ground beef and cook until browned, about 5 minutes.
3. Add remaining ingredients, stir, cover, and simmer for about 20 minutes, until flavors are combined. Serve.

CALORIES 162
FAT 8G
CARBOHYDRATES 6G
PROTEIN 17G

CHAPTER 7
Chicken and Turkey

Most people know that lean chicken and turkey are good choices for daily and weekly meals. However, you may not realize that you can take those healthy choices to a higher level by switching out fat-laden ingredients with lighter, more nutrient-rich components, or by adding fiber-filled and vitamin- and mineral-rich foods that metabolize certain nutrients found in protein-rich foods. These recipes will help you do just that while helping you reach new metabolism-boosting heights in the process!

Lemon Chicken

SERVES 4

1½ pounds skinless chicken thighs and breasts, breasts preferably boneless
Fine zest of 2 lemons
Juice of 2 lemons
2 tablespoons distilled white vinegar
1 tablespoon fresh oregano leaves
1 yellow onion, sliced
Pinch sea salt
Pinch black pepper
Pinch paprika

Paprika is rich in capsaicin, a compound that provides an instant boost to your metabolism and is found typically in richly colored foods such as peppers.

1. Place chicken parts in 9" × 13" inch baking dish. In a small bowl, mix together lemon zest, juice, vinegar, oregano, and onion. Pour over the chicken. Cover and marinate for 4 hours or overnight in the refrigerator, turning occasionally.
2. When ready to cook, sprinkle with salt, pepper, and paprika. Preheat oven to 300°F. Cover the baking dish with foil and bake for 30 minutes. Uncover and continue to cook until the juices are clear and chicken is cooked through, about 30 more minutes. Serve hot.

CALORIES 246
FAT 7G
CARBOHYDRATES 11G
PROTEIN 13G

Chicken Marsala

SERVES 4

1 tablespoon butter
4 skinless, boneless chicken breasts
Pinch sea salt
Pinch black pepper to taste
2 shallots, chopped
½ cup Marsala wine
½ cup low-sodium chicken broth
1 16-ounce can diced tomatoes
¼ cup chopped fresh Italian flat-leaf parsley

Some studies show that free-range organic chicken has a higher nutritional value than its non-free-range counterparts. This may be due to the more natural diet the chickens are provided and the idea that free-range chickens get more exercise and are therefore leaner. Either way, chicken is one of the leanest proteins you can enjoy.

1. In heavy skillet, melt butter on medium heat. Add chicken and brown on both sides, about 5 minutes each. Sprinkle with salt and pepper and remove from skillet.
2. Add shallots, wine, broth, and tomatoes to skillet. Simmer over medium heat until liquid is partially reduced, about 10 minutes. Return chicken to skillet, spoon sauce onto it, cover, and simmer over low heat until chicken is tender and cooked through, about 15–20 minutes. When serving, place chicken on warmed plates and spoon sauce over top. Sprinkle with parsley.

CALORIES 195
FAT 4G
CARBOHYDRATES 8G
PROTEIN 28G

Indian Chicken Paprika

SERVES 6

PROTEIN CALCIUM

3 chicken thighs, skin removed
3 boneless, skinless chicken breasts
Pinch black pepper
¼ cup plain, all-purpose flour
1 tablespoon olive oil
¼ cup diced yellow onion
1 cup hot water
Juice of ½ lemon
2 tablespoons cornstarch
2 cups nonfat plain yogurt
2 teaspoons paprika
½ teaspoon curry powder

Cooking with yogurt adds a creamy texture and flavor to your food without adding the fat from heavy cream products. Yogurt is rich in protein, calcium, and B vitamins. It is also a source of probiotics—live organisms that aid in the digestive process.

1. Season the chicken with pepper. Roll chicken in flour, coating well. In large skillet over medium heat, heat oil. Add chicken and brown on both sides, about 10–15 minutes total. Add the onion, water, and lemon juice. Cover and cook over low heat until tender, about 40 minutes, adding a little water if needed. Transfer chicken to oven-safe dish, cover, and keep in oven at 200°F.

2. In a medium bowl, mix together the cornstarch and 2 tablespoons of the yogurt. Blend well and then add remaining yogurt. Stir into skillet. Simmer over low heat, stirring occasionally, until thickened, about 5 minutes. Add paprika and curry. Place chicken on serving plates and spoon sauce over.

CALORIES 207
FAT 6G
CARBOHYDRATES 13G
PROTEIN 25G

BURN IT UP

Chicken contains fewer calories than red meat, making it a more healthy option. Cutting back on red meat may help lower your risk of serious illness later in life, including heart disease, stroke, diabetes, and certain forms of cancer. It will also help lower your caloric intake, thus boosting your metabolism. When you do eat red meat, make sure it's lean and well cooked.

Skillet Chicken and Rice with Mushrooms

SERVES 6

Nonstick cooking spray
1 pound skinless chicken thighs
1 pound boneless, skinless chicken breasts
3 cups sliced cremini mushrooms
Juice of 1 lemon
3 stalks celery, sliced
1 cup long-grain white rice
1 medium white onion, chopped
1 chicken bouillon cube
1 teaspoon poultry seasoning
Lemon pepper to taste
2½ cups water

Although high in carbohydrates, rice has metabolism-boosting nutrients such as potassium and niacin. Rice is also a source of iron, manganese, and selenium.

1. Spray heavy skillet with nonstick cooking spray. Heat skillet over medium heat and add chicken. Brown chicken on both sides, about 15 minutes total. Remove the chicken from the skillet and set aside.
2. Return skillet to heat and add mushrooms, lemon juice, celery, rice, onion, bouillon, poultry seasoning, lemon pepper, and water. Stir to combine. Place chicken on top, cover, and simmer over low heat until juices are clear and chicken is cooked through, about 30 minutes. Rice will be tender. Serve hot.

CALORIES 208
FAT 3G
CARBOHYDRATES 27G
PROTEIN 18G

Chicken with Sweet and Sour Sauce

SERVES 8

1 tablespoon canola oil
4 large boneless chicken breasts, skin removed, cut into 1-inch pieces
1 can pineapple chunks, drained, juice reserved
2 stalks celery, chopped
1 red bell pepper, seeded and chopped
¼ cup firmly packed brown sugar
½ cup apple cider vinegar
2 tablespoons low-sodium soy sauce
1 tablespoon ketchup
1½ teaspoons Worcestershire sauce
½ teaspoon freshly chopped gingerroot
2 tablespoons cornstarch
2 tablespoons cold water
Special equipment needed: Pressure cooker

Traditional sweet and sour chicken or pork is loaded with sugar, which, if not burned by the body as energy, turns to fat. This recipe uses only ¼ cup, which is then divided among 8 servings.

1. In the bottom of a pressure cooker, heat oil over medium heat. Add the chicken pieces and brown on both sides, about 5 minutes total. Measure out 1 cup of the reserved pineapple juice and combine with the celery, bell pepper, brown sugar, vinegar, soy sauce, ketchup, Worcestershire, and ginger. Mix well and pour over the chicken. Secure the lid on the pressure cooker. Bring to high pressure on high heat. Adjust the heat to maintain a high pressure for 8 minutes. Reduce the pressure using the quick release method.

2. Remove the chicken and vegetables and place on a warm platter or hold in a 200°F oven.

3. In a small bowl, stir together the cornstarch and water. Then stir into the hot liquid. Place over high heat and cook until the mixture boils, stirring frequently, about 5 minutes. Add the pineapple chunks and heat through, about 5 more minutes. Pour sauce over warmed chicken and serve.

CALORIES 199
FAT 4G
CARBOHYDRATES 22G
PROTEIN 18G

Baked Chicken Breast Stuffed with Crab

PROTEIN

SERVES 6

¼ pound cooked crabmeat
¼ cup finely chopped water chestnuts
2 tablespoons plain bread crumbs
2 tablespoons low-fat mayonnaise
1 tablespoon minced fresh Italian flat-leaf parsley
½ teaspoon Dijon mustard
6 boneless, skinless chicken breasts
Nonstick cooking spray
2 tablespoons Worcestershire sauce
2 scallions, minced

A hidden food gem, crab is low in calories but high in essential vitamins and minerals, such as calcium, iron, niacin, and magnesium, that provide maximum metabolism-boosting impact with few calories and virtually no fat.

1. In a small bowl, combine crab, water chestnuts, bread crumbs, mayonnaise, parsley, and mustard. Mix well.

2. Place 1 chicken breast between 2 pieces of plastic wrap and pound lightly with flat surface of meat pounder until ⅛-inch thick. Repeat with remaining chicken.

3. Spoon equal amounts of crab mixture onto half of each chicken breast. Fold in sides and roll up. Secure with toothpicks. Arrange chicken, seam side down, in a large baking dish that has been sprayed with nonstick cooking spray. Brush chicken with Worcestershire sauce.

4. Bake about 25 minutes until chicken is done and juices are clear. Sprinkle with scallions and serve.

CALORIES 201
FAT 6G
CARBOHYDRATES 4G
PROTEIN 31G

Chili Pepper Chicken with Rice

SERVES 6

1 8-ounce can tomato sauce

½ cup orange juice

1 medium white onion, chopped

2 tablespoons golden raisins or golden currants

2 tablespoons chopped pimiento

1 serrano chili pepper, seeded and diced

1 teaspoon chopped fresh oregano leaves

½ teaspoon chili powder

1 clove garlic, minced

Two dashes Tabasco sauce or other hot sauce

6 skinless, boneless chicken breasts

2 teaspoons cornstarch

1 teaspoon water

¼ cup chopped fresh Italian flat-leaf parsley leaves

3 cups hot cooked white rice

Rice is high in fiber, but if you really want to see your metabolism soar, try eating whole-grain brown rice. It's contains even more fiber than white rice and has even more fat-burning potential.

1. In a large skillet over medium heat, combine tomato sauce, orange juice, onion, raisins, pimiento, chili pepper, oregano, chili powder, garlic, and Tabasco sauce. Bring to a boil, cover, reduce heat to low, and simmer for 5 minutes.

2. Next, add the chicken and return to a boil. Cover, reduce heat to low, and simmer until juices run clear and chicken is cooked through, about 15–20 minutes.

3. Meanwhile, in a small bowl, combine cornstarch and water. Mix well. Stir into the chicken mixture and stir until thickened and bubbly, about 5 minutes. Cook and stir for 2 minutes longer.

4. Toss the parsley into the hot rice. Spoon rice onto platter or plates and serve chicken mixture over rice.

CALORIES 274

FAT 2G

CARBOHYDRATES 34G

PROTEIN 30G

BURN IT UP

One of the most popular ways to boost your metabolism is by dining on green and red chilies. Studies have shown that people tend to eat less food when they are flavored with these antioxidant-rich peppers, which also have a positive impact on your body's cholesterol levels.

Chicken Teriyaki

SERVES 2

2 tablespoons teriyaki sauce
1 tablespoon water
2 cloves garlic, minced
1 teaspoon minced fresh gingerroot
2 boneless chicken breasts, skin removed, cut into ¼-inch wide strips
10- to 12-inch wooden skewers, soaked in water for 30 minutes
½ tablespoon sesame seeds, toasted

Teriyaki chicken can be high in sugar and sodium, but combining it here with fresh garlic and ginger keeps flavor high and sugar to a minimum.

1. In a medium bowl, combine the teriyaki sauce, water, garlic, and ginger. Mix well. Add chicken and toss to coat. Let stand for 10 minutes at room temperature, stirring occasionally.
2. Preheat broiler. Drain chicken and thread onto skewers. Place on broiler pan and broil for 3 minutes, turn and broil an additional 2–3 minutes, until chicken is cooked through.
3. Sprinkle chicken with sesame seeds and serve.

CALORIES 152
FAT 2G
CARBOHYDRATES 4G
PROTEIN 29G

Pecan-Crusted Chicken Tenders

SERVES 6

¾ cup crushed corn flakes
¼ cup finely chopped pecans
1 tablespoon chopped fresh Italian flat-leaf parsley
1 clove garlic, chopped
Sea salt to taste
4 boneless, skinless chicken breasts, sliced into 1-inch wide strips
¼ cup nonfat milk

Nuts are high in fat but also contain protein your body needs. When you choose protein, always reach for healthy options, such as fish, skinless chicken, lean pork, tofu, nuts, beans, eggs, and low-fat dairy products.

1. Preheat oven to 400°F. In medium, shallow dish, combine corn flakes, pecans, parsley, garlic, and salt. toss well. Dip chicken in milk, then roll in the crumb mixture.
2. Place dipped chicken on a parchment paper–lined baking sheet and bake until chicken is cooked through, about 8 minutes. Serve hot.

CALORIES 214
FAT 6G
CARBOHYDRATES 10G
PROTEIN 29G

Cider Lime Chicken

SPICY PROTEIN

1 tablespoon olive oil
4 boneless chicken breast halves, skin removed
Fine zest of 1 lime
Juice of 2 limes
¼ cup apple cider
2 teaspoons cornstarch
½ cup low-sodium chicken broth
Sea salt as needed
Black pepper as needed

Lime juice is an excellent source of vitamin C, which has antioxidant properties that lower the risk of heart disease and assist with the synthesis of carnitine, a compound that helps break down fat. This metabolic-friendly recipe is low in fat and calories and is great before or after a workout.

1. Preheat oven to 350°F. Heat the oil in a heavy skillet over medium heat. Add chicken and brown on both sides, about 5 minutes each side. Transfer chicken to oven-safe baking dish or baking sheet, cover with foil and place in oven until done, about 10 minutes.
2. Meanwhile, in a medium bowl, combine ½ the lime zest, lime juice, cider, and cornstarch. Mix well. Add to the skillet and stir in broth. Cook over medium heat until thickened and hot, about 10 minutes. Continue to cook, stirring about 3 minutes longer.
3. Slice chicken into 1-inch-thick strips and place on serving plates. Spoon sauce over chicken and sprinkle with remaining zest.

CALORIES 161
FAT 2G
CARBOHYDRATES 7G
PROTEIN 27G

BURN IT UP

Studies suggest that black pepper may boost your metabolism in addition to helping protect against oxidative damage. The active chemical in black pepper (piperine) triggers parts of the brain and the nervous system which, in turn, boosts your metabolism and burns calories.

Chicken with Artichoke Hearts over Parmesan Pasta

CALORIES	530
FAT	13G
CARBOHYDRATES	61G
PROTEIN	41G

HIGH FIBER ANTIOXIDANTS

SERVES 6

6 boneless, skinless chicken breasts
2 teaspoons paprika
2 tablespoons butter
2 scallions, chopped
¼ cup water
¼ cup dry white wine such as sauvignon blanc
1 cup sliced cremini mushrooms
2 14-ounce cans artichoke hearts, unmarinated and drained
1 pound egg noodles, cooked and drained
¼ cup grated Parmesan cheese
1 teaspoon chopped fresh Italian flat-leaf parsley

Though high in carbs, egg noodles are a good source of iron, selenium (a powerful antioxidant), and thiamine (a water-soluble vitamin). All of these have metabolism-boosting properties.

1. Dust the chicken with the paprika. In a heavy skillet, melt butter over medium heat. Add chicken and brown on both sides, about 5 minutes each side. Add the scallions, water, and wine, cover, and simmer over low heat for 45 minutes.
2. Add the mushrooms and artichoke hearts. Cook slowly until chicken is done and mushrooms are tender, about 15 minutes, uncovered.
3. Toss noodles with Parmesan. Place on serving plate, top with chicken and sprinkle with parsley. Serve.

Chicken Enchiladas

PROTEIN SPICY

SERVES 6

Nonstick cooking spray
5 boneless, skinless chicken breasts
1 cup low-sodium chicken broth
2 tablespoons olive oil
1 white or yellow onion, chopped
2 cloves garlic, chopped
2 tablespoons plain flour
1 4-ounce can diced green chili peppers, drained
1 28-ounce can diced tomatoes
12 6-inch corn tortillas
1 cup shredded Parmesan cheese

Corn tortillas are good for you. They are low in saturated fat and cholesterol and are a good source of phosphorus, which helps with bone and teeth formation.

1. Preheat oven to 350°F. Spray medium baking dish with nonstick spray. In a saucepan, combine the chicken breasts and broth. Place over low heat and simmer gently until chicken is tender and cooked through, about 15 minutes. Remove the chicken and save the broth. Chop chicken into bite-sized pieces. Set aside.
2. In skillet over medium heat, heat oil. Add the onion and sauté until just tender, about 5 minutes. Add the garlic and flour. Cook, while stirring, for 1 minute. Stir in ½ cup of the broth and cook, stirring occasionally, until mixture thickens, about 7

minutes. Add the chilies and tomatoes; simmer about 10 minutes.

3. Dip a tortilla into the sauce and place in prepared baking dish. Place a spoonful each of cheese, chicken, and sauce in a line down middle of tortilla. Fold in sides and roll up. Place seam side down in dish. Repeat using all of the tortillas. Spoon remaining enchilada sauce over filled tortillas. Top with remaining cheese. Bake until cheese is melted and enchiladas are heated through, about 20 minutes. Serve hot.

CALORIES 381

FAT 12G

CARBOHYDRATES 35G

PROTEIN 33G

Jamaican Chicken

SUPERFOOD

SERVES 6

1 yellow onion, quartered, plus 1 onion, diced
1 jalapeño pepper, seeded and diced
2 to 3 cloves garlic, minced
⅓ cup orange juice
¼ cup low-sodium soy sauce
1 tablespoon peanut oil
2 tablespoons red wine vinegar
1 teaspoon chopped fresh thyme leaves
1 teaspoon ground allspice
½ teaspoon ground cinnamon
½ teaspoon curry powder
Salt to taste
Pepper to taste
2 pounds boneless, skinless chicken breasts and thigh

Jamaican cuisine is traditionally rich in metabolism-boosting spices.

1. In a food processor, process the onion, jalapeño, and garlic until puréed. Add the orange juice, soy sauce, oil, vinegar, thyme, allspice, cinnamon, curry powder, salt, and pepper. Process until smooth. Place the chicken pieces in a shallow dish and pour the puréed ingredients over them. Cover and refrigerate for 2 hours, turning occasionally.

2. Heat grill or grill pan. Remove the chicken from the marinade. Place on the grill and cook, turning once, until the chicken is done and juices run clear when pierced, 8–10 minutes on each side, or bake in a 325°F oven until done, about 40 minutes. Serve hot.

CALORIES 211

FAT 6G

CARBOHYDRATES 5G

PROTEIN 33G

New Orleans-Style Jambalaya

SERVES 8

1 tablespoon butter
2 large white or yellow onions, chopped
2 cups minced celery
1 green bell pepper, chopped
3 ounces turkey sausage, diced
1½ pounds skinless, boneless chicken breasts, cut into 1-inch chunks
2 cloves garlic, minced
2 bay leaves
2 teaspoons chopped fresh oregano leaves
1 teaspoon chopped fresh thyme leaves
1 teaspoon sea salt
1 teaspoon cayenne pepper
1 teaspoon black pepper
1 23-ounce can diced tomatoes
1 8-ounce can tomato sauce
4 cups low-sodium chicken broth
2½ cups long-grain white rice
1 pound medium shrimp, peeled and deveined
1 red bell pepper, chopped
1 white or yellow onion, minced
½ cup chopped fresh Italian flat-leaf parsley leaves

With all the protein from the turkey sausage, chicken, and shrimp in this recipe, the only thing missing is an energizing run! You can be sure that you'll have all the energy, nutrients, and fiber you need to get through your day!

1. In a large stockpot or quart boiler, melt the butter over medium heat. Add the chopped onion and celery and sauté until vegetables begin to soften, about 3 minutes. Add the green bell pepper, sausage, chicken, garlic, bay leaves, oregano, thyme, salt, cayenne pepper, and black pepper. Cook, stirring, for 5 minutes.
2. Add the tomatoes, tomato sauce, broth, and rice. Reduce the heat to low, cover, and cook until rice is tender, 20–30 minutes.
3. Add the shrimp, stir, and cook until the shrimp turn pink, another 5–10 minutes.
4. Garnish with red bell pepper, minced onion, and parsley before serving.

CALORIES 488
FAT 8G
CARBOHYDRATES 62G
PROTEIN 38G

BURN IT UP

Parsley is rich in flavonoids known for their antioxidant content and helping prevent free-radical damage (a major metabolism buster) to your body's cells. Parsley's dark green color also provides needed oxygenating chlorophyll, which increases the antioxidant capacity of your blood.

Tacos of Lean Turkey with Pistachios

SERVES 6

1 head iceberg lettuce
8 prepared taco shells
1 pound cooked turkey breast meat, shredded
1 pound tomatoes, chopped
1 large green bell pepper, chopped
¼ cup low-fat sour cream
¼ cup pistachios, chopped
1 cup bottled salsa, mild or hot
1 teaspoon grated lime zest
2 tablespoons lime juice

Pistachios are a great source of healthy fats and high in fiber. They are also rich in metabolism-boosting minerals such as copper, phosphorus, potassium, magnesium, and vitamin B6.

1. Shred the lettuce and divide among 4 plates. Stand 2 taco shells upright in the center of each bed of lettuce. Fill the shells with the turkey, tomatoes, and bell pepper, dividing evenly. Top with the sour cream and pistachios, again dividing evenly.
2. In a bowl, stir together the salsa, lime zest, and lime juice. Spoon over the tacos and serve.

CALORIES 231
FAT 9G
CARBOHYDRATES 21G
PROTEIN 27G

BURN IT UP

The mineral chloride aids in the metabolic process by combining with hydrogen in the stomach to produce hydrochloric acid, one of the most powerful digestive enzymes. This acid breaks down the food we eat and helps to balance pH levels and the amount of carbon dioxide being expelled from the body. Chloride is found in salt, but for a healthier option, choose kelp, olives, tomatoes, lettuce, or rye.

Turkey Tetrazzini

PROTEIN CALCIUM

SERVES 4

Nonstick cooking spray
1 tablespoon butter
½ pound cremini mushrooms, sliced
2 tablespoons all-purpose flour
Salt to taste
Pepper to taste
2 cups nonfat milk
1 teaspoon Worcestershire sauce
½ cup shredded low-fat Swiss cheese
1 green bell pepper, seeded and chopped
4 scallions, minced
2 cups diced cooked turkey breast
½ pound fettuccini noodles, cooked and drained
⅓ cup grated Parmesan cheese

Though this recipe may seem fairly high in calories and carbs, don't be discouraged. Any balanced diet should be just that—balanced—and this recipe keeps things level with a serving of lean protein, calcium, and good carbs.

1. Preheat oven to 350°F. Spray a 2-quart baking dish with nonstick cooking spray. In a skillet, melt the butter over medium heat. Add the mushrooms and sauté, stirring occasionally, until tender, about 5–7 minutes. Add the flour, salt, and pepper and stir until well blended. Slowly pour in the milk, stirring constantly. Add the Worcestershire sauce, and simmer, stirring occasionally, until the sauce thickens, about 5 minutes. Add the Swiss cheese, bell pepper, and scallions and mix well. Add the turkey and fettuccini, mixing well.
2. Transfer to the prepared baking dish and sprinkle with the Parmesan cheese.

3. Bake, uncovered, until flavors have blended, about 20 minutes. Serve immediately.

CALORIES 537
FAT 16G
CARBOHYDRATES 57G
PROTEIN 41G

Oven-Baked Turkey Cutlets with Lime

PROTEIN

SERVES 6

Nonstick cooking spray
2 large limes: 1 zested and juiced, 1 sliced
Fine zest of ½ orange
⅓ cup plain nonfat yogurt
1 tablespoon canola oil
2 teaspoons fresh gingerroot, peeled, chopped
1 teaspoon ground cumin
1 teaspoon ground coriander
1 teaspoon sea salt
1 clove garlic, crushed
1½ pounds lean turkey cutlets
Fresh cilantro sprigs for garnish

Nonfat yogurt is fat free but still rich in essential vitamins and minerals such as riboflavin, calcium, and phosphorus. Acidophilus—a bacteria that helps your immune system—is also found in yogurt.

1. Preheat oven to 375°F. Prepare baking dish by spraying with nonstick spray. Place lime zest, juice, and orange zest in a large bowl. Add yogurt, oil, ginger, cumin, coriander, salt, and garlic to bowl with zest and juice. Mix until blended.

2. Add the turkey cutlets to the bowl with the yogurt mixture, stirring to coat the cutlets, but do not marinate, as their texture will become mealy.

3. Transfer turkey cutlets to a prepared baking dish. Cover with foil and bake for 10 minutes. Uncover and cook an additional 5 minutes or until done. Serve with lime wedges. Garnish with cilantro sprigs.

CALORIES 229
FAT 4G
CARBOHYDRATES 8G
PROTEIN 28G

Sautéed Turkey with Mushroom Sauce

SUPERFOOD PROTEIN

SERVES 6

1 tablespoon cornstarch
2 tablespoons cold water
1 tablespoon unsalted butter
2 teaspoons cornmeal
Salt to taste
Freshly ground black pepper to taste
1½ pounds boneless, skinless turkey breast
4 shallots, chopped
1 clove garlic, minced
½ pound shiitake mushrooms, stemmed and
   brushed clean
½ cup white grape juice
Fine zest of ½ orange
¼ teaspoon ground nutmeg
¾ cup low-sodium chicken broth
½ cup nonfat milk
½ cup chopped fresh Italian flat-leaf parsley
   leaves

White grape juice has vitamin C, and its natural sugars give your body an energy boost.

1. Combine cornstarch and water to form smooth paste. Preheat the oven to 325°F.

2. Over medium heat, melt the butter in oven proof skillet. Dust the turkey with cornmeal, salt, and pepper.

3. Sauté the turkey on each side until just browned, about 3 minutes each. Add the shallots, garlic, and mushrooms to skillet. Sauté, stirring constantly.

4. Add the grape juice, orange zest, nutmeg, chicken broth, and milk. Cover the turkey with sauce. Transfer to oven, cover, and bake for 35–40 minutes or until done.

5. Remove the turkey from the skillet, leaving the sauce. Slice turkey and arrange on a serving platter or individual plates.

6. Return skillet to stove top and, over medium heat, whisk the flour and water mixture into the sauce until it thickens. Pour sauce over turkey and sprinkle with parsley.

CALORIES 200
FAT 4G
CARBOHYDRATES 10G
PROTEIN 31G

Grilled Turkey Thighs with Fresh Herbs

SERVES 6

¼ cup olive oil
¼ cup freshly squeezed lemon juice
1 tablespoon chopped fresh thyme leaves
1 tablespoon chopped fresh basil leaves
1 teaspoon cayenne pepper
1 teaspoon onion powder
½ teaspoon garlic powder
2 to 2½ pounds turkey thigh, bone in, skin on

Fresh thyme and basil are not just for flavor, they are packed with antioxidants, are high in fiber, and are naturally low in calories.

1. Preheat oven to 350°F. Then, heat the grill or grill pan.
2. In a small bowl, whisk together the olive oil, lemon juice, thyme, basil, cayenne pepper, onion powder, and garlic powder.
3. Brush both sides of the turkey with olive oil mixture and place on grill or grill pan. Brush every few minutes with olive oil mixture and cook until turkey has nice grill marks and color on both sides.
4. Transfer to baking sheet or baking dish and finish cooking in the oven until turkey is cooked through, about 15–20 minutes. Slice and serve.

CALORIES 312
FAT 21G
CARBOHYDRATES 2G
PROTEIN 27G

BURN IT UP

Spicy cayenne pepper is one of the all-time best metabolism enhancers. It serves as a potent stimulant for the whole body and a tonic for the nervous system. Recent research has suggested that cayenne can also ease the severe pain of shingles and migraines. So spice up your meals and feel good about it.

Turkey Tenderloin with Dijon Glaze

SERVES 6

> 1 pound turkey tenderloin
> ½ cup orange juice
> Juice of 1 lemon
> 2 tablespoons Dijon mustard
> ¼ cup honey
> 2 garlic cloves, chopped
> Sea salt and black pepper to taste

Turkey tenderloins have all the nutrition of turkey breasts and are great for roasting, grilling, or slicing into medallions or cutlets.

1. Preheat grill to medium-high heat. Butterfly tenderloin by cutting in half lengthwise, being careful not to cut all the way through. Spread tenderloin open, cover with plastic wrap and pound out using a meat mallet to about ½ inch thick.
2. In a bowl, mix remaining ingredients and blend well. Transfer turkey to large Ziploc bag and pour in mustard mixture. Knead the bag pressing the marinade into the turkey. Let stand at room temperature for 10 minutes.
3. Place turkey on grill for 5 minutes, brushing with any leftover marinade. Turn turkey and cook for 4–6 minutes on second side, until thoroughly cooked. Discard any remaining marinade. Slice and serve hot.

CALORIES 227
FAT 5G
CARBOHYDRATES 2G
PROTEIN 22G

Turkey Chili

SERVES 12

> ¼ cup cooking oil
> 2½ pounds lean ground turkey
> 4 sweet red onions, chopped
> 6 cloves garlic, chopped
> 4 Italian green peppers, seeded, and chopped
> 2 large red bell peppers, seeded and chopped
> 2 yellow peppers, seeded, and chopped
> 4 jalapeño peppers, seeded, and chopped
> 2 tablespoons chili powder, or to taste
> 1 tablespoon dry English-style mustard
> 1 teaspoon cinnamon
> 1 teaspoon Dutch-process cocoa powder
> ½ cup strong cold coffee
> 3 14-ounce cans red kidney beans, drained and rinsed
> 2 28-ounce cans Italian plum tomatoes
> Salt to taste
> Black pepper to taste
> 1 teaspoon liquid smoke, or to taste

Caffeine is actually good for your metabolism. Its natural properties instantly increase your energy and help you burn more calories.

1. Heat the oil over medium heat in a stockpot or quart boiler. Add the turkey, breaking it up with a wooden spoon. Add the onions, garlic, and peppers and sauté until tender, about 8 minutes. Then, add the chili powder and stir to combine.
2. Separately, in a small bowl, blend the dry mustard, cinnamon, and cocoa powder with the coffee. Whisk with a fork until smooth. Add to the turkey mixture, stir in remaining ingredients and cover. Reduce heat to low and simmer, stirring occasionally and

adding water, if needed to prevent sticking and drying. Simmer about 2 hours. When ready, serve hot.

CALORIES 355
FAT 14G
CARBOHYDRATES 36G
PROTEIN 25G

Turkey Picadillo

SUPERFOOD SPICY

SERVES 6

2 tablespoons olive oil
1½ pounds lean ground turkey
1 clove fresh garlic, minced
½ teaspoon all-purpose seasoning
1 yellow onion, chopped
1 large tomato, diced
1 tablespoon tomato paste
2 teaspoons cumin
Fine zest of 1 lemon
¼ cup chopped fresh cilantro leaves
¼ cup golden raisins
1 cup baking potatoes, peeled and cut into
    1-inch cubes
1 cup water

All-purpose seasoning is a tasty and powerful blend of herbs and spices that work together to increase your metabolism.

1. In large skillet over medium heat, heat 1 tablespoon olive oil. Add turkey, remaining olive oil, garlic, and all-purpose seasoning to skillet. Cook on medium high for 5–8 minutes, using a spatula to stir and chop turkey meat.

2. Add onions, tomatoes, tomato paste, cumin, lemon zest, and cilantro to skillet. Cook for 5 minutes on medium heat.

3. Add raisins, potatoes, and water. Simmer for another 8–10 minutes or until potatoes are tender.

CALORIES 222
FAT 11G
CARBOHYDRATES 14G
PROTEIN 25G

Cream Cheese Turkey Scallopini

SERVES 5

PROTEIN

1 tablespoon olive oil
2 pounds boneless, skinless turkey breasts
Black pepper to taste
2 yellow onions, chopped
1 stick unsalted butter
½ cup plain flour
4 cups low-fat milk
2 cups nonfat sour cream
8 ounces low-fat cream cheese

Scallopini are very thinly sliced pieces of protein—such as the lean turkey in this recipe. If your chicken (or veal or turkey) cutlets are thicker than you like, lightly pound with a meat pounder to about ¼–½ inch thick.

1. Preheat oven to 400°F. Grease a large roasting pan with oil. Slice the turkey into thin "scaloppini-like" portions, and season with pepper.
2. Place onions and turkey in roasting pan. Cover and roast for 20 minutes. Uncover and continue roasting for another 10–15 minutes.
3. While turkey is roasting, make the cheese sauce by melting butter in large saucepan over medium heat. Sprinkle in flour and stir with a wooden spoon. Whisk in the milk and sour cream, stirring constantly. Simmer until the sauce thickens, about 10 minutes. Remove from heat and stir in cream cheese.
4. To serve, place roasted turkey on platter and drizzle with cheese sauce. Serve remaining sauce on the side.

CALORIES 340
FAT 11G
CARBOHYDRATES 27G
PROTEIN 32G

BURN IT UP

Like avocados and nuts, olive oil contains essential fatty acids. Fats slow down the entry of carbohydrates into the bloodstream and help you to feel full. You should receive 25–35 percent of your daily calories from fats.

Risotto with Walnut-Crusted Turkey

SERVES 8

ANTIOXIDANTS SUPERFOOD

2 tablespoons olive oil
Sea salt to taste
Black pepper to taste
1½ pounds boneless turkey, cut into
    1-inch pieces
1 egg, beaten
1 cup finely chopped walnuts
4 cloves garlic, minced
1½ cups Arborio rice
¾ cup pinot grigio or sauvignon blanc
4 cups chicken broth, plus 1 to 2 cups,
    if needed
½ bunch fresh Italian parsley,
    chopped
½ cup Parmesan cheese, grated
1 tablespoon butter, unsalted

Walnuts, which are low in saturated fat, contain omega-3 fatty acids and are attributed to lowering cholesterol and decreasing stress.

1. Preheat oven to 375°F. Lightly grease a baking pan with 1 tablespoon of the oil. Season the turkey with salt and pepper. Dip turkey in the egg, and lightly coat with nuts. Heat 1 tablespoon of the oil in a large saucepan. Lightly brown the turkey on each side, about 3 minutes per side. Transfer turkey to baking dish and bake for about 10 minutes, or until cooked through.

2. Add the garlic and rice; stir for 1 minute. Pour in the wine and stir until completely absorbed. Add the broth ½ cup at a time, stirring frequently and allowing each addition to be completely absorbed before adding the next. (You will be able to tell because the rice will begin to make that "sticking" sound). Continue until all broth is absorbed and rice is tender. This process will take about 20 minutes. Remove from heat; add cooked turkey along with parsley, cheese, and butter.

CALORIES 339
FAT 13G
CARBOHYDRATES 39G
PROTEIN 24G

CHAPTER 8

Beef, Pork, and Lamb

Beef and pork don't have to be heavy proteins that are difficult to digest! With a tweak here or there, it's easy to adjust your game plan by adding nutrient rich, fiber filled foods. Soon, you'll find that what are traditionally considered to be heavy, protein-filled meals are now deliciously light and metabolically friendly.

Filet Mignon with Mushrooms, Onions, and Red Wine Reduction

SERVES 10–12

4 tablespoons unsalted butter

4 cups finely chopped mushrooms such as cremini, morel, or shiitake

6 shallots, peeled and minced

4 cloves garlic, peeled and minced

1 tablespoon Worcestershire sauce

¼ cup chestnut flour, mixed with salt and pepper to taste

½ cup dry red wine, divided

4 sage leaves, torn in small pieces

1 6-pound filet mignon, fat trimmed

½ cup chestnut flour

1 tablespoon coarse salt

1 teaspoon black pepper

1 cup beef broth

2 tablespoons olive oil

Protein-rich filet mignon is one of the leanest cuts of beef, and you can make this meal even more healthy by substituting flavorful chestnut flour for lower-fiber white flour.

1. Melt the butter and sauté the mushrooms, shallots, and garlic until the vegetables are soft and the mushrooms are wilted. Add the Worcestershire sauce. Add ¼ cup flour seasoned with salt and pepper and blend; stir in ½ cup red wine and sage. Reduce to about 1½ cups.

2. Preheat oven to 350°F. Make a trough down the middle of the filet mignon using the end of a wooden spoon or knife. Stuff the mushroom mixture into the filet. If there are extra mushrooms, save for the sauce.

3. Coat the outside of the filet with ½ cup chestnut flour, salt, and pepper. Place the remaining ½ cup red wine and beef broth in the bottom of a roasting pan with the filet. Sprinkle with olive oil and roast in oven for 20 minutes per pound.

CALORIES 321

FAT 10G

CARBOHYDRATES 9G

PROTEIN 21G

BURN IT UP

Red wine, in moderation, can have quite the positive impact on your health. Studies have shown that red wine may inhibit the formation of fat cells and help prevent obesity by affecting the gene SIRT1. Red wine is rich in antioxidants that can help raise HDL ("good") cholesterol and protect against heart disease.

Marinated Beef with Sautéed Spinach

`PROTEIN` `ANTIOXIDANTS` `SUPERFOOD`

SERVES 4

2 cloves garlic, minced
2 tablespoons sugar
½ teaspoon salt, or to taste
1 teaspoon red pepper flakes, or to taste
2 tablespoons canola oil
1½ pounds filet mignon, trimmed and cut into
   ½-inch slices
¼ cup dry white wine
¼ cup white wine vinegar
2 teaspoons sugar
2 tablespoons fish sauce
2 tablespoons canola or peanut oil
4 cups fresh baby spinach, washed and dried,
   stems removed
1 tablespoon butter
For garnish: soy sauce, chopped scallions, lemon
   and lime slices

Filled with protein and vitamin A, this recipe gets its main metabolic strength from filet mignon, superfood spinach, and spicy red pepper flakes.

1. In a large bowl or glass baking dish, mix together the garlic, 2 tablespoons sugar, salt, pepper flakes, and 2 tablespoons oil. Add the slices of filet mignon, turning to coat. Cover and refrigerate for 2 hours.
2. Mix together the wine, vinegar, 2 teaspoons sugar, and fish sauce; set aside. Heat a nonstick pan over very high heat and add 2 tablespoons oil. Quickly sauté the filets until browned on both sides, about 2 minutes per side. Arrange the meat over a bed of spinach.

3. Add the wine mixture and butter to the pan and deglaze, reducing quickly. Pour over the spinach and meat. Serve with soy sauce, chopped scallions, and slices of lemon or lime on the side.

`CALORIES` 298
`FAT` 5G
`CARBOHYDRATES` 8G
`PROTEIN` 19G

Stir-Fried Beef

`SUPERFOOD`

SERVES 4

3 tablespoons peanut oil
2 tablespoons shredded gingerroot
½ cup shredded red hot chili peppers
½ pound sliced beef
3 tablespoons soy sauce
1 tablespoon sugar substitute like Splenda
1 tablespoon red wine

Stir-fry can often be high in both calories and fat, but this leaner version is filled with energy-boosting protein, ginger, and spicy peppers.

1. Heat the peanut oil in a heavy skillet or wok.
2. Add the gingerroot and chili peppers. Then add the sliced beef, soy sauce, sugar substitute, and wine. Stir ingredients until blended and beef is browned.

`CALORIES` 255
`FAT` 21G
`CARBOHYDRATES` 4G
`PROTEIN` 12G

Soy-Marinated Flank Steak

SUPERFOOD

1 teaspoon sea salt
1 teaspoon coarse ground black
  pepper
1½ pounds flank steak
1 clove garlic, chopped
¼ cup garlic-flavored olive oil
6 tablespoons cider vinegar
2 teaspoons low-sodium soy sauce

Balance this meal with a nutrient-rich vegetable side such as Asian Stir Fry with Rice and Vegetables (Chapter 12).

1. Sprinkle salt and pepper liberally on both sides of steak. Make small slits with sharp knife over steak on both sides so the salt and pepper can soak in and season the meat. Place all other ingredients in a plastic bag, seal, and shake well.
2. Add the flank steak to the plastic bag and let it sit for 2 hours. Transfer flank steak to grill and cook to desired doneness.
3. Transfer steak to cutting board and slice diagonally across the grain, making very thin slices, about ⅛ inch thick.

CALORIES 448
FAT 28G
CARBOHYDRATES 2G
PROTEIN 48G

BURN IT UP

Soy sauce is made with soybeans, wheat, and salt and is filled with metabolism-boosting iron. It actually also contains protein and acts as a tenderizer for other proteins such as beef.

Beef Fajitas with Red and Green Bell Peppers

HIGH FIBER ANTIOXIDANTS

SERVES 4

1 pound extra-lean beef round steaks, cut into thin strips
1 envelope fajita seasoning mix
½ tablespoon olive oil
1 small onion, diced
1 green bell pepper, sliced
1 small red bell pepper, sliced
½ cup water
1 11-ounce packet corn tortillas

Corn tortillas are higher in fiber than their flour-filled counterparts, so your body has to work harder, thus burning more calories, to digest them. If you have the choice, always go the high-fiber route.

1. Sprinkle steak strips with fajita seasoning in a medium bowl, making sure to cover all sides.
2. Heat oil in heavy skillet over medium heat. Add onion and pepper and sauté until tender, about 4 minutes. Add steak to vegetables and add water. Cover and simmer for 3 hours.
3. When ready to serve, place fajita mixture in center of tortillas, fold in half and serve.

CALORIES 610
FAT 26G
CARBOHYDRATES 58G
PROTEIN 31G

Thai Beef Satay

PROTEIN CALCIUM SUPERFOOD

SERVES 4

1 pound beef tenderloin, cut into 2-inch strips
15–20 wooden skewers, soaked in water for 20 minutes
1 cup plain nonfat yogurt
1 teaspoon minced garlic
2 teaspoons curry powder
Juice of 1 lemon

Yogurt is high in protein, potassium, phosphorus, and amino acids, all of which boost your immune system and help protect against cancer.

1. Thread beef chunks onto skewers. Separately, combine the yogurt, garlic, curry powder, and lemon juice together in a small bowl. Coat the beef skewers with the yogurt mixture. Place skewers with beef and marinade into the refrigerator for several hours to let the marinade soak in.
2. When ready to cook, heat grill or grill pan over medium heat and add skewers. Cook until cooked through but tender, about 2–3 minutes on each side.

CALORIES 328
FAT 22G
CARBOHYDRATES 6G
PROTEIN 26G

Mexican Beef Tacos

SERVES 4

½ tablespoon canola oil
1 pound extra-lean ground beef
1 1¼-ounce packet low-sodium taco seasoning mix
¼ cup water
8 hard taco shells
4 ounces shredded Mexican cheese
½ head iceberg lettuce, shredded
1 tomato, diced
1 small onion, diced
½ cup nonfat sour cream

Tacos are a great way to boost your metabolism as they combine lean protein with other metabolism-boosting ingredients such as antioxidant-filled tomatoes and calcium-rich cheese and sour cream. Make your tacos even leaner with low-fat ground turkey or shredded chicken, or skip the traditional and add protein-filled, low-fat black beans.

1. Heat oil in heavy skillet over medium heat and add in beef. Cook until beef is browned. Add taco seasoning and water to taste, about ¼ cup.
2. Warm taco shells in oven at 325°F for 10 minutes. Spoon seasoned beef into warm taco shell. Layer the remaining ingredients on top of beef as desired.

CALORIES   483
FAT   19G
CARBOHYDRATES   29G
PROTEIN   45G

Traditional Prime Rib of Beef

SERVES 10

1 3-pound beef rib roast
½ teaspoon garlic powder
Sea salt to taste
Black pepper to taste
1 small onion, chopped
3 stalks celery, chopped
1 14-ounce can low-sodium beef broth

For maximum metabolism-boosting potential, pair this protein-rich entrée with a nutrient-rich side such as Wild Rice with Fresh Herbs (Chapter 12).

1. Preheat oven to 350°F. Rub garlic powder, salt, and black pepper on beef.
2. Place roast, onion, celery, and beef broth into roasting pan. Bake uncovered for about 2 hours or until beef reaches 145°F.
3. Let rest for 5–10 minutes before serving to allow juices to settle. Slice and serve with any remaining pan juices.

CALORIES   455
FAT   39G
CARBOHYDRATES   2G
PROTEIN   23G

Beef Stroganoff

SERVES 4

1 pound very lean flank steak
1 tablespoon olive oil
1 large onion, finely chopped
1 clove garlic, finely chopped
2 cups cremini mushrooms, sliced
1 tablespoon cornstarch
2 tablespoons sherry wine
1 cup low-sodium beef broth
Sea salt to taste
Black pepper to taste
1 cup fat-free sour cream
2 cups cooked egg noodles
½ cup finely chopped Italian flat-leaf parsley
   leaves

One key ingredient to this recipe is the antioxidant-rich parsley leaves. The antioxidants help protect your body's cells while the parsley also provides fiber essential to digesting this hearty meal.

1. Thinly slice steak. Then, in heavy skillet over medium heat, heat oil and add onions and garlic. Sauté until onion is tender and garlic is fragrant. Add steak and mushrooms. Cook until meat is browned.
2. Separately, combine cornstarch, sherry, and broth in a small bowl to make a paste. Pour paste into meat mixture and let simmer for 5 minutes. Add salt, pepper, and sour cream. Add cooked noodles and serve garnished with parsley.

CALORIES 488
FAT 22G
CARBOHYDRATES 38G
PROTEIN 33G

Spicy Three-Pepper Burgers

SERVES 4

½ teaspoon sea salt
1 teaspoon freshly ground black pepper
1 teaspoon cayenne pepper
½ teaspoon red pepper flakes
2 teaspoons low-sodium soy sauce
1 tablespoon Worcestershire sauce
16 ounces ground round or sirloin beef
4 whole wheat hamburger buns

If some spice is good, lots of spice is better! The peppers in this recipe are instant metabolism enhancers and also aid in digestion.

1. Place all ingredients except beef and buns in large mixing bowl and mix well to combine. Add beef and mix together until well combined. Form into 4½-inch-thick patties.
2. Heat grill or grill pan over medium heat. Place burgers and cook until done, about 3–4 minutes per side. When cooked through, transfer to wheat buns and serve.

CALORIES 204
FAT 11G
CARBOHYDRATES 1G
PROTEIN 25G

Indian Curried Lamb Kebabs

SERVES 4

1 cup plain nonfat yogurt
Juice of ½ lime
2 cloves garlic, mashed
2 tablespoons curry powder
1 teaspoon freshly grated gingerroot
Sea salt to taste
Freshly ground black pepper to taste
1 teaspoon dried mint leaves or 1 tablespoon fresh mint, minced
1 pound lean lamb, well trimmed, cut in 1-inch pieces
8 6-inch wooden skewers soaked in water for at least 30 minutes

Lamb is full of red blood cell–building and immune system–boosting zinc and iron, as well as the B vitamins essential to a high metabolism.

1. Combine all ingredients to create marinade, then add lamb. Marinate for 4 hours or overnight.
2. When ready to cook, heat grill or grill pan over medium heat. Dry lamb on paper towels, then string on skewers. Broil for about 2 minutes per side for medium doneness.

CALORIES 243
FAT 9G
CARBOHYDRATES 8G
PROTEIN 32G

Herb-Crusted Rack of Lamb

SERVES 4–6

2 racks of lamb, 1½ to 2 pounds each, most of the fat removed
2 teaspoons sea salt
Freshly ground black pepper to taste
1 cup cornmeal
4 tablespoons finely chopped fresh rosemary leaves
3 tablespoons minced fresh Italian flat-leaf parsley leaves
2 tablespoons minced chives
2 tablespoons minced garlic
½ cup olive oil
6 sprigs fresh mint and lemon wedges to garnish

Nutrient-rich fresh herbs such as rosemary, parsley, chives, and mint provide substantial amounts of vitamins, minerals, and antioxidants and the fiber-rich cornmeal adds flavor and texture to this metabolism-boosting favorite.

1. Preheat the broiler to 450°F. Rub the lamb with salt and pepper. Place on a broiler pan, bones side up. Broil for 5 minutes. Turn and continue to broil for another 5 minutes.
2. While the lamb is broiling, mix the rest of the ingredients together. Press the herb mixture into the meat and change the setting from broil to bake. Bake the lamb at 450°F for another 10–12 minutes. Slice into chops and serve.

CALORIES 288
FAT 4G
CARBOHYDRATES 8G
PROTEIN 16G

Lamb with Eggplant and Mint Yogurt

HIGH FIBER ANTIOXIDANTS

¼ cup olive oil

8 small eggplants, about 4–5 inches in length

½ cup minced onion

4 cloves garlic, minced

½ pound lean ground lamb

Sea salt to taste

Black pepper to taste

½ cup fresh tomato, finely chopped

3 tablespoons chopped fresh mint

¼ teaspoon ground coriander

Juice of ½ lemon

For garnish: yogurt, extra mint leaves, and finely chopped tomato

Eggplant is rich in fiber, potassium, B vitamins, and antioxidants. As a healthy alternative to frying, simply slice eggplant in half lengthwise and bake on parchment paper–lined baking sheet for about 15 minutes.

1. Heat oil over medium-high heat. Add eggplant and fry until just tender, about 3 minutes. Remove from oil and set aside on paper towels to drain. When cool enough to handle, make a slit from top to bottom but do not cut through.
2. Then, over moderate heat, add the onion, garlic, lamb, salt, pepper, tomato, and herbs to the skillet. Stir to blend and break up the lamb. Add lemon juice to flavor. Set aside to cool for 15 minutes.
3. Preheat oven to 400°F. Place the eggplants on a baking sheet that has been covered with aluminum foil. Spread the eggplants open and fill with lamb stuffing. Bake for 10 minutes.
4. Serve with a dollop of yogurt on each eggplant and garnish with mint and chopped tomato.

CALORIES 300
FAT 4G
CARBOHYDRATES 8G
PROTEIN 18G

BURN IT UP

Garlic, one of the world's most popular culinary herbs, has a long history as a medicinal plant. Among its many attributes, garlic is known to lower cholesterol levels, thin the blood, kill bacteria, boost the immune system, lower blood sugar levels, reduce the risk of certain types of cancer, and fire up the metabolic furnace. Bottom line: those who wish to maintain their health and age well should eat lots of garlic.

Sautéed Pork Meatballs with Asian Pears

`HIGH FIBER` `ANTIOXIDANTS`

SERVES 4

1 pound ground pork
1 yellow onion, finely chopped
2 teaspoons fresh oregano leaves, chopped
1 egg, lightly beaten
Sea salt and black pepper to taste
1 cup Italian-seasoned bread crumbs, plus an additional ½ cup if needed
2 tablespoons olive oil
2 Asian pears, cored and diced
¼ cup apple juice

Pears are rich in fiber and vitamins C and K, the former of which is an antioxidant that works to protect your body's cells.

1. Preheat oven to 400°F. Line baking sheet with parchment paper.
2. In bowl, combine pork, onion, oregano, egg, salt, and pepper. Mix well. Add in bread crumbs as needed to bind ingredients. Form mixture into 1½- to 2-inch balls. Place meatballs on baking sheet. Bake for about 15 minutes. Remove from oven and set aside.
3. When meatballs are cooked but not done, heat oil in large saucepan over medium heat, add meatballs, pears, and apple juice. Cover and reduce heat. Simmer for about 8 minutes or until meatballs are cooked through. Serve meatballs with a side of pasta tossed with salt, pepper, and olive oil.

CALORIES 267
FAT 5G
CARBOHYDRATES 16G
PROTEIN 37G

Skillet Pork Roast with Prepared Horseradish

`SUPERFOOD`

SERVES 6

2 tablespoons olive oil
1½ pounds boneless pork roast, cut into 1- to 2-inch cubes
1 yellow onion, chopped
1 carrot, peeled and chopped
1 rib celery, chopped
2 cups water
2 cans beef broth
Sea salt and lemon pepper to taste
¼ cup cider vinegar
¼ cup prepared horseradish

The spicy horseradish found in this recipe is high in flavor and fat free! It also, contains potassium, calcium, and other essential vitamins. You'll get the most out of horseradish if you eat it raw, but you'll still benefit from eating it cooked.

In large saucepan, heat oil over medium heat. Add in pork and cook until browned, about 3 minutes. Add in vegetables and cook until onions are softened, about 3 minutes. Add water, beef broth, salt, lemon pepper, vinegar, and horseradish and bring to a boil. Reduce the heat, cover, and simmer for 1½ hours or until pork is tender.

CALORIES 210
FAT 6G
CARBOHYDRATES 4G
PROTEIN 34G

Oven-Baked Pork Chops with Cinnamon-Glazed Peaches and Roasted Vegetables

SERVES 4

SUPERFOOD SPICY

Nonstick cooking spray
5 carrots, washed and peeled
10-ounce package frozen sliced peaches, thawed
2 teaspoons brown sugar
¼ teaspoon ground cinnamon
Pinch ground cloves
¼ teaspoon freshly ground black pepper
1 teaspoon chopped fresh thyme leaves
1 teaspoon chopped fresh rosemary leaves
½ teaspoon chopped fresh oregano leaves
1 teaspoon lemon pepper
4 6-ounce boneless pork chops
8 cloves garlic, crushed plus 1 clove
4 large Yukon gold potatoes, washed and sliced
10-ounce package frozen whole green beans, thawed
Extra-virgin olive spray oil

The peaches in this recipe are considered a superfood because they are low in calories; naturally fat free; and high in fiber, vitamins A and C, niacin, and potassium.

1. Preheat oven to 425°F. Treat a large roasting pan or jelly roll pan with nonstick spray. Place the carrots, peaches, brown sugar, cinnamon, and cloves in a medium-size bowl; stir to mix. Set aside.
2. Mix the pepper, thyme, rosemary, oregano, and lemon pepper granules together and use a mortar and pestle or the back of a spoon to crush them. Rub the pork chops with the one clove of garlic.
3. Evenly spread the sliced potatoes and green beans across the prepared baking pan. Place the crushed garlic cloves and pork chops atop the vegetables. Spray lightly with the spray oil. Sprinkle with the herb mixture. Spread the carrot and peach mixture atop the pork chops and vegetables.
4. Bake for 30 minutes or until the meat, potatoes, and carrots are tender.

CALORIES 463
FAT 14G
CARBOHYDRATES 38G
PROTEIN 42G

BURN IT UP

Researchers at the U.S. Agricultural Research Service have theorized that a substance called MHCP—found in cinnamon—may help fat cells become more responsive to the insulin needed to increase glucose (sugar) metabolism. Instead of butter, try sprinkling cinnamon on your whole-grain bread or oatmeal to save fat calories and boost your metabolism. You can also sprinkle cinnamon in your coffee, tea, or yogurt.

Roasted Pork Tenderloin with Blackberry Glaze

SUPERFOOD PROTEIN SPICY

SERVES 4

1 tablespoon olive oil
1 tablespoon coarse-grain mustard
1½-pound pork tenderloin
1 tablespoon kosher salt
1 teaspoon ground black pepper
1 shallot, minced
½ cup blackberries, fresh or frozen
1 tablespoon balsamic vinegar
½ cup blackberry preserves

The antioxidant-rich blackberries found in this recipe are high in fiber and vitamin C and are a natural metabolism enhancer. The spicy mustard also helps this dish pack a metabolism-boosting punch.

1. Preheat a grill or grill pan over high heat. Rub 1 teaspoon olive oil and coarse-grain mustard on the tenderloin, then sprinkle with the kosher salt and black pepper.
2. Place tenderloin on heated pan and sear on all sides for a total of about 10 minutes. Place the tenderloin on foil; cover and let rest about 10 minutes before slicing.
3. Meanwhile, sauté the shallots until tender in remaining olive oil. Remove from heat and stir in the blackberries, balsamic vinegar, and blackberry preserves.
4. Slice tenderloin in ½-inch-thick slices and arrange on a platter. Spoon the blackberry sauce over and serve.

CALORIES 382
FAT 12G
CARBOHYDRATES 31G
PROTEIN 35G

Roasted Pork Loin with Dried Plums

HIGH FIBER

SERVES 4

2 pounds pork tenderloin
1 tablespoon chopped fresh rosemary leaves
1 tablespoon chopped fresh tarragon
1 teaspoon chopped fresh thyme leaves
Sea salt to taste
Black pepper to taste
2 tablespoons olive oil
Nonstick cooking spray
½ cup coarsely chopped shallots
2 cloves garlic, minced
¼ cup brandy
½ cup low-sodium chicken broth
½ cup pitted dried plums, quartered
½ tablespoon cornstarch
1 tablespoon nonfat milk
2 tablespoons nonfat sour cream

The dried plums, or prunes, are high in fiber, vitamin A, iron, and other minerals. They are also linked to reducing heart disease.

1. Preheat oven to 450°F. Coat pork with rosemary, tarragon, and thyme, and season lightly with salt and pepper. Drizzle with the olive oil.
2. Spray bottom of roasting pan with nonstick spray. Then, sprinkle shallots and garlic in bottom of pan. Place prepared pork on top of shallot and garlic mixture. Roast for 10 minutes, uncovered.
3. Reduce oven temperature to 300°F. Cover roast and cook about 40 minutes or until pork is cooked through, just pink. Remove roast from oven and keep warm in foil. Place roasting pan on stove top. Add brandy and scrape any brown bits. Add chicken

broth, stir, and then transfer to a saucepan. Simmer over low heat until reduced by half. Strain the sauce and return to pan.

4. Add the dried plums and simmer about 10 minutes over low heat. Mix the cornstarch and milk. Add the sour cream to the cornstarch mixture then stir into the sauce. Simmer until sauce thickens slightly. Season with additional salt and pepper if needed.

5. Slice the pork roast, arrange on platter, and spoon plum sauce over top. Serve.

CALORIES 287
FAT 24G
CARBOHYDRATES 11G
PROTEIN 67G

Herb-Crusted Pork Tenderloin with Dijon Mustard

SPICY PROTEIN

SERVES 4

2 pounds pork tenderloin, fat trimmed
1 tablespoon Dijon mustard
1 package low-sodium onion soup mix
2 teaspoons chopped fresh rosemary leaves
2 garlic cloves, minced
1 teaspoon chopped fresh marjoram leaves

Rich protein is the core of this dish. The spicy mustard contains phytonutrients and the antioxidant selenium and will instantly boost your metabolism.

1. Preheat oven to 375°F. Rub top of tenderloin with Dijon mustard. Then, coat both sides with the soup mix. Place on aluminum foil, mustard side up. Top with rosemary, garlic, and marjoram. Cover with foil and place on baking sheet or in baking dish.

2. Bake for about 40 minutes or until pork is cooked through but slightly pink. Remove from oven, let rest 10 minutes, then slice and serve.

CALORIES 330
FAT 10G
CARBOHYDRATES 9G
PROTEIN 49G

Baked Pork Chops with Long-Grain Rice

CALCIUM

SERVES 4

2 tablespoons olive oil
4 6-ounce bone-in pork chops, fat trimmed
½ cup cooked brown rice
1 10-ounce can light or reduced-fat cream of mushroom soup
1 cup nonfat sour cream

High levels of fiber, selenium, manganese, and protein are all found in the brown rice used in this recipe. The sour cream is rich in calcium and will help strengthen bones, regulate blood pressure, secrete hormones and digestive enzymes, assist with weight loss, and boost your metabolism.

1. Heat oil in heavy skillet over medium-high heat. Add pork chops and brown on each side, about 2–3 minutes per side.

2. Spray baking dish with nonstick spray and preheat oven to 350°F. Add rice to

baking dish, then add pork chops. In separate bowl, combine soup and sour cream. Mix to combine. Pour over pork chops and rice. Cover with foil and bake for 40 minutes or almost done. Remove foil and bake an additional 5 minutes or until cooked through. Remove from oven and serve.

CALORIES 510
FAT 34G
CARBOHYDRATES 17G
PROTEIN 35G

Pan-Grilled Pork Chops with Artichoke Hearts and Lemon

SUPERFOOD

SERVES 2

1 teaspoon olive oil
Sea salt to taste
Black pepper to taste
2 rib or loin pork chops
1 10-ounce package frozen artichoke hearts, thawed
½ lemon, zested and juiced
½ cup chicken broth

Artichokes are a true superfood! They are high in fiber, filled with vitamin C and magnesium, and have over 400 milligrams of potassium which may reduce the risk of stroke.

1. Heat the oil in a large nonstick pan over medium flame. Sprinkle salt and pepper on the pork chops. Brown on each side, about 2 minutes each side. Add the artichokes and toss to coat.

2. Reduce heat to medium low, add the lemon zest and juice, then add broth, cover and cook for 5 minutes at a simmer. Turn and cook for another 5 minutes or until done.

CALORIES 455
FAT 25G
CARBOHYDRATES 18G
PROTEIN 35G

Scandinavian Pork with Caraway Seeds

HIGH FIBER PROTEIN

SERVES 2

1 teaspoon olive oil
Sea salt to taste
Black pepper to taste
1 teaspoon Wondra flour
8 ounces pork tenderloin, trimmed of fat
2 medium red onions, chopped
¼ cup low-sodium chicken broth
8 ounces sauerkraut, drained
1 teaspoon caraway seeds

High-fiber sauerkraut may improve the immune system and balance the bacteria in the intestinal tract. It is also linked to the prevention of cancer growth. In Germany, people often drink sauerkraut juice to cure an upset stomach.

1. Heat the oil in a frying pan over medium heat. Sprinkle the pork tenderloin with salt, pepper, and flour. Sauté the pork over medium heat for 4 minutes; turn the pork and add onions.

2. Continue to sauté until the pork is lightly browned on both sides and the onions have softened slightly.

3. Add the chicken broth, sauerkraut, and caraway seeds. Cover and simmer for 25 minutes. Pork should be slightly pink.

CALORIES 309
FAT 15G
CARBOHYDRATES:4G
PROTEIN 32G

Wontons of Pork with Asian Cabbage

PROTEIN ANTIOXIDANTS SUPERFOOD

SERVES 4

¼ cup peanut oil plus another ¼ cup for later use
2 tablespoons sesame oil
6 scallions, coarsely chopped
1 tablespoon minced fresh gingerroot
3 cloves garlic, minced
¼ cup low-sodium soy sauce plus 2 tablespoons for later use
½ head Napa (Chinese) cabbage sliced thinly crosswise, rinsed, and drained
½ cup sweet onion, finely chopped
½ pound lean ground pork
2 ounces raisins
1 ounce pine nuts, toasted
Salt to taste
Black pepper to taste
24 wonton wrappers
Nonstick spray

Pine nuts and peanut oil are low in saturated fats and contain healthy polyunsaturated and monounsaturated fats. In addition, raisins are a good source of vitamins and minerals and contain virtually no fat.

For Napa Cabbage:
Heat ¼ cup of the peanut oil and the sesame oil in large skillet over medium heat. Add scallions, ginger, and ⅓ of the garlic. Sauté until fragrant, about 1 minute. Add ¼ cup of the soy sauce and mix well. Toss with cabbage and set aside.

For Wontons:
1. Make the stuffing by sautéing the onion and remaining garlic in the remaining peanut oil. When softened, mix in pork, stirring to break up lumps.

2. Mix in the remaining soy sauce, raisins, pine nuts, salt, and pepper.

3. Divide the pork stuffing among wonton wrappers and moisten edges with a bit of water before folding in triangles. At this point, wontons can be stored in refrigerator for a day or frozen for a month.

4. Steam wontons in a steamer prepared with nonstick spray for 10 minutes.

5. Serve over prepared cabbage.

CALORIES 435
FAT 32G
CARBOHYDRATES 25G
PROTEIN 30G

Stuffed Rosemary Pork Chops with Apples

`HIGH FIBER`

SERVES 4

¼ cup olive oil plus another ¼ cup for later use
2 Granny Smith apples, cored and chopped
2 yellow onions, chopped
2 tablespoons chopped fresh rosemary leaves
¼ cup chopped fresh Italian parsley leaves
½ cup gluten-free cornbread crumbs
Sea salt to taste
Black pepper to taste
4 thick-cut pork rib chops
4 garlic cloves, chopped
Zest and juice of 1 lemon
½ cup chicken broth
½ cup dry white wine
1 teaspoon cornstarch mixed in 1 tablespoon water

Apples have a wealth of nutrients and also contain pectin, a fiber that has been linked to cholesterol reduction and is also said to help in the management of diabetes by producing galacturonic acid, which may lower the body's need for insulin.

1. In large saucepan, heat ¼ cup of the olive oil. Add apples, half the onion, and all of the herbs and sauté until softened, about 5 minutes. Add cornbread crumbs and season with salt and pepper. Mix to combine. Remove from heat and let cool slightly.
2. Make a slit in the side of each pork chop, not cutting all the way through. Then stuff 2 tablespoons of mixture into pork chops.
3. Lightly coat stuffed chops with 1 tablespoon of the olive oil. Heat remaining olive oil in saucepan over medium heat. Add the stuffed chops and brown on each side. Add the remaining ingredients, except for the cornstarch-water mixture, and cover. Simmer for 20 minutes over low heat, or until chops are cooked through.
4. Place the chops on a warm platter and add the cornstarch-water mixture to the remaining liquid in the saucepan. Stir to thicken. Season with salt and pepper as desired. Spoon sauce over chops when serving.

`CALORIES` 315
`FAT` 8G
`CARBOHYDRATES` 12G
`PROTEIN` 41G

Cornmeal-Crusted Pork Tenderloin with Dried Apricots, Cranberries, and Golden Currants

`HIGH FIBER` `ANTIOXIDANTS`

SERVES 6

6 dried apricots, chopped
½ cup dried cranberries
¼ cup golden currants or white raisins
1 cup warm water
Juice of ½ lemon
1½ pounds pork tenderloins
1 tablespoon Worcestershire sauce
1 tablespoon chopped fresh Italian flat-leaf parsley
1 cup cornmeal
Sea salt and black pepper to taste
¼ cup olive oil

Dried fruits have essential vitamins and minerals but are also naturally high in the fiber that gives you that "full" feeling, helping you eat less while increasing your metabolism.

1. Place dried fruit in a mixing bowl with warm water and lemon juice. Let stand until most water is absorbed.
2. Preheat oven to 350°F. Make a tunnel through the center of each tenderloin by using the handle of a wooden spoon or long knife. Stuff the fruit into the tunnels. Sprinkle tenderloins with Worcestershire. Make a paste with parsley, cornmeal, salt, pepper, and olive oil. Spread it on the pork and roast for 30 minutes or until cooked through. The crust should be golden brown and the pork a healthy, cooked pink.

CALORIES 297
FAT 5G
CARBOHYDRATES 28G
PROTEIN 32G

Pork Medallions with Fresh Spinach Leaves and Water Chestnuts

HIGH FIBER

SERVES 4

¼ cup potato flour
Pinch nutmeg
¼ teaspoon ground cloves
Sea salt and black pepper to taste
1½ pounds pork tenderloin, fat trimmed, pork sliced into ½- to 1-inch medallions
¼ cup olive oil
1 yellow onion, chopped
Juice from 1 lemon
1 teaspoon Worcestershire sauce
1 large bunch fresh spinach, washed, dried, stems trimmed
½ cup sliced water chestnuts, drained

What exactly are water chestnuts? They are fibrous aquatic vegetables that grow in marshes that happen to be high in potassium.

1. In large mixing bowl, combine flour, nutmeg, cloves, salt, and pepper, and mix well. Coat pork with flour mixture.
2. Heat olive oil in large saucepan over medium heat. Add onions and sauté until tender, about 5 minutes. Add pork medallions and sauté about 3 minutes, turn and sauté an additional 3 minutes. Add lemon juice, Worcestershire sauce, spinach, and water chestnuts, and sauté an additional 3–4 minutes, until pork is cooked through and spinach leaves are wilted.

CALORIES 325
FAT 19G
CARBOHYDRATES 4G
PROTEIN 42G

CHAPTER 9
Seafood and Fish

Seafood and fish are commonly thought of as light and lean, but many people don't know what to do with them. Here you will discover how different types of fish can become more metabolically friendly just by adding a super spice here or an antioxidant-rich ingredient there. These flavorful fish recipes will have you running to the docks for more!

Shrimp Scampi

1½ pounds jumbo shrimp in shell
¼ cup lemon juice
¼ cup water
1 pound linguini pasta
2 teaspoons unsalted butter
2 tablespoons extra-virgin olive oil
4 cloves garlic, smashed
½ cup Italian flat-leaf parsley leaves,
   chopped
Parmesan cheese for garnish
   (optional)

For increased fiber in your diet, use whole wheat linguini pasta instead of traditional pasta.

1. Peel the shrimp. Place the shrimp in the refrigerator. In a large saucepan, bring the shrimp shells, water, and lemon juice to a boil. Reduce heat and simmer for 20 minutes, covered. Strain and reserve broth.
2. Fill large quart boiler ¾ full with water, bring to a boil and add linguini. Cook until al dente and drain. While pasta is cooking, heat a large sauté pan and add the butter, oil, shrimp, and garlic. Stir occasionally until shrimp are done, about 3 minutes.
3. Remove the shrimp to a warm platter. Immediately add the parsley and shrimp shell broth to the pan. When the linguini is cooked, drain it and pour into a bowl. Pour the shrimp and broth over the pasta.

CALORIES 287
FAT 9G
CARBOHYDRATES 24G
PROTEIN 27G

BURN IT UP

Rice bran oil, avocado oil, flaxseed oil, nut oils, grapeseed oil, and extra-virgin olive oil (found in this recipe) all contain medium-chain saturated fats, which are quickly metabolized in the liver and aren't readily stored as body fat. Browse through a natural foods store or food co-op and really look at the oils lining their shelves. Read labels and browse the Internet for information about these fats and oils.

Baked Stuffed Shrimp with Herbs

SUPERFOOD PROTEIN

SERVES 4

1 tablespoon unsalted butter
2 cloves garlic, smashed
2 tablespoons Parmesan cheese
6 tablespoons seasoned bread crumbs
Juice of ½ lemon
1 teaspoon chopped fresh oregano leaves
Sea salt to taste
1 teaspoon freshly ground black pepper
16 jumbo shrimp, peeled and butterflied
Fresh chopped Italian flat-leaf parsley leaves for garnish

To butterfly shrimp, cut along the back of the shrimp and gently pull into a butterfly shape, keeping the shrimp intact. This makes it possible to remove the dark, black vein that is found in shrimp. Cook until the shrimp turn just pink. Don't overcook, as they become tough in texture.

1. Preheat the oven to 500°F. Melt the butter in a saucepan over medium heat. Sauté the garlic for about 4 minutes.
2. Stir in the next 6 ingredients and mix well. Place the shrimp on a baking pan. Mound the stuffing on each. Bake for about 6 minutes or until the shrimp have turned pink and the stuffing is lightly brown.

CALORIES 125G
FAT 5G
CARBOHYDRATES 9G
PROTEIN 10G

Barbeque Shrimp

PROTEIN

SERVES 4

1 cup barbeque sauce
1 tablespoon lemon juice
16 jumbo shrimp, peeled and cleaned
4 8-inch wooden skewers, soaked in water for 30 minutes

Nutrient-rich shrimp are deliciously lean and boost your metabolism with their protein and essential vitamins and minerals. A tasty side dish to serve with this recipe is Creamy Buttermilk Potatoes (see Chapter 12).

1. Set your grill or broiler on high. Mix the sauce with lemon juice. Coat the shrimp.
2. String the shrimp on the skewers. Grill or broil for 2 minutes per side and serve.

CALORIES 95
PROTEIN 9G
CARBOHYDRATES 9G
FAT 2G

Sautéed Shrimp with Crushed Red Pepper and Cilantro

SUPERFOOD ANTIOXIDANTS

SERVES 4

1 tablespoon olive oil
½ cup chopped sweet onion
3 cloves garlic, minced
4 ripe tomatoes, diced
2 chipotle peppers, finely chopped
Sea salt to taste
Freshly ground black pepper to taste
1 teaspoon red pepper flakes
1 tablespoon minced cilantro leaves
1 pound medium shrimp, peeled and deveined

An easy way to devein shrimp is to use a plastic deveiner. They can be found at most kitchen stores and are very inexpensive. Plus, they save you time in the kitchen, as the deveiner removes both the dark vein and the shrimp shell.

1. Heat the oil in a large sauté pan over medium heat. Sauté the onion and garlic. Stir in the tomatoes, peppers, salt, pepper, pepper flakes, and cilantro. Cook until slightly thickened.
2. Add the shrimp and cook for about 3 minutes, flipping shrimp to cook thoroughly. Serve immediately.

CALORIES 221
FAT 6G
CARBOHYDRATES 10G
PROTEIN 30G

Curried Shrimp Salad with Avocado and Lemon Aioli

ANTIOXIDANTS SUPERFOOD

SERVES 4

1 fennel bulb, shaved on a mandolin
2 avocados, peeled, sliced, and formed into ½-inch balls
1 green apple, peeled, cored, and diced
1 tablespoon lemon juice
3 tablespoons olive oil
4 tablespoons low-fat mayonnaise
Sea salt to taste
Black pepper to taste
1 teaspoon curry powder, or to taste
16 jumbo shrimp

Avocados are high in good, unsaturated fats and also contain vitamin K, which improves your blood's ability to clot and plays a role in bone health.

Arrange the shaved fennel, avocado balls, and diced apple on serving plates. Whisk the next 6 ingredients together for a quick dressing. Drizzle half of it over the salads, about a teaspoonful each. Brush the rest of the dressing on the shrimp and preheat your grill or grill pan over medium heat. Grill the shrimp for about 1½ minutes per side. Arrange the shrimp on the plates and serve.

CALORIES 433
FAT 38G
CARBOHYDRATES 18G
PROTEIN 10G

Shrimp with Tomatillos and Jicama

HIGH FIBER

1 pound frozen salad shrimp
4 tomatillos, peeled and chopped
1 cup jicama, peeled and julienne cut
1 bunch green onions, trimmed and chopped
2 tablespoons chopped fresh Italian flat-leaf parsley or cilantro leaves
Nonstick cooking spray
2 large ripe peaches, halved
4 cups mixed greens
1 cup chimichuri sauce

Tomatillos are a member of the tomato family. They grow with the fruit of the tomato encased in a thin husk layer that must be removed before cooking. Tomatillos are an excellent source of many vitamins and minerals including potassium and vitamin C.

1. Thaw the shrimp under cool running water. Drain and dry on paper towels. Mix shrimp with the tomatillos, jicama, green onions, and parsley or cilantro. Keep chilled.
2. Spray the top of the stove grill pan with nonstick spray and place over high heat. Grill the peaches. Turn when they sizzle.
3. Arrange the greens on serving plates. Spoon the shrimp salad over the greens. Tip a peach half against each salad. Spoon chimichuri sauce over all.

CALORIES 373
FAT 25G
CARBOHYDRATES 21G
PROTEIN 19G

BURN IT UP

Try eating different fruits every day to get different types of dietary fiber. Fiber-filled fruits that will help boost your metabolism include bananas, blueberries, cantaloupes, cranberries, grapefruits, honeydew melons, lemons, limes, mangoes, oranges, papayas, peaches (found in this recipe), pineapples, raspberries, tomatoes, tangerines, and watermelons.

Broiled Oysters with Pancetta

SERVES 2

8 oysters on the half shell, open
Sea salt to taste
Black pepper to taste
4 tablespoons freshly squeezed lemon juice
4 green onions, peeled and minced
4 teaspoons seasoned bread crumbs
4 slices pancetta, minced

Oysters are rich in protein, vitamins B12 and C, and minerals such as riboflavin, niacin, phosphorus, iron, zinc, copper, manganese, and selenium. When opening, or shucking, an oyster, use a shucker—a special knifelike tool—and wear "steel" gloves to protect your hand in case the "knife" slips. You can also fold a clean kitchen towel to use as a protective mitt.

Preheat the broiler. Arrange the oysters on a baking sheet or foil. Sprinkle with salt, pepper, lemon juice, green onions, and bread crumbs. Dot with pancetta. Place under broiler until pancetta is crisp. Serve hot.

CALORIES 315
FAT 28G
CARBOHYDRATES 9G
PROTEIN 8G

Steamed Mussels with Balsamic Tomatoes

SERVES 6

4 cloves garlic, chopped
½ cup sweet red or white onion, diced
1 tablespoon olive oil
3 cups canned plum tomatoes, drained
½ cup balsamic vinegar
Sea salt to taste
Black pepper to taste
3 pounds mussels in their shells, scrubbed

The mussels in this recipe pack a ton of vitamins, including A, B12, and C, and minerals such as calcium, iron, potassium, zinc, phosphorus, manganese, and selenium.

1. In a large pan, sauté the garlic and onion in the oil until softened. Add the tomatoes and vinegar. Salt and pepper to taste. Bring to a boil and reduce heat to a simmer.
2. Cover partially and cook until you have 2 cups of sauce, stirring occasionally for about 60 minutes.
3. Heat ½ cup of water over high heat in another large pot. Add the mussels. Cook, stirring until they are all open. Remove the mussels to a large bowl as they open.
4. Pour tomato sauce over each portion. Serve with hot crusty Italian bread or over whole wheat pasta.

CALORIES 252
FAT 7G
CARBOHYDRATES 17G
PROTEIN 28G

Mussels with Lemon Butter and Capers

SERVES 4

2 pounds mussels, well scrubbed and checked for liveliness
½ cup dry white wine
½ cup unsalted butter
Juice of ½ lemon
½ teaspoon Dijon mustard
¼ teaspoon freshly ground black pepper
Salt to taste
½ bunch Italian flat-leaf parsley, stemmed and chopped
¼ cup capers, drained

In addition to having many vitamins and minerals, mussels contain more omega-3 fatty acids than any other shellfish. These omega-3s work to reduce inflammation, improve skin, and may help prevent many diseases.

1. Heat a large quart boiler over high heat and add mussels and white wine.
2. In a small bowl on the side, whisk the rest of the ingredients together to make a sauce.
3. Serve the mussels in large bowls with the sauce on the side. Reserve mussel liquid for making soups or other sauces.

CALORIES 199
FAT 17G
CARBOHYDRATES 4G
PROTEIN 8G

BURN IT UP

England's Oxford Polytechnic Institute discovered that eating a teaspoon of hot mustard—not the mellow yellow, but the spicy browns—with your meal will boost your metabolism 20–25 percent for several hours after eating.

Broiled Salmon with Fresh Dill

SERVES 4

1 teaspoon chopped fresh dill
4 salmon fillets
¼ cup orange juice
1 tablespoon lemon juice
2 tablespoons olive oil

This mineral-rich salmon is one of the best foods on the planet. It's lean, full of protein, and is metabolically friendly as well as being easily digestible and full of nutrients.

1. Sprinkle dill on salmon. Place in a large glass baking dish. Separately, in small bowl, combine orange juice, lemon juice, and olive oil; pour over salmon. Cover and refrigerate for 1 hour.
2. When ready to cook, preheat grill or grill pan. Remove salmon from marinade and place on grill. Cook for about 3 minutes on each side, turning once. Brush salmon with remaining marinade as it grills. Serve immediately. Discard any unused marinade.

CALORIES 323
FAT 18G
CARBOHYDRATES 2G
PROTEIN 64G

Grilled Halibut with Fresh Bell Peppers and Broccoli

SERVES 4

1 10-ounce can low-sodium chicken broth
3 tablespoons lemon juice
4 tablespoons olive oil
4 4-ounce halibut steaks
1 red pepper, cut in quarters
1 green pepper, cut in quarters
2 cups fresh broccoli florets

Fish, in general, is easier to digest than beef, chicken, or pork due to its low fat content. This is a metabolism booster that helps give you the energy you need.

1. Mix chicken broth, lemon juice, and olive oil in a medium bowl. Brush each halibut steak with the chicken broth mixture on both sides. Heat grill to medium and place steaks on grill, turning every 3 minutes until done.
2. Add vegetables to a vegetable pan over grill, tossing gently as they cook. Serve vegetables and halibut together.

CALORIES 290
FAT 17G
CARBOHYDRATES 9G
PROTEIN 28G

Oven-Baked Halibut with Herbs and Lemon

SERVES 4

2 lemons, sliced
1 pound fresh halibut
1 tablespoon olive oil
Sea salt to taste
Black pepper to taste
½ cup chopped Italian flat-leaf parsley leaves
2 tablespoons chopped fresh basil leaves
2 tablespoons chopped fresh thyme leaves

This recipe calls for a whopping ½ cup of fresh Italian flat-leaf parsley leaves which can be equated nutritionally to equal amounts of spinach. Parsley adds flavor to foods while adding only minimal amounts of fat and calories.

1. Preheat oven to 375°F. Place the lemon slices in a baking dish.
2. Rub the fish on both sides with olive oil, salt, pepper, parsley, basil, and thyme.
3. Place the halibut over the lemons and bake for about 15 minutes or until the fish flakes and cooks through.

CALORIES 168
FAT 6G
CARBOHYDRATES 4G
PROTEIN 24G

Fillet of Sole with Tarragon and Tomatoes

SERVES 4

4 tablespoons olive oil
4 4-ounce sole fillets
4 tablespoons chopped fresh tarragon leaves
1 10-ounce can tomatoes in juice

Sole is a light, flaky fish that is low in calories and fat, yet rich in vitamins B6, B12, and D. Sole is a flat fish that is commonly found in the seafood section, both fresh and frozen, at most supermarkets.

1. Preheat oven to 400°F. Rub olive oil on sole fillets. Sprinkle fresh tarragon on sole fillets.
2. Pour tomatoes and juice in a baking dish.
3. Place fillets in dish and bake for 20 minutes or until fish flakes.

CALORIES 285
FAT 16G
CARBOHYDRATES 4G
PROTEIN 32G

Seared Scallops with Shallots and Lime

SERVES 4

4 teaspoons olive oil, divided
1½ pounds scallops
2 teaspoons minced garlic
2 small shallots, chopped
1 lime

Scallops are naturally low in fat and carbohydrates while remaining high in protein. This helps make them a deliciously healthy, metabolism-boosting food.

1. In a deep skillet, heat 2 teaspoons olive oil for 4 minutes. Drain juices from scallops and pat dry with a paper towel. Add the scallops and sear them on each side for about 3 minutes, until scallops have a golden brown texture. Remove scallops from skillet and set aside in a bowl.
2. Separately, mix 2 teaspoons olive oil, garlic, shallots, and juice from 1 lime in a small bowl.
3. Pour lime marinade over scallops, mixing lightly. Place scallops in the refrigerator for about 1 hour. Serve cold or warm.

CALORIES 238
FAT 6G
CARBOHYDRATES 19G
PROTEIN 31G

BURN IT UP

Consume a variety of vegetables to obtain different sources of fiber. Mature vegetables tend to contain more lignin while those harvested at an earlier growth stage have higher contents of pectin and hemicellulose. Eat as much as you want of these vegetables without feeling guilty: asparagus, beets, broccoli, cabbage, carrots, cauliflower, celery, chicory, chili peppers, cucumber, and the spicy garlic found here.

Broiled Cajun Scallops

SERVES 4

Nonstick cooking spray
4 tablespoons lemon juice
2 teaspoons chili powder
½ teaspoon ground cumin
½ teaspoon cayenne pepper
14 scallops

Scallops are edible bivalves similar to oysters and clams. There are large scallops called sea scallops as well as smaller bay scallops. Both can be sautéed, grilled, or steamed.

1. Preheat broiler. Spray baking sheet with light cooking spray. Mix the lemon juice, chili powder, cumin, and cayenne pepper in a small saucepan over medium heat and let simmer about 3 minutes.
2. Dry scallops and transfer to a medium bowl. Pour mixture from saucepan over scallops and toss gently with a wooden spoon. Evenly distribute scallops onto a baking sheet. Broil 5–10 minutes or until scallops are opaque.

CALORIES 65
FAT 1G
CARBOHYDRATES 5G
PROTEIN 10G

Pan-Grilled Crab Cakes

SERVES 4

1 egg
1 teaspoon Old Bay seasoning
1 teaspoon light mayonnaise
Sea salt to taste
Black pepper to taste
1 teaspoon Worcestershire sauce
¼ cup fresh Italian flat-leaf parsley, chopped
½ onion, finely chopped
1 pound lump crabmeat, cooked
1 tablespoon olive oil

Crab is low in fat, rich in calcium, and a terrific source of vital minerals such as zinc, phosphorus, and selenium.

1. Beat the egg in a medium bowl. Add the Old Bay seasoning, mayonnaise, salt, pepper, Worcestershire sauce, parsley, and onion. Add the crabmeat and mix together thoroughly. Make into cakes, about 2 inches in diameter.
2. Heat olive oil on medium in a large skillet. Add the crab cakes and cook until golden brown on both sides, about 2 minutes per side.

CALORIES 165
FAT 7G
CARBOHYDRATES 2G
PROTEIN 26G

Manhattan Clam Chowder

SERVES 6

3 strips turkey bacon
1 large onion, diced
1 green bell pepper, cored and diced
1 rib celery, diced
3 cloves garlic, minced
2 16-ounce cans diced tomatoes
4 cups clam juice
1 cup water
4 white potatoes, diced
1 large carrot, diced
24 cherrystone clams, steamed and chopped
½ teaspoon chopped fresh oregano leaves
½ teaspoon red pepper flakes
Sea salt to taste
Black pepper to taste
¼ cup minced fresh Italian flat-leaf parsley leaves

Manhattan clam chowder is tomato based and lower in fat, calories, and carbohydrates than the equally flavorful New England clam chowder. This antioxidant-rich chowder is one of the tastiest metabolism-boosting treats that you can enjoy.

1. In a heavy soup pot over medium-high heat, fry bacon until crisp; remove to paper towels to drain. Add onions, green pepper, celery, and garlic to bacon fat; sauté 3 minutes.
2. Stir in tomatoes, clam juice, and water; bring to a boil. Reduce heat to medium; add potatoes and carrots. Simmer, uncovered, 30 minutes, stirring occasionally.
3. Add clams, oregano, and red pepper flakes; simmer 15 minutes.
4. Remove from heat. Season with salt and pepper; add parsley.

CALORIES 73
FAT 2G
CARBOHYDRATES 12G
PROTEIN 2G

Shrimp and Pork Dumplings

SERVES 4

1 pound raw shrimp, peeled and deveined
1 egg
1 tablespoon dry sherry
2 teaspoons low-sodium soy sauce
1 teaspoon sugar
1 tablespoon cornstarch
1 cup lean ground pork
2 scallions, chopped
3 cups canola oil for frying

The shrimp and pork combination found here provides a high-protein and low-fat metabolism boost that will instantly increase your fat-burning potential.

1. Adding slowly, place all ingredients, except the cooking oil, in a food processor. Pulse, and scrape the sides often. Roll mixture into small balls. Heat the oil to hot but not smoking.
2. Carefully drop balls by the teaspoonful into the oil. When golden, after about 3–4 minutes, drain on paper towels. Transfer to platter and serve.

CALORIES 210
FAT 11G
CARBOHYDRATES 23G
PROTEIN 7G

Lobster Bisque

SERVES 4

½ cup butter
½ cup flour
1 minced shallot
6 cups lobster broth
2 tablespoons tomato purée
2 cups whole milk
¼ cup sherry
1 tablespoon brandy
2 lobster tails, finely chopped
1 tablespoon chopped fresh tarragon
Sea salt to taste
Black pepper to taste

Cooking with lobster tails is an easy way to work with lobster. They are easier to prepare and give you the most lobster meat for the least amount of work. Lobster tails are readily available at most supermarkets and are usually previously frozen.

1. Melt butter in a soup pot over medium-high heat. Add flour; stir until mixture forms a paste. Cook until bubbly, but not browned.
2. Add shallot and cook 1 minute; carefully add broth. Whisk until flour is dissolved and mixture is slightly thickened. Stir in tomato purée. Bring to a boil; reduce heat to medium.
3. Simmer until broth is reduced by ⅓, about 20–30 minutes.
4. Stir in milk, sherry, and brandy; simmer, without boiling, 20 minutes.
5. Add chopped lobster meat and tarragon. Remove from heat; add salt and pepper. Serve in creamed soup bowls with baguette slices.

CALORIES 380
FAT 27G
CARBOHYDRATES 10G
PROTEIN 16G

BURN IT UP

Chromium, a mineral, helps the body metabolize fat and convert blood sugar into energy, and makes insulin work more efficiently. Several recent studies have also shown that chromium protects the heart by lowering serum cholesterol levels and triglycerides. Sources rich in chromium include seafood, like the lobster found here.

New Orleans Seafood Gumbo

SERVES 8

⅔ cup canola oil
⅔ cup granulated flour
2 onions, diced
2 cups sliced okra
10 cups fish stock (or clam juice also works)
1 green bell pepper, cored and diced
1 rib celery, diced
3 cloves garlic, minced
2 tomatoes, diced
2 bay leaves
½ teaspoon cayenne pepper
½ teaspoon garlic powder
½ teaspoon onion powder
1 teaspoon chopped fresh thyme leaves
1 pound medium shrimp, peeled and deveined
1 pound peeled crawfish tails
1 dozen oysters
1 pound lump crabmeat
Sea salt to taste
Black pepper to taste
¼ cup minced fresh parsley
¼ cup minced green onion

Because of the variety of ingredients, seafood gumbo is a natural metabolism booster with hearty minerals, vitamins, protein, and fiber. A traditionally spicy dish, gumbo uses a wide variety of herbs and spices to complement the varying flavors of the seafood. Feel free to substitute your favorite seafoods. Two-inch chunks of fish such as halibut, or oysters, or mussels taste great!

1. In a heavy soup pot over medium heat, combine oil and flour; stir until mixture forms a smooth paste. Continue to cook, stirring constantly, until roux turns a toasty brown. Add 1 onion to roux; stir until onion turns translucent. Add okra; stirring, continue to cook 3 minutes.

2. Slowly add hot broth; stir until flour mixture is dissolved. Bring mixture to a boil. Cook 10 minutes.

3. Reduce heat to medium; add remaining onion, green pepper, celery, and garlic. Stir in tomatoes, bay leaves, cayenne, garlic powder, onion powder, and thyme. Simmer 1½ hours, adding more stock if needed.

4. Add shrimp, crawfish, oysters, and crabmeat; continue to simmer, stirring occasionally, 20 minutes.

5. Add salt and pepper; stir in parsley and green onion. Serve over steamed rice.

CALORIES 110
FAT 5G
CARBOHYDRATES 14G
PROTEIN 5G

Shrimp and Scallop Kebabs with Citrus Marinade

SERVES: 4

½ pound sea scallops
12 large shrimp, peeled and deveined (about ½ pound total)
1 teaspoon finely shredded orange zest
½ cup orange juice
1 teaspoon peeled and grated fresh ginger
¼ teaspoon cayenne pepper
2 tablespoons soy sauce
1 clove garlic, minced
12 fresh or frozen snow peas
1 orange, cut into 8 wedges

Snow peas are low in fat, low in carbohydrates, rich in vitamins A and C, and full of iron and many other metabolism-boosting minerals. As a rule of thumb, fresh is always best, as it maintains a vegetable's crisp texture and the highest amount of vitamins and minerals. However, fresh snow peas can sometimes be expensive or just not available. For those occasions, frozen snow peas are a good substitute.

1. Halve any large scallops. Place the scallops and shrimp in a lock-top plastic bag set in a deep bowl. In a small bowl, stir together the orange zest, orange juice, ginger, cayenne pepper, soy sauce, and garlic. Pour over the seafood. Seal the bag. Marinate in the refrigerator for 30 minutes.
2. Preheat grill. Drain the seafood, reserving the marinade. If using fresh snow peas, cook in boiling water for about 2 minutes, then drain. If using frozen snow peas, thaw and drain well. Wrap 1 snow pea around each shrimp. Thread the shrimp onto four 10- to 12-inch-long skewers alternately with the scallops and orange wedges.
3. Place the skewers on the grill rack and cook about 5 minutes. Turn, brush with the reserved marinade, and cook until shrimp are pink and the scallops are opaque, about 4 minutes longer. Serve warm.

CALORIES 141
FAT 2G
CARBOHYDRATES 11G
PROTEIN 20G

Oven-Baked Parmesan-Crusted Sole

ANTIOXIDANTS

SERVES: 4

Nonstick cooking spray
1½ pounds sole fillets
4 cups fresh bread crumbs
½ medium onion, minced
1 tablespoon lemon juice
½ teaspoon chopped fresh marjoram leaves
½ teaspoon sea salt
1 teaspoon pepper
2 tablespoons butter, melted
1 tomato, coarsely chopped
2 tablespoons grated Parmesan cheese

Naturally thin sole fillets are delicious baked or fried, however, baking is a healthier option as you skip the fat in the oil needed for frying. Due to the fact that sole is a thin fish, a meal of baked sole can be made in minutes!

1. Preheat oven to 400°F. Spray a large baking dish in which all the fillets fit snugly with nonstick cooking spray. Arrange the sole in a single layer in the prepared baking dish.
2. In a small dish, stir together the bread crumbs, onion, lemon juice, marjoram, salt, pepper, and butter. Spread the mixture over the fish. Top with the tomato and sprinkle with the Parmesan cheese.
3. Bake until the fish is opaque throughout and flakes easily when tested with a fork, about 10 minutes. Serve immediately.

CALORIES 367
FAT 11G
CARBOHYDRATES 27G
PROTEIN 38G

Shrimp and Lobster Salad with Citrus Chili Pepper Sauce

PROTEIN

SERVES 4

1 cup low-fat mayonnaise
1 teaspoon Dijon mustard
Juice of ½ lime
Fine zest of ½ lime
1 teaspoon low-sodium soy sauce
1 tablespoon chili sauce
1 teaspoon minced garlic
Sea salt to taste
Black pepper to taste
1 1½-pound lobster, cooked, removed from shell, and chopped
1½ pounds cleaned and cooked shrimp
¼ cup mixed, snipped fresh dill and chopped fresh Italian flat-leaf parsley
1 tablespoon capers
4 cups shredded iceberg lettuce

Shrimp and lobster are dinner favorites. These types of seafood are rich in protein and minerals and low in fat, thus making them healthy options. But don't overdo it; shrimp and lobster are both high in cholesterol.

1. Mix together the mayonnaise, mustard, lime juice and zest, soy sauce, chili sauce, minced garlic, salt, and pepper.
2. Just before serving, mix the sauce with the seafood. Garnish with snipped fresh dill and chopped parsley, sprinkle with capers, and serve over a bed of lettuce.

CALORIES 169
FAT 8G
CARBOHYDRATES 11G
PROTEIN 11G

Spicy Baked Salmon with Pineapple

ANTIOXIDANTS PROTEIN

SERVES 6

1 clove fresh garlic, minced
½ teaspoon all-purpose seasoning
2 cups crushed pineapple
¼ red onion, chopped
1 tablespoon freshly squeezed lemon juice
½ teaspoon jalapeño peppers, finely chopped
1 teaspoon chili powder
Nonstick cooking spray
6 4- or 5-ounce salmon fillets

This pineapple mixture is filled with bromelain, a metabolism-boosting enzyme primarily found in pineapple. Bromelain helps aid in digestion and has healing properties; it is well known for helping reduce inflammation.

1. Mix all ingredients except salmon fillets in a bowl.
2. Spray a 9" × 13" baking dish with nonstick spray. Place salmon in the dish. Pour mixture over the fish; cover with foil.
3. Bake at 350°F for 15 minutes or until fish flakes easily.

CALORIES 220
FAT 5G
CARBOHYDRATES 15G
PROTEIN 29G

Seafood Medley with Tomatoes and Red Onion

SERVES 4

PROTEIN ANTIOXIDANTS

¼ cup water

¼ cup dry white wine

1 teaspoon lemon juice

16 medium shrimp, raw, peeled, and deveined

16 medium sea scallops

½ pound fillet of bluefish, turbot, scrod, or halibut, skinless

1 pound Alaskan crab legs, cut in 2-inch lengths, cracked

½ pound mussels, scrubbed

1 cup low-fat Italian dressing

2 teaspoons capers

Black pepper to taste

1 cup fresh Italian flat-leaf parsley, pulled from stems

½ teaspoon coriander seeds, cracked

1 teaspoon lemon zest

12 grape tomatoes

½ red onion, thinly sliced

This medley has all kinds of seafood favorites, including shrimp, scallops, bluefish, crab, and mussels. Feel free to swap ingredients in or out depending on your likes, dislikes, and dietary needs.

1. Set a large bowl next to the stove. Place a large stock pot on stove top and mix in the water, wine, and lemon juice; bring to a boil over high heat. Poach the shrimp and sea scallops for 5 minutes. Remove and transfer to the bowl.

2. Place the bluefish, turbot, scrod, or halibut into the water and allow to simmer for 4 minutes. Add to the bowl of seafood.

3. Drop the crab leg pieces into the boiling water. Remove after 1 minute. Place in the bowl.

4. Add mussels to the boiling water and poach until they open. Place in the bowl.

5. Add the dressing and remaining ingredients to the seafood and toss gently to coat. Cover and refrigerate for 2 hours. Serve chilled or at room temperature.

CALORIES 553

FAT 33G

CARBOHYDRATES 6G

PROTEIN 58G

BURN IT UP

Here's reality: some foods are very good for your body (and your metabolism); some are not. Eat foods that improve your health, such as:

- Omega-3 fatty acids found in fish, flax oil, and spinach
- Colorful vegetables that are rich in antioxidants
- Whole foods such as brown rice, whole wheat bread and pasta, and legumes
- Lean protein from organic meats, fish, soy, and legumes

Pan-Grilled Mahi Mahi with Fresh Cilantro and Citrus

SERVES 6

Nonstick cooking spray
1 tablespoon olive oil
1 clove fresh garlic, minced
½ teaspoon all-purpose seasoning
½ cup yellow onions, sliced
½ cup chopped fresh cilantro leaves
2 teaspoons chopped fresh Italian
    flat-leaf parsley leaves
¼ cup freshly squeezed orange juice
¼ cup freshly squeezed lemon juice
½ teaspoon cumin
6 3- to 5-ounce mahi mahi fillets
4 lemon slices
4 orange slices

Mahi mahi, or dorado, is known as a dolphin-fish but is not related to the more commonly known dolphin. Mahi mahi like warmer waters and can be found in both tropical and subtropical water areas. They are very high in protein and contains minerals such as selenium and niacin, which not only boost your metabolism, but also help balance your overall health.

1. Coat a large skillet with nonstick spray. Mix all ingredients except fish, lemon slices, and orange slices. Add fish to skillet, coat with mixture, and top with lemon and orange slices.
2. Cover and cook on medium heat for 15–20 minutes or until fish flakes easily.

CALORIES 160
FAT 3G
CARBOHYDRATES 5G
PROTEIN 27G

BURN IT UP

Parsley is loaded with compounds that purify your blood and expel toxins from your body. It is also dense in vitamins A, C, and K, iodine, iron, and chlorophyll—all metabolism boosters! Actually, parsley has higher vitamin C than citrus and is an excellent ingredient to battle inflammation.

CHAPTER 10

Pasta, Polenta, and Grains

When you think of pasta, a gigantic vision of a pile of carbohydrates on your plate likely comes to mind. But it doesn't have to be that way. You can combine the carb-rich foods that you love with fiber-rich combinations that will help you maximize your energy levels throughout the day while being efficiently digested and processed through your body. So grab a fork and dig in!

Spaghetti with Traditional Marinara and Fresh Vegetables

SERVES: 8

2 cups small onions, cut into eighths
2 cups peeled and chopped tomatoes
1 cup thinly sliced yellow squash
1 cup thinly sliced zucchini squash
1½ cups green beans, cut into ½-inch lengths
⅔ cup water
2 tablespoons minced fresh parsley
1 clove garlic, minced
½ teaspoon chili powder
¼ teaspoon sea salt
⅛ teaspoon black pepper
1 6-ounce can tomato paste
1 pound spaghetti
½ cup grated Parmesan cheese

Carbs are needed for energy and should be consumed during the most active part of your day, so this dish is a great lunch option.

1. In a large saucepan, combine all the ingredients except the tomato paste, spaghetti, and cheese. Place over low heat and cook, stirring often, for 10 minutes, then stir in the tomato paste. Cover and simmer over low heat to allow flavors to combine, about 20 minutes.
2. Meanwhile, cook the spaghetti in boiling unsalted water until al dente. Drain and place in a large bowl.
3. Spoon the sauce over the spaghetti and then sprinkle the Parmesan over the top. Serve immediately.

CALORIES 289
FAT 3G
CARBOHYDRATES 55G
PROTEIN 12G

BURN IT UP

The good news for all you spaghetti lovers out there is that spaghetti squash is the perfect substitution for pasta. It has a mild flavor, tastes great with tomato sauce, twirls like spaghetti, and is great for your metabolism! One cup of spaghetti squash contains only 42 calories and 0.4 grams of fat.

Penne with Chicken, Asparagus, and Fresh Rosemary

SERVES: 4

1 tablespoon olive oil
1 clove garlic, minced
2 shallots, minced
½ teaspoon chopped fresh rosemary leaves
¾ pound skinless chicken breast meat, cut into bite-sized strips
2 cups chopped asparagus
½ cup reduced-sodium, fat-free chicken broth
¼ cup dry white wine
2 tablespoons chopped fresh Italian flat-leaf parsley leaves
½ pound penne
Sea salt to taste
Black pepper to taste
2 tablespoons grated Parmesan cheese

Remember, exercise can help boost your metabolism, and this high-carb meal is a perfect energy booster before a workout or high-intensity activity such as tennis, jogging, or swimming.

1. In a large, deep skillet, heat the oil over medium heat. Add garlic, shallots, and rosemary and cook for 1 minute. Add the chicken and sauté, tossing well, until lightly browned, about 3 minutes. Add the asparagus, broth, wine, and parsley. Simmer to heat through.
2. Meanwhile, cook the penne in boiling salted water until al dente. Drain.
3. Add the penne to the skillet with the chicken. Raise the heat to high and boil, stirring, until the liquid reduces enough to glaze the pasta lightly. Season with salt and pepper. Transfer to a warmed platter, sprinkle with the Parmesan, and serve.

CALORIES	330
FAT	4G
CARBOHYDRATES	52G
PROTEIN	20G

Sesame Fettuccini with Broccoli

SERVES: 6

2 cups broccoli florets
¼ pound eggless fettuccine, broken up
1 tablespoon olive oil
3 tablespoons grated Parmesan cheese
1 teaspoon sesame seeds, toasted
⅛ teaspoon garlic powder
Black pepper to taste

Sesame seeds add flavor and crunch to your recipes. They are also high in minerals such as calcium, iron, and zinc.

1. In a large saucepan, cook the broccoli and pasta in boiling salted water until the pasta is al dente, stirring once or twice. Drain and place in a bowl.
2. Add the oil to the pasta mixture and toss well. Add the cheese, sesame seeds, garlic powder, and pepper. Toss gently to coat. Serve immediately.

CALORIES	118
FAT	4G
CARBOHYDRATES	17G
PROTEIN	5G

Penne with Fresh Herbs and Zucchini

SERVES: 4

2 teaspoons butter
1 clove garlic, minced
4 zucchini, sliced
2 teaspoons chopped fresh rosemary leaves
Sea salt to taste
Black pepper to taste
1 pound uncooked penne pasta
2 tablespoons chopped fresh Italian flat-leaf parsley leaves
⅓ cup grated Parmesan cheese

Pasta provides instant energy that can last all day. However, pasta dishes are best complemented with lean proteins such as chicken or fish that can help you feel fuller for longer.

1. In a large skillet or shallow saucepan, melt the butter over medium heat. Add the garlic and zucchini and cook until crisp and tender, about 5–7 minutes. Add the rosemary and season with salt and pepper. Raise the heat and cook for a few minutes to blend the flavors. Remove from the heat.
2. Meanwhile, cook the pasta in boiling salted water until al dente. Drain thoroughly and add to the zucchini mixture. Return the pan to the heat and toss until the shells are well coated with sauce, 2–3 minutes. Add the parsley and cheese and toss again. Serve at once.

CALORIES 495
FAT 6G
CARBOHYDRATES 91G
PROTEIN 19G

Orzo with Red Bell Pepper and Fresh Basil

SERVES: 4

2 cups minced fresh basil leaves
½ cup minced fresh Italian flat-leaf parsley leaves
4 cloves garlic, minced
½ teaspoon sea salt
¼ cup olive oil
1 pound orzo pasta, cooked, drained, and cooled
1 red bell pepper, chopped

Orzo is a carb-rich pasta that is also rich in minerals, like selenium, that maintain healthy cells. It also has a lot of manganese, which functions in carbohydrate and fat metabolism.

1. In a serving bowl, stir together the basil, parsley, garlic, salt, and oil.
2. Add the orzo and red pepper and mix well.
3. Chill for 1 hour. Toss all before serving.

CALORIES 564
FAT 16G
CARBOHYDRATES 90G
PROTEIN 16G

Pasta with Spinach and Pine Nuts

SERVES: 4

Pesto:
1 10-ounce package spinach, stemmed
4 cloves garlic, cut up
Sea salt to taste
Black pepper to taste
2 tablespoons olive oil

Pasta:
1 pound corkscrew, or other, pasta
½ cup low-fat mayonnaise
2 tablespoons olive oil
2 tablespoons pine nuts
Diced pimiento

Traditional pesto is filled with fat and calories from oil, nuts, and cheese. This version focuses on fresh spinach with fresh pine nuts as garnish.

1. To make the pesto, combine spinach, garlic, salt, and pepper in a food processor. Process to chop finely. With the machine running, gradually add the ¼ cup oil in a thin, steady stream, processing until the pesto is the consistency of thin mayonnaise. Set aside.
2. Cook the pasta in boiling salted water until al dente. Drain, then transfer to a large bowl. Add the mayonnaise and olive oil. Mix well.
3. Add the pesto to the pasta and stir and toss until well mixed. Cover and chill before serving. Garnish with the pine nuts and pimiento.

CALORIES 419
FAT 14G
CARBOHYDRATES 52G
PROTEIN 23G

Fettuccine with Shrimp and Artichokes

SERVES: 4

½ pound eggless fettuccine
½ avocado, pitted, peeled, and cut into chunks
1 8-ounce can marinated artichoke hearts, drained
1 large tomato, diced
2 cloves garlic, minced
1 tablespoon olive oil
2 scallions, thinly sliced
½ pound cooked shrimp
2 tablespoons grated Parmesan cheese

Cooking anything to "al dente" means to cook "to teeth," or to where the pasta, or other food product, is tender and firm but not mushy. Other foods that taste delicious cooked "al dente" are sliced carrots, asparagus spears, and broccoli.

1. Cook the fettuccine in boiling salted water until al dente. Drain and place in a bowl.
2. Add all the remaining ingredients except the Parmesan cheese and toss well.
3. Serve warm or chilled. Top with the Parmesan just before serving.

CALORIES 495
FAT 6G
CARBOHYDRATES 91G
PROTEIN 19G

Macaroni with Ground Turkey and Light Cream Sauce

CALCIUM SPICY

SERVES: 10

1 teaspoon olive oil
1 large onion, finely chopped
1½ pounds lean ground turkey
1 cup water
¾ cup dry white wine
1 6-ounce can tomato paste
½ cup bulgur
¾ teaspoon cinnamon
¾ teaspoon nutmeg
¾ teaspoon allspice
1½ teaspoons sea salt, plus more to taste
½ teaspoon black pepper, plus more to taste
2 cups nonfat cottage cheese
2 tablespoons all-purpose flour
1 cup reduced-sodium, fat-free chicken broth
1 12-ounce can evaporated skim milk
¾ cup plus 2 tablespoons freshly grated Parmesan cheese
1 pound elbow macaroni
1 teaspoon olive oil
Nonstick cooking spray
2 tablespoons chopped fresh Italian flat-leaf parsley leaves

The cottage cheese in this recipe is a great low-fat protein option that provides you with a much needed, metabolically friendly energy boost.

1. In a large nonstick skillet, heat oil over medium heat; add onion and sauté until softened, about 5 minutes. Add ground turkey and cook, breaking it up with a wooden spoon, until no longer pink, about 5 minutes. Drain off fat. Add water, wine, tomato paste, bulgur, spices, 1 teaspoon of the salt, and ½ teaspoon of the pepper. Simmer, uncovered, over low heat, stirring occasionally, until the bulgur is tender, about 20 minutes. Taste and adjust seasonings.

2. In a food processor or blender, purée cottage cheese until completely smooth. Set aside. In a small bowl, stir together flour and ¼ cup cold chicken broth until smooth. In a medium-sized heavy saucepan, combine evaporated skim milk and the remaining chicken broth. Heat over medium heat until scalding. Stir the flour mixture into the hot milk mixture and cook, stirring constantly, until thickened, about 2 minutes.

3. Remove from the heat and whisk in the puréed cottage cheese and the ½ cup of grated cheese. Season with salt and a generous grinding of pepper to taste. To prevent a skin from forming, place wax paper or plastic wrap directly over the surface and set aside.

4. In a large pot of boiling salted water, cook macaroni until al dente, 8–10 minutes. Drain and return to the pot. Toss with ¼ cup of the grated cheese, oil, and ½ teaspoon of the salt.

5. Preheat oven to 350°F. Spray a 9" × 13" baking dish with nonstick cooking spray. Spread half of the pasta mixture over the bottom of the prepared dish. Top with one third of the cream sauce. Spoon all of the meat sauce over, spreading evenly. Cover with another third of the cream sauce. Top with the remaining pasta mixture and cover

with the remaining cream sauce. Sprinkle with the remaining 2 tablespoons of the grated cheese. Bake for 40–50 minutes, or until bubbling and golden. Sprinkle with parsley, and serve.

CALORIES 470
FAT 14G
CARBOHYDRATES 52G
PROTEIN 32G

Mostaccioli with Mushrooms and Artichokes

HIGH FIBER

SERVES: 1

1 artichoke
1 lemon, halved
2 tablespoons olive oil
1 cup sliced cremini mushrooms
2 tablespoons dry white wine
¼ cup thinly sliced scallions
½ teaspoon chopped fresh basil leaves
Sea salt to taste
¼ pound mostaccioli pasta
1 tablespoon grated Parmesan cheese
Cracked pepper to taste

Fiber- and mineral-rich foods such as scallions, basil, and artichokes help metabolize natural carbs found in mostaccioli pasta.

1. Bend back the outer leaves of the artichoke until they snap off easily near base. The edible portion of the leaf should remain on the artichoke base or heart. Continue to snap off and discard the thick, dark leaves until central core of pale green leaves is reached. Cut off the top 2 inches of artichoke; discard. Cut off the stem; reserve. Using a paring knife, trim the dark green outer layer from the artichoke bottom and the stem. Rub all cut surfaces with a lemon half to prevent discoloration. Quarter the artichoke lengthwise. Scoop or cut out the prickly center petals and choke and discard. Rub again with a lemon half. Cut the artichoke and stem lengthwise into very thin slices.

2. Heat the oil over medium heat in a large skillet. Add the artichoke and mushrooms and sauté for 2 minutes. Add the wine, scallions, and basil; cover and simmer until the liquid has evaporated and the artichokes are tender, about 5 minutes. Season with salt.

3. Meanwhile, cook the pasta in boiling salted water until al dente. Drain and place in a bowl. Spoon the sauce over the pasta and sprinkle with Parmesan and pepper.

CALORIES 365
FAT 15G
CARBOHYDRATES 50G
PROTEIN 12G

Penne Pasta with Tri-Colored Bell Pepper and Pistachios

SERVES: 4

1 tablespoon butter
1 yellow onion, sliced into thin wedges
¼ cup finely diced green bell pepper
¼ cup finely diced yellow bell pepper
¼ cup finely diced red bell pepper
2 tablespoons minced garlic
¼ pound prosciutto, sliced ⅛ inch thick and then diced
1 cup pistachios, coarsely chopped
1½ teaspoons chopped fresh rosemary leaves
3 tablespoons extra-virgin olive oil
1 pound penne pasta

Protein-rich prosciutto and pistachios are essential to this metabolism-positive entrée, or side dish, as protein helps build calorie and fat-burning muscle. For added fiber, which helps to naturally breakdown proteins, opt for fiber-rich whole wheat penne pasta.

1. In a skillet, melt the butter (or margarine) over low heat. Add the onion and sauté until nearly tender. Add all the bell peppers, the garlic, prosciutto, pistachios, rosemary, and olive oil. Continue to cook, stirring, until thoroughly heated.
2. Meanwhile, cook the penne in boiling salted water until al dente. Drain and place in a bowl. Spoon the sauce over the top and serve.

CALORIES 408
FAT 17G
CARBOHYDRATES 45G
PROTEIN 15G

Pasta with Tuna, Olives, and Tomato

SERVES: 4

¼ cup low-fat Italian dressing
¼ cup chopped fresh basil
2 cloves minced garlic
¼ teaspoon red pepper flakes
2 cups small shell pasta, cooked, drained, and chilled
1 6-ounce can water-packed albacore tuna, drained and flaked
¾ cup diced tomato
½ avocado, peeled and diced
¼ cup thinly sliced red onion
2 tablespoons chopped black olives
4 red leaf lettuce leaves

This recipe is full of superfoods like tuna, tomatoes, and avocado that are rich not only rich in protein, but in essential vitamins and minerals as well.

1. In a small bowl, stir together the dressing, basil, garlic, and red pepper flakes to form a dressing.
2. In a large bowl, combine the pasta, tuna, tomato, avocado, red onion, and olives. Add dressing and toss well. Line 4 plates with the lettuce leaves.
3. Spoon the pasta mixture on the lettuce, dividing evenly. Serve at once.

CALORIES 236
FAT 6G
CARBOHYDRATES 23G
PROTEIN 15G

Penne Pasta with Spinach, Pistachio, and Honey Dijon

SERVES: 4

1½ cups frozen peas
6 ounces penne pasta
2 tablespoons honey
2½ tablespoons Dijon mustard
3 tablespoons red wine vinegar
1 egg white
1½ teaspoons chopped fresh oregano
  leaves
½ teaspoon garlic powder
2 cups spinach leaves, torn
2 cups halved cherry tomatoes
½ cup pistachio nuts

Using egg whites instead of the whole egg cuts down on fat, calories, and cholesterol. Honey gives this dish added sweetness even though it is more easily broken down than granulated sugar.

1. Place the peas in a sieve and rinse with running hot water to thaw; drain well and set aside. Cook the pasta in boiling salted water until al dente.
2. Meanwhile, in a small bowl, stir together the honey, mustard, vinegar, egg white, oregano, and garlic powder to form a dressing.
3. When the pasta is ready, drain and place in a bowl. Add the spinach, tomatoes, peas, pistachios, and the dressing. Toss well and serve warm.

CALORIES 358
FAT 9G
CARBOHYDRATES 56G
PROTEIN 14G

BURN IT UP

Peas contain pantothenic acid, or vitamin B5. This compound is utilized in the formation of coenzymes, which are equally important in about a hundred metabolic reactions. These processes include energy production; fatty acid catabolism; fatty acid synthesis; and cholesterol, phospholipid, and steroid hormone production.

Fusilli with Chili Pepper Chicken and Almonds

CALORIES 415
FAT 12G
CARBOHYDRATES 51G
PROTEIN 17G

PROTEIN ANTIOXIDANTS

SERVES: 4

2 boneless, skinless chicken breasts, halved
3 ounces fresh cilantro leaves
4 cloves garlic, chopped
½ cup slivered blanched almonds
4 serrano chili peppers, seeded and diced
2 tablespoons olive oil
1 cup low-fat mayonnaise
1 pound fusilli pasta, cooked, drained, and chilled

High-protein chicken is surrounded by good carbs from fusilli (or corkscrew) pasta. Other pastas that would be delicious in this recipe are penne or farfalle (bowtie). For added fiber, remember that you can use whole wheat pastas or be creative and use a combination of both whole wheat and traditional.

1. Preheat oven to 375°F. Place the chicken breasts in a baking pan. Bake until cooked through and tender, 15–20 minutes. Remove from the oven, let cool, and shred the meat. Place in a bowl, cover, and chill.
2. In a food processor or blender, combine the cilantro, garlic, almonds, and chilies. Process until finely chopped. With the motor running, add the oil in a thin, steady stream, processing until the pesto is the consistency of a thick paste.
3. Place the pesto in a bowl. Whisk in the mayonnaise. In a large bowl, combine the chilled pasta, shredded chicken, and the pesto. Stir to mix well. Cover and chill for 1 hour before serving.

Baked Chicken Ziti with Fresh Pineapple and Mint

SPICY PROTEIN

SERVES: 4

1 pound skinless chicken breast
1 tablespoon olive oil
¼ cup dry white wine
¼ teaspoon cayenne pepper
6 scallions, cut on the diagonal into 1-inch lengths
1½ cups pineapple juice
1 tablespoon soy sauce
1 tablespoon peeled and grated fresh ginger
1 tablespoon honey
1 tablespoon fresh orange juice
1 tablespoon butter
½ pound ziti pasta
1 10-ounce can mandarin oranges, drained
1 tablespoon chopped fresh mint

Ginger, a major ingredient here, has been shown to increase thermogenesis—a fancy way to say it fires up your body's furnace—which equals a boost in your body's ability to metabolize food.

1. Preheat oven to 350°F. Place the chicken in a baking dish and brush with the oil. Sprinkle with wine, and season with the cayenne pepper. Cover with foil and bake until cooked through and tender, about 15 minutes. Do not overcook. During the last 2–3 minutes, add the scallions to the pan. Remove from the oven, let cool slightly,

and cut the chicken into bite-sized pieces. Reserve the scallions.

2. While the chicken is cooking, combine the pineapple juice, soy sauce, ginger, and honey in a small saucepan. Bring to a boil over medium-high heat and cook until reduced by half, about 20 minutes. Add the orange juice. Remove from the heat and whisk in the butter (or margarine).

3. Meanwhile, cook the pasta in boiling salted water until al dente. Drain and transfer to a large warmed bowl. Top with the scallions, pour the sauce over the pasta, and toss well. Carefully fold in the mandarin oranges and mint. Serve at once.

CALORIES 513

FAT 9G

CARBOHYDRATES 73G

PROTEIN 35G

Three-Cheese Fusilli with Fresh Herbs

PROTEIN

SERVES: 4

1 15-ounce container part-skim ricotta cheese
¼ cup nonfat cottage cheese
⅔ cup low-fat milk
¼ cup grated Parmesan cheese
1 tablespoon olive oil
¾ cup chopped onion
4 cloves garlic, minced
½ cup chopped fresh basil leaves
¼ cup chopped fresh chives
¼ cup chopped fresh Italian flat-leaf parsley leaves
Sea salt to taste
Black pepper to taste
1 pound fusilli pasta

The high-protein cheeses used here are also lower in fat and calories than their full-fat counterparts. Flavorful recipes like this one prove that nonfat and skim milk products are healthier for you and still taste as good as, if not better than, full-fat products. And, although the cheeses here have little to no fat, they still give this recipe a creamy texture that is pleasing to your taste buds.

1. In a food processor or blender, combine the ricotta cheese, cottage cheese, milk, and Parmesan. Process until smooth. In a large, deep skillet, heat the oil over medium heat. Add the onion and sauté until nearly browned, about 10 minutes. Add the garlic and cook until softened.

2. Add the ricotta mixture and fold in the basil, chives, and parsley. Cook until heated through. Season with salt and pepper.

3. Meanwhile, cook the pasta in boiling salted water until al dente. Drain and add to the skillet. Toss well so that the pasta is coated with the sauce. Transfer to a warmed bowl and serve.

CALORIES 614

FAT 11G

CARBOHYDRATES 96G

PROTEIN 27G

Vermicelli with Anchovies, Capers, and Lemon

SERVES: 4

2 tablespoons olive oil
½ cup chopped yellow onion
1 clove garlic, minced
1 16-ounce can plum tomatoes, drained
1 anchovy fillet, finely chopped
2 tablespoons butter
1 pound vermicelli noodles
3 tablespoons capers
1 6½ ounce can water-packed tuna, drained and flaked
2 tablespoons chopped fresh parsley
Fresh lemon slices

This protein-rich dish boosts your metabolism by building muscle tissue, which, in turn, burns a higher volume of calories.

1. In a large, deep skillet, heat the oil over medium heat. Add onion and sauté until soft, about 5–7 minutes. Add the garlic and sauté briefly. Add the tomatoes, break them up with a wooden spoon, cover, and simmer until soft, about 10 minutes.

2. Place the anchovies in a small bowl and mash them with a spoon. Add butter to the anchovies and mash together with a fork.

3. Meanwhile, cook the pasta in boiling salted water until al dente. Scoop out ½ cup of the cooking water. Drain the pasta.

4. Stir enough of the reserved cooking water into the anchovy butter to make it thick and smooth and no longer a paste. Add the capers to the skillet and stir to blend. Add the tuna fish and heat through over medium heat. Add the pasta to the sauce and toss until the pasta is coated. Transfer to a warmed bowl, sprinkle with the parsley, garnish with lemon slices, and serve.

CALORIES 623
FAT 15G
CARBOHYDRATES 92G
PROTEIN 28G

BURN IT UP

You're eating a complete protein when you dine on fish. In other words, you're getting all of the amino acids your body requires for proper nutrition. But if you want an extra helping of calcium to help maintain your skeleton, munch on fish with small, soft, edible bones such as canned anchovies, sardines, chum salmon, or jack mackerel.

Penne Pasta with Basil Cream Sauce

PROTEIN CALCIUM

SERVES 4

1 teaspoon Jane's Krazy Mixed-Up Salt or other salt seasoning
1 pound penne pasta, uncooked
1 teaspoon olive oil
2 cups nonfat sour cream
1 tablespoon chopped fresh basil
½ pound canned crab meat, drained

Basil is high in vitamin A and fiber—much like its equally dark green herb neighbors cilantro and Italian flat-leaf parsley. If you prefer cilantro to basil, feel free to substitute here. Also, lighter angel hair pasta would be a good replacement for heartier penne pasta should your taste buds prefer.

1. Fill large quart boiler ¾ full with water and add ½ tablespoon of seasoning. Bring to a boil and add pasta. Add a drizzle of olive oil. Cook until al dente, then drain.
2. In large saucepan over medium heat, add sour cream and basil. Heat until just bubbling. Reduce heat and add in drained crabmeat. Cook until heated. Toss with pasta and serve.

CALORIES 239
FAT 8G
CARBOHYDRATES 8G
PROTEIN 17G

Lentils with Cannellini Beans, Fresh Herbs, and Red Bell Pepper

PROTEIN HIGH FIBER

SERVES: 6

3 red bell peppers
1 19-ounce can white beans, drained and rinsed
2 cups well-drained cooked lentils
½ cup diced celery
¼ cup chopped fresh basil
¼ cup chopped fresh parsley
⅓ cup balsamic vinegar
Sea salt to taste
Black pepper to taste

Lentils are a great source of protein and fiber, and contain essential minerals and vitamins.

1. Preheat a broiler. Grill the bell peppers under the broiler for 15 minutes, turning once or twice, until the skin is blackened and blistered. Remove from the broiler and, when cool enough to handle, pull away the blackened skin. Then remove the skins and seeds and cut into narrow strips.
2. Combine the peppers, beans, lentils, celery, basil, and parsley in a medium bowl. Add vinegar and mix thoroughly. Season with salt and pepper.
3. Chill for at least one hour before serving.

CALORIES 197
FAT 1G
CARBOHYDRATES 36G
PROTEIN 13G

Risotto with Asparagus and Red Bell Pepper

HIGH FIBER | SUPERFOOD

SERVES 6

1 tablespoon olive oil
1 yellow onion, chopped
3 cloves garlic, minced
½ cup asparagus tips, coarsely chopped
½ cup chopped red bell pepper
1½ cups Arborio rice
¼ cup dry white wine
3½ cups vegetable or chicken broth
½ pound cooked shrimp, peeled and deveined
½ bunch fresh Italian parsley, chopped
¼ cup Parmesan cheese
Sea salt and black pepper to taste

Arborio rice is a short, thick-grain rice that is from the Arborio region of Italy. Its high starch content makes it ideal for absorbing moisture, and it is primarily used for making risotto, or reboiled rice, which is creamy in texture. Rich Arborio rice is a good source of iron.

1. In large saucepan, heat oil over medium heat and add onion. Cook for 3 minutes.
2. Add the garlic, asparagus, and red bell pepper and cook an additional 1 minute.
3. Add the rice and stir into the mixture, combining well.
4. Pour in the wine and let reduce by half.
5. Add the broth, ½ cup at a time, stirring each until liquid is fully incorporated before adding more. Continue the process until all liquid is used. Remove from heat.
6. Stir in shrimp, parsley, and cheese. Season with salt and pepper and serve.

CALORIES	452
FAT	1.3G
CARBOHYDRATES	52G
PROTEIN	32G

Cheese Ravioli with Tomato Sauce

ANTIOXIDANTS | PROTEIN

SERVES 4

1 9-ounce package refrigerated or frozen cheese ravioli
¾ cup prepared tomato sauce
½ cup grated Parmesan cheese

The acidic and antioxidant-rich tomato sauce, which is naturally low in fat, helps break down the fats and proteins in these delicious ravioli.

Bring large pot of water to a boil. Add ravioli and return to a boil over high heat. Reduce heat to medium, cover, and simmer for 5 minutes until ravioli are hot, stirring occasionally. Drain pasta. Return pasta to stock pot. Stir in tomato sauce, mixing gently so as not to break ravioli. Cook until heated, about 1–2 minutes. Top with grated Parmesan cheese and serve.

CALORIES	498
FAT	6G
CARBOHYDRATES	85G
PROTEIN	14G

Whole Wheat Fettuccine with Cream Sauce

SERVES 4

6 slices turkey bacon, chopped
1½ cups nonfat sour cream
4 egg yolks
1 cup Parmesan cheese
4 cups cooked whole wheat fettuccine noodles
Sea salt to taste
Black pepper to taste
2 tablespoons chopped fresh Italian
flat-leaf parsley leaves

This flavorful sauce is also delicious over cooked chicken breasts or tossed with other pasta such as penne or farfalle (bowtie). Another healthy substitution to whole wheat pasta is spinach pasta. Look for the lightly green colored pasta at the grocery store.

1. Cook the bacon in a sauté pan until crispy. Add 1 cup sour cream and turn off the heat.
2. Whisk egg yolks, ⅓ cup sour cream, and Parmesan cheese in a bowl.
3. Ladle about ½ cup of the warm sour cream from the pan into the egg yolk mixture so the yolks will not curdle when you add them to the pan.
4. Pour the yolk mixture into the pan with the bacon and sour cream; stir to combine. Cook for a few minutes while stirring over medium-low heat, then add cooked fettuccine and toss to coat with sauce.
5. Remove from heat, season with salt and pepper, and toss in chopped parsley.

CALORIES 755
FAT 55G
CARBOHYDRATES 42G
PROTEIN 26G

BURN IT UP

If you crave carbohydrates, you should reach for a complex carbohydrate instead of a simple one. Complex carbs take longer to break down into absorbable sugars. In addition, some complex carbohydrates have the benefit of being high in fiber, so you stay feeling full longer, and they are usually low in calories and fat. Good sources of complex carbs include nuts, vegetables, beans, whole grains, whole-wheat pasta, and brown rice.

Italian Pasta Fagiole

SERVES 8

16-ounce package ziti pasta
2 tablespoons olive oil
2 cloves garlic, minced
1½ cups sugar snap peas
1½ cups diced cooked extra-lean ham
1 cup cooked navy beans
¼ cup sun-dried tomatoes packed in oil, drained and chopped
1½ cups low-fat, reduced-sodium chicken broth
½ teaspoon kosher or sea salt
¼ teaspoon cracked black pepper
¼ cup grated Parmesan cheese

Antioxidant and lycopene rich sun-dried tomatoes are the key ingredient in this metabolic-friendly recipe. They work with the fiber-filled navy beans to send your metabolism through the roof.

1. Cook the pasta according to package directions.
2. Meanwhile, heat a large skillet over medium heat and add the olive oil.
3. Sauté the garlic for 2 minutes, being careful not to burn it.
4. Add the peas and stir-fry for about 3 minutes.
5. Stir in the ham, beans, tomatoes, broth, salt, and pepper and simmer for 5 minutes.
6. Toss the stir-fried bean mixture with the pasta and Parmesan cheese.

CALORIES 380
FAT 8G
CARBOHYDRATES 57G
PROTEIN 20G

Stir-Fry Chicken Lo Mein

SERVES 4

⅛ teaspoon low-sodium chicken base
½ cup water
2 10-ounce packages frozen Chinese vegetables
1 tablespoon freeze-dried shallots
1 pound cooked boneless, skinless chicken breast and thighs
⅛ cup or to taste hoisin sauce
1 pound no-salt-added oat bran pasta
1 teaspoon lemon juice
⅛ teaspoon mustard powder
1 teaspoon cornstarch
¼ teaspoon toasted sesame oil
4 thinly sliced scallions
Low-sodium soy sauce

The oat bran pasta found here is high in fiber and rich in minerals such as thiamine, magnesium, phosphorus, and manganese.

1. Add the chicken base and water to a medium sauté pan and heat over medium-low heat. Stir well to combine. Add the vegetables and freeze-dried shallots and cook an additional 3–4 minutes, or until vegetables are tender. Add the chicken and stir to combine. Transfer all to a bowl, cover and set aside.
2. Fill large quart boiler ¾ full with water. Bring to a boil and add the pasta, lemon juice, and mustard powder, but do not add salt.
3. While the pasta cooks, mix the cornstarch with a tablespoon of water in a small cup or bowl. Bring ½ cup of the pasta water to a boil over medium heat in the sauté pan. Whisk in the cornstarch mix; cook for at least 1 minute, stirring constantly.

4. Once the mixture thickens, remove from heat; add the toasted sesame oil to the broth mixture, then whisk again. Add the vegetable and chicken mixture to the broth mixture. Toss to coat. Cook until heated through, about 5 minutes.

5. Drain the pasta; add it to the chicken-vegetable mixture and stir to combine. Serve topped with scallions and soy sauce, if desired.

CALORIES 406

FAT 5G

CARBOHYDRATES 45G

PROTEIN 44G

Whole Wheat Pasta with Bleu Cheese and Walnuts

SUPERFOOD PROTEIN

SERVES 4

¼ cup chopped dry-toasted walnuts
4 teaspoons olive oil
2 cloves garlic, minced
½ cup nonfat cottage cheese
2 ounces crumbled bleu cheese
Skim milk, as needed (optional)
4 cups cooked whole wheat pasta
¼ cup freshly grated Parmesan cheese
Freshly ground black pepper

Nuts are high in protein, essential oils, and good, unsaturated fats. Walnuts in particular are one of the most nutritious nuts of all.

1. To toast walnuts, place in a heavy skillet over medium-low heat. Shake skillet occasionally to "toss" the nuts. Cook until slightly fragrant and nuts become lightly browned. Do not walk away from stove while toasting as nuts can go from lightly browned to burnt in a matter of seconds.

2. Heat the olive oil in a large nonstick skillet. Add the garlic and sauté for 1 minute. Lower the heat, stir in the cottage cheese, and bring it to temperature. Atdd the bleu cheese and stir to combine; thin the sauce with a little skim milk, if necessary.

3. Toss with the pasta and divide into 4 equal servings. Top each serving with 1 tablespoon of the Parmesan cheese, freshly ground black pepper to taste, and toasted walnuts.

CALORIES 309

FAT 11G

CARBOHYDRATES 38G

PROTEIN 16G

Parmesan Polenta with White Fish

SPICY HIGH FIBER

1½ tablespoons olive oil
½ serrano chili pepper, seeded and
   diced
1 quart vegetable broth
1½ cups cornmeal or masa meal
¾ pound white fish such as cod or
   tilapia
Sea salt and black pepper to taste
3 ounces Parmigiano-Reggiano
   cheese or Parmesan
2 tablespoons extra-virgin olive oil,
   for drizzling when serving
1 tablespoon apple cider vinegar

Masa meal is naturally high fiber and is also rich in minerals such as niacin and folate.

1. Heat ½ tablespoon olive oil in a stockpot on medium. Lightly sauté the serrano pepper, then add the broth and bring to a boil.
2. Whisk in the cornmeal slowly and cook for about 20–30 minutes, stirring frequently and adding more broth if necessary.
3. While polenta cooks, heat 1 tablespoon of the oil in large saucepan over medium heat. Add in fish and season with salt and pepper. Cook until light and flaky, about 3 minutes per side.
4. When polenta is cooked, remove from heat and stir in cheese until thoroughly combined.
5. To serve, spoon out generous dollop of polenta on each serving plate and arrange the fish on top. Drizzle with the vinegar.

CALORIES 265
FAT 12G
CARBOHYDRATES 32G
PROTEIN 15G

BURN IT UP

Be honest, you probably don't take vitamin C until you have a cold. Many fruits and vegetables are great sources of vitamin C—a guaranteed metabolism booster! These fruits and veggies include hot chili peppers—like the ones found here—cantaloupe, sweet peppers, dark green leafy vegetables, tomatoes, and oranges.

Tabouli with Fresh Tomatoes, Mint, and Lemon

SERVES 6

½ cup medium bulgur wheat
1½ cups water
⅓ cup lemon juice
2 tablespoons chopped fresh mint
1 teaspoon sea salt
1 teaspoon black pepper
¼ cup extra-virgin olive oil
1 cup chopped fresh Italian flat-leaf parsley leaves
½ cup chopped green onions
2 large tomatoes, diced
1 tablespoon minced garlic

Bulgur wheat consists of whole wheat berries that have been steamed, dried, cracked, and rehydrated. It's high in fiber and protein, and contains essential vitamins and minerals such as potassium.

1. Soak the bulgur in the water for at least 2 hours. Drain the excess water and put the bulgur in a large bowl. Add the remaining ingredients to the bulgur and mix well.
2. Let sit at room temperature for 60 minutes or refrigerate overnight. Serve chilled or at room temperature.

CALORIES 142
FAT 10G
CARBOHYDRATES 13G
PROTEIN 2G

BURN IT UP

Pantothenic acid, or vitamin B5, helps the body break down carbohydrates, fats, and various amino acids. Pantothenic acid can be found in corn, eggs, cheese, meat, peanuts, liver, soy products, broccoli, tomatoes, and whole grains.

CHAPTER 11
Vegetarian

There's no reason why vegetarian dishes can't pack the same nutritional punch as their carnivorous counterparts. In this chapter, you'll experience protein-rich grains, nuts, and more that will give you the protein you need to increase fat-burning muscle, the fiber you need for proper digestion, and the nutrient-rich foods that will give your body the overall metabolic balance it needs.

Veggie Burgers of Lentils, Sunflower Seeds, and Fresh Herbs

SERVES 8

1½ cups vegetable broth
½ cup water
¾ cup medium bulgur wheat
⅓ cup dried red lentils
1½ cups chopped cremini mushrooms
1 minced shallot
½ teaspoon celery salt
1½ teaspoons chopped fresh oregano leaves
½ teaspoon chopped fresh thyme leaves
1½ teaspoons chopped fresh sage leaves
¼ teaspoon onion powder
¼ teaspoon Hungarian paprika
1 teaspoon Dijon mustard
1 teaspoon sea salt
1 cup sunflower seeds, shelled and toasted
½ cup whole wheat flour
2 teaspoons instant yellow miso
1 tablespoon low-sodium soy sauce
1 tablespoon Worcestershire sauce
2 tablespoons dry plain or Italian-style bread crumbs
1 tablespoon olive oil

Lentils and bulgur have high fiber, good carbs, and natural protein that will keep you full and give you slow-releasing energy to see you through your day.

1. Place broth, water, bulgur, and lentils in a medium saucepan over medium low heat. Bring to a simmer, cover, and let simmer for about 30 minutes. Set aside.
2. Meanwhile, in a large mixing bowl, combine mushrooms, shallots, celery salt, herbs, onion powder, paprika, mustard, salt, sunflower seeds, and wheat flour. Mix well.
3. Add to the bulgur mixture the miso, soy sauce, and Worcestershire. Stir to combine and then add this mixture to the mushroom mixture. Stir to combine and then add the bread crumbs.
4. Mold mixture into 8 equal portions, pressing down to flatten slightly and then rounding by hand to form patties. Cover with plastic wrap and refrigerate for 3 hours or overnight.
5. When ready to cook, heat oil in a nonstick pan over medium heat. Cook patties until warmed and browned, about 3 minutes per side. Serve on hot hamburger buns, whole wheat rolls, or alone with ketchup or your sauce of choice.

CALORIES 268
FAT 14G
CARBOHYDRATES 29G
PROTEIN 11G

Falafel Pita Pockets

SERVES 6

1 cup dried garbanzo beans
½ cup chopped red onion
3 cloves garlic, peeled
1 teaspoon sea salt
1 teaspoon black pepper
1 teaspoon ground cumin
Pinch cayenne pepper
1 teaspoon baking powder
3 tablespoons all-purpose flour
3 tablespoons whole wheat flour
2 cups canola oil
3 rounds of whole wheat pita bread
6 tablespoons hummus
1 cup chopped fresh tomatoes
1 cup shredded iceberg lettuce
½ cup chopped cucumbers
6 tablespoons plain yogurt
2 tablespoons chopped fresh Italian flat-leaf
   parsley

Pita bread is high in fiber and low in fat. It's a versatile, healthy alternative to loaf bread and other specialty breads.

1. Soak the garbanzo beans in 3 cups of water overnight. Drain the garbanzo beans and put them in a food processor with the red onion, garlic, salt, pepper, cumin, and cayenne pepper. Pulse until everything is combined and the texture is fine but not a paste. Sprinkle the baking powder and flours over the mixture and pulse again until well combined. Refrigerate for 3 hours.
2. Heat the oil in a deep fryer or large pot to 375°F. Shape falafel mixture into small balls and fry 4–5 at a time. Drain on paper towels.

3. Cut the pita rounds in half and open them to create a bread pocket out of each half. For each sandwich, spread the inside of a pita pocket with hummus, stuff a few falafel into it, and top with tomatoes, lettuce, and cucumbers. Drizzle yogurt over the top and sprinkle with parsley.

CALORIES 449
FAT 24G
CARBOHYDRATES 52G
PROTEIN 12G

Portobello Panini of Tomato, Bell Pepper, and Basil

SERVES: 4

1 tablespoon low-fat mayonnaise
½ teaspoon lemon juice
2 cloves garlic, minced
4 large portobello mushrooms
4 teaspoons olive oil
1 tomato, sliced
1 red bell pepper, sliced
1 red onion, thinly sliced
⅔ cup fresh basil leaves, minced
4 leaves green leaf lettuce

The meaty portobello mushrooms in this recipe are as rich in minerals and protein as they are in flavor and texture; you can always consider substituting them for meat. They are also rich in fiber and minerals such as selenium, zinc, and manganese.

1. Preheat broiler. In a small bowl, mix together the mayonnaise, lemon juice, and

garlic. Separately, brush the mushrooms with the oil and place on a broiler pan. Broil until tender, about 5 minutes.

2. Spread the mayonnaise mixture on top of one broiled mushroom. Repeat with remaining mushrooms. Then top with the tomato, red pepper, onion, basil, and lettuce. Serve.

CALORIES 215
FAT 4G
CARBOHYDRATES 37G
PROTEIN 8G

Whole Wheat Veggie Loaf Sandwich

HIGH FIBER

SERVES 8

1 cup vegetable broth
¾ cup kasha
¼ cup olive oil
¾ cup shredded carrots
1 cup diced onion
½ cup diced celery
¼ cup grated Parmesan cheese
2 tablespoons chopped fresh Italian flat-leaf parsley
1 tablespoon Dijon mustard
1 tablespoon Worcestershire sauce
1 egg, beaten
1 teaspoon sea salt
½ teaspoon black pepper
1 cup finely chopped pecans
2 tablespoons tomato paste
1 tablespoon brown sugar
½ cup sliced red onions
1 tablespoon grated Parmesan cheese per sandwich
2 slices whole wheat bread per serving

The red onions found in this recipe have essential minerals, like chromium, and vitamin B6, which may promote positive bone development and help lower blood sugar levels.

1. Preheat oven to 350°F. Spray a loaf pan with oil. Bring the vegetable broth to a boil in a saucepan and add the kasha. Cover, turn down the heat, and simmer for 15 minutes. Add the olive oil to the sauté pan and sauté the carrots, onion, and celery in it for 5 minutes. Transfer them to a large bowl.

2. Add the Parmesan cheese, parsley, Dijon mustard, Worcestershire sauce, egg, salt, and pepper and mix together with a wooden spoon. Add the cooked kasha and pecans and combine thoroughly. Add a little beef broth if it seems too dry.

3. Press the mixture into the oiled loaf pan. Spread the tomato paste on top of the loaf, sprinkle the brown sugar over the tomato paste, scatter the red onions across, and bake 30 minutes. Remove the meatless loaf from the loaf pan and cut into slices.

4. Per sandwich: sprinkle 1 tablespoon Parmesan cheese on each meatless loaf slice and brown in a skillet, then sandwich it between 2 slices of bread. Add lettuce, mayonnaise, ketchup, or any other sandwich ingredients you like.

CALORIES 396
FAT 23G
CARBOHYDRATES 40G
PROTEIN 13G

Baguette Stuffed with Grilled Vegetables and Creamy Dijon

HIGH FIBER ANTIOXIDANTS

SERVES: 6

Dressing:

1 cup plain nonfat yogurt
3 tablespoons Dijon mustard
Black pepper to taste
2 tablespoons nonfat cottage cheese
⅓ teaspoon Tabasco sauce
2 tablespoons minced shallot
1 clove garlic, minced
1 teaspoon lemon juice

Sandwiches:

Nonstick cooking spray
1 small eggplant, cut into ¼-inch thick rounds
1 medium-sized yellow squash, cut into ¼-inch thick rounds
1 medium-sized zucchini, cut into ¼-inch thick rounds
1 medium onion
1 tablespoon Italian seasoning
¼ teaspoon cayenne pepper
2 baguettes
1 large tomato, sliced
Black pepper to taste
2 tablespoons chopped jalapeño pepper
8 fresh basil leaves
8 arugula leaves
2 red bell peppers, roasted and quartered

Arugula is high in vitamins A and K and is rich in minerals. Its high-fiber content makes it perfect for increasing your metabolism.

1. To make the dressing, combine all the ingredients and blend until smooth. Transfer to a bowl, cover, and refrigerate.
2. Preheat broiler. Spray a baking sheet with nonstick cooking spray. Arrange the eggplant, yellow squash, zucchini and onion in a single layer on the baking sheet. Sprinkle the Italian dressing and cayenne pepper over all of the rounds. Broil for about 5 minutes on each side, or until browned, turning once. Remove the baking sheet, but leave the broiler on.
3. Cut each of the baguettes in half lengthwise and scoop out the soft inner dough. Place the baguette halves in the broiler and toast for 2 minutes on each side. Put a few slices of tomato into the well in each baguette half. Dust with black pepper and sprinkle with the jalapeño pepper. Place 4 basil leaves, 4 arugula leaves, and 4 pieces of roasted pepper onto the bottom half of each baguette. Layer slices of eggplant, yellow squash, zucchini, and onion on top. Coat the inside of the remaining half of each baguette with the dressing and place it on top of the vegetables. Cut each baguette crosswise into 3 equal pieces and serve.

CALORIES 286
FAT 3G
CARBOHYDRATES 53G
PROTEIN 11G

Oven-Baked Eggplant with Fresh Herbs and Parmesan

SERVES: 8

HIGH FIBER ANTIOXIDANTS SUPERFOOD

1 28-ounce can tomatoes, coarsely chopped, juices reserved

1 onion, sliced

½ pound green beans, sliced

½ pound okra, cut into ½-inch lengths

¾ cup finely chopped green bell peppers

2 tablespoons lemon juice

1 tablespoon chopped fresh basil leaves

1½ teaspoons fresh oregano leaves, chopped

3 medium zucchini, cut into 1-inch cubes

1 eggplant, peeled and cut into 1-inch chunks

2 tablespoons grated Parmesan cheese

Eggplant is high in fiber, and rich in B vitamins, potassium, and other metabolically important minerals.

1. Preheat oven to 325°F. In a baking dish, combine the tomatoes and their liquid, onion, green beans, okra, bell peppers, lemon juice, basil, and oregano. Cover with foil or a lid. Bake for 15 minutes.

2. Mix in the zucchini and eggplant, cover, and continue to bake, stirring occasionally, until the vegetables are tender, about 1 hour.

3. Sprinkle the top with Parmesan cheese just before serving.

CALORIES 82

FAT 1G

CARBOHYDRATES 17G

PROTEIN 4G

BURN IT UP

Because organic foods are not subjected to pesticides, they retain more of their natural nutrients and fewer free radicals. This maintains cellular health, which in turn helps your body burn foods more efficiently, effectively boosting your metabolism. If you have to economize, opt for organic fruits and vegetables whose skin you eat—like the tomatoes and green beans found in this recipe.

Vegetarian Chili with Cocoa Habañero

`SPICY` `PROTEIN`

SERVES: 6

1 green bell pepper, cut into 1-inch pieces, seeds reserved
1 red bell pepper, cut into 1-inch pieces, seeds reserved
1 cup very coarsely chopped onion
3 cloves garlic, minced
1 teaspoon ground cumin
1½–3 tablespoons chili powder, to taste
¼ teaspoon finely chopped habañero pepper
½ teaspoon cocoa powder
½ teaspoon brown sugar
1 8-ounce can tomato sauce
1–2 16-ounce cans dark kidney beans, drained
1½ cups water or tomato juice
Sea salt to taste
Black pepper to taste

The protein-filled beans in this recipe also have the fiber your body needs to process nutrients. The spicy chili powder, habañero peppers, and cocoa all help boost your metabolism while bringing great taste to the table.

1. In a large nonstick saucepan, combine all the ingredients, including the bell pepper seeds. Bring to a boil, cover, reduce the heat to low, and simmer. Stir occasionally to loosen the bottom for 35–50 minutes, until heated through.
2. Adjust the seasoning and serve piping hot.

`CALORIES` 122
`FAT` 1G
`CARBOHYDRATES` 22G
`PROTEIN` 7G

Baked Cheese and Corn Zucchini

`ANTIOXIDANTS` `PROTEIN`

SERVES: 4

Nonstick cooking spray
2 medium zucchini
1 cup frozen corn kernels
½ cup low-fat small-curd cottage cheese
⅛ teaspoon sea salt
⅛ teaspoon black pepper
2 tablespoons chopped scallions
¼ cup grated Parmesan cheese

Naturally low in calories and fat, zucchini is also high in the vitamin C that acts as an antioxidant and promotes resistance to infection, among other qualities.

1. Preheat oven to 400°F. Spray an 8-inch-square baking dish with nonstick cooking spray. Cut each zucchini in half lengthwise. Using a teaspoon, scoop out the seeds from each half.
2. In a bowl, mix together the corn, cottage cheese, salt, pepper, and scallions. Spoon the mixture into the squash halves, mounding it slightly. Top with the Parmesan cheese. Place the squash in the prepared baking dish. Bake, uncovered, until the squash is tender and the cheese topping has melted, about 15 minutes. Serve immediately.

`CALORIES` 100
`FAT` 3G
`CARBOHYDRATES` 12G
`PROTEIN` 8G

Caribbean Spiced Coconut Rice over Plantains

SERVES: 6

1 tablespoon olive oil
2 teaspoons minced garlic
1 cup coarsely chopped onions
1 hot red chili pepper, seeded and
    chopped, or 1 generous pinch red
    pepper flakes
1 cup diced red bell pepper
1 cup coarsely chopped plum
    tomatoes
2–2¼ cups boiling water
1½ cups long-grain brown rice
½ cup unsweetened grated dried
    coconut
½ teaspoon dried thyme or oregano,
    crumbled
1 teaspoon sea salt, or to taste
1 cup cooked peas, either pigeon or
    black-eyed
¼ cup finely minced fresh coriander
2 very ripe plantains, peeled, cut on
    the diagonal into thin slices

Plantains are a member of the banana family, yet are starchier, less sweet, and most often cooked before eaten. They are rich in vitamin A, potassium, and fiber. Handle them in the same way you would bananas.

1. Heat the oil in a pressure cooker over medium-high heat. Add the garlic, onions, and chili pepper or pepper flakes and cook, stirring frequently, for 1 minute. Add the bell pepper, tomatoes, boiling water, rice, coconut, oregano or thyme, and salt. Secure the lid in place. Adjust the heat to maintain high pressure and cook for 25 minutes. Allow the pressure to reduce naturally. This will take about 10 minutes.
2. Remove the lid, tilting away from you to allow excess pressure to escape. Add the cooked peas and coriander. Stir well to distribute all the ingredients.
3. Serve topped with the plantains.

CALORIES 359
FAT 8G
CARBOHYDRATES 68G
PROTEIN 8G

BURN IT UP

When you choose to fry or make a food that is higher in fat, use natural fats like cold-pressed olive peanut oil, and canola oil. Using natural fats like these will ensure that even your baked and fried foods will have little or no artificial trans fat.

Baked Tomatoes Stuffed with Parmesan Mushrooms

SERVES: 2

2 large tomatoes
2 tablespoons chopped fresh Italian flat-leaf parsley
2 tablespoons chopped onion
2 tablespoons chopped cremini mushrooms
2 cloves garlic, minced
¼ teaspoon chopped fresh thyme leaves
1 tablespoon chopped fresh basil leaves
¼ cup seasoned dried bread crumbs
Sea salt to taste
Black pepper to taste
1 teaspoon olive oil

It has been said that mushrooms have no nutritional value; however, cremini mushrooms are good sources of vitamins and minerals such as riboflavin and zinc, which function in metabolizing carbohydrates, fat, and protein, as well as the proper function of cells.

1. Preheat oven to 350°F. Slice the top off each tomato, reserving the "lids." Scoop out the pulp and reserve in a bowl. To the tomato pulp, add the parsley, onion, mushrooms, garlic, thyme, and basil and blend. Add the bread crumbs, salt, pepper, and oil and mix well.
2. Fill the tomato shells with this mixture. Replace the lids. Bake until mixture is heated through. Serve immediately.

CALORIES 138
FAT 3G
CARBOHYDRATES 25G
PROTEIN 5G

Baked Vegetable Tamale

SERVES: 8

Vegetable Filling:
Nonstick cooking spray
1 14-ounce can pinto beans, drained
1 white onion, chopped
½ green bell pepper, diced
2 jalapeño peppers, seeded and chopped
2 cups canned tomatoes drained and chopped,
½ red bell pepper, diced
1½ cups shredded low-fat sharp Cheddar cheese
8 pitted black olives, sliced
¾ teaspoon minced garlic
¾ teaspoon ground cumin
¾ teaspoon chili powder

Tamale Topping:
½ cup plus 1 tablespoon all-purpose flour
1 cup yellow cornmeal
1½ teaspoons baking powder
½ teaspoon baking soda
⅛ teaspoon sea salt
½ cup plain low-fat yogurt
1 egg, at room temperature
2 teaspoons butter, melted and cooled
1 tablespoon snipped fresh chives (optional)

Pinto beans, like most beans, are naturally high in protein and fiber. You can also use other beans such as kidney beans or a combination of both.

1. Preheat oven to 375°F. Spray an 8-inch square baking pan with nonstick cooking spray. Combine all of the filling ingredients in the prepared pan. Toss until well mixed; set aside.
2. To make the topping, in a medium bowl, combine the flour, cornmeal, baking

powder, baking soda, and salt; stir until evenly mixed. In a small bowl, beat together the yogurt, egg, and butter. Add to the flour mixture and stir just until the dry ingredients are moistened. Spoon the mixture evenly on top of the vegetable filling. If desired, sprinkle evenly with the chives.

3. Bake until the filling is hot and bubbly, the topping is lightly browned, and a toothpick inserted into the center of the topping comes clean, 35–40 minutes. Let stand for 5 minutes before cutting into slices.

CALORIES 215
FAT 3G
CARBOHYDRATES 33G
PROTEIN 14G

Whole Wheat Lo Mein with Vegetables

CALCIUM SUPERFOOD

SERVES: 6

3 tablespoons soy sauce
2 tablespoons oyster sauce
1 tablespoon Asian sesame oil
½ teaspoon sugar
4 quarts water
½ pound fresh Chinese wheat noodles
1 tablespoon peanut oil
8 cloves garlic, chopped
1 cup chopped celery
1 6-ounce can bamboo shoots, drained
1 cup shredded Napa cabbage
1 cup chopped bok choy
1 cup bean sprouts
4 cups loosely packed, coarsely chopped spinach

Native to Asia, bamboo shoots are available fresh or canned, although they are much easier to find canned. They are rich in vitamin A, riboflavin, and calcium, among other essential nutrients, and will help rev your metabolic engine.

1. In a small bowl, combine the soy sauce, oyster sauce, sesame oil, and sugar; stir well. Set aside.

2. In a large saucepan, bring the water to a boil. Add the noodles, boil for 3 minutes, and drain. Rinse under cold water and drain again. Set aside.

3. In a wok or large, deep skillet, heat the peanut oil over high heat. Add the garlic, celery, bamboo shoots, Napa cabbage, bok choy, and bean sprouts. Stir-fry for 1 minute.

4. Add the cooked noodles, mix well, and then add the spinach. Stir-fry to mix. Add the sauce and stir and toss to mix well and heat through. Serve immediately.

CALORIES 195
FAT 6G
CARBOHYDRATES 29G
PROTEIN 8G

Vegetarian Quiche with Cheddar Cheese

SERVES 6

CALCIUM PROTEIN HIGH FIBER

1 9-inch frozen pie shell
1 15-ounce can chickpeas
3 egg whites, well beaten
½ cup skim milk
2 tablespoons flour
½ cup chopped onion
½ cup shredded low-fat Cheddar
  cheese

Chickpeas are terrific on salads and in vegetable sautés, and are the primary ingredient in many traditional hummus recipes such as the Pita Pocket with Hummus and Cucumber found in Chapter 4.

1. Preheat oven to 400°F. Bake the pie shell for 7 minutes, remove from heat, and turn the oven down to 350°F.
2. Purée the chickpeas, egg whites, and skim milk in a blender. Add in the flour if the mix is too watery.
3. Move mixture to a medium bowl, and add the onion. Pour into the partially baked pie shell. Sprinkle the cheese over the top evenly.
4. Bake for 35 minutes and serve warm.

CALORIES 455
FAT 22G
CARBOHYDRATES 52G
PROTEIN 12G

BURN IT UP

Once the victim of a bad rap, nutritional research has shown that an egg has protein (in the white) and fat (in the yolk), but no carbohydrates. The egg white has few other nutrients, while the yolk has a high amount of vitamin B12 and folate. Nutritionists used to think that eggs contained too much fat and cholesterol, but new research shows that the cholesterol in an egg doesn't contribute to higher levels of cholesterol in the blood.

Vegetarian Spiced Chili over Brown Rice

SERVES: 4

1 tablespoon olive oil
2 large onions, chopped
5 cloves garlic, minced
1 green bell pepper, chopped
2 jalapeño peppers, seeded and finely chopped
1 35-ounce can tomatoes in purée, drained and chopped
1 teaspoon ground coriander
Pinch ground cloves
Pinch ground allspice
2 teaspoons chopped fresh oregano leaves
1 tablespoon brown sugar
2 tablespoons chili powder
2 tablespoons ground cumin
2 cups cooked kidney beans
2 cups water
1 cup brown rice

Sometimes referred to as a pimento plant, allspice is part of the pepper family. It has been used to aid in digestion and is a popular remedy for arthritis and sore muscles.

1. In a large skillet, heat the oil over medium heat. Add the onions, garlic, bell pepper, and jalapeño pepper and sauté until vegetables are tender, about 10 minutes. Add the tomatoes, coriander, cloves, allspice, oregano, brown sugar, chili powder, cumin, and beans. Bring to a boil, cover, reduce the heat to low, and cook until the flavors are blended, about 30 minutes.
2. Meanwhile, in a saucepan, bring the water to a boil. Add the rice, reduce the heat to low, cover, and cook until the rice is tender and the liquid is absorbed, 20–30 minutes. To serve, spoon the rice onto individual plates. Serve the chili over the rice.

CALORIES 472
FAT 6G
CARBOHYDRATES 93G
PROTEIN 16G

Yellow Squash and Mushrooms with Goat Cheese

SERVES 4

2 tablespoons olive oil
1 yellow onion, chopped
3 yellow squash, sliced
1 zucchini squash, sliced
2 cups cremini or button mushrooms, cleaned and sliced
1 red bell pepper, seeded and chopped
Sea salt to taste
Lemon pepper to taste
4 ounces goat cheese

Goat cheese has bone-strengthening phosphorus, vitamin B12, and zinc, and is a great alternative for people who cannot have cow's milk products.

1. In large sauté pan over medium heat, add olive oil. Heat oil until fragrant, then add onion and sauté for 3 minutes.
2. Add both squash, mushrooms, and peppers. Season with salt and pepper. Cover and reduce heat to medium low. Simmer for about 5–6 minutes.
3. Uncover, stir, and stir in goat cheese. Cook until heated through. If there's too

much liquid, cook uncovered about 1–2 minutes longer. Or leave liquid and serve over brown or white rice.

CALORIES 122
FAT 3G
CARBOHYDRATES 14G
PROTEIN 11G

Frittata with Red Onion, Green Beans, and Tofu

PROTEIN CALCIUM

SERVES 8

2 tablespoons butter, unsalted
½ cup chopped red onion
½ cup diced firm tofu
¼ cup chopped asparagus spears
½ cup coarsely chopped broccoli florets
½ red bell pepper, seeded and diced
½ cup chopped fresh green beans
Sea salt to taste
Black pepper to taste
6 eggs
1 tablespoon fresh cilantro, leaves chopped
Fine zest of 1 lemon
¼ cup Monterey jack cheese, shredded

Tofu is made from soy beans and is often overlooked as a viable, delicious protein even though it is easily metabolized in the body.

1. In large oven-proof saucepan over medium heat, heat butter. Add in onion and tofu and sauté about 1 minute. Continue cooking and add asparagus, broccoli, red bell pepper, and green beans. Season with salt and pepper and cook about 2–3 minutes.

2. In separate bowl, whisk eggs until combined. Add in cilantro and lemon zest, and whisk again. Pour egg mixture over vegetables, tilting pan to coat evenly. Top with cheese.

3. Preheat broiler. Reduce heat, cooking slowly for about 5 minutes, or until eggs are setting. To finish cooking, place saucepan under broiler for about 1 minute to finish cooking and brown very slightly on top.

CALORIES 225
FAT 15G
CARBOHYDRATES 23G
PROTEIN 21G

Tortillas with Spicy Jalapeño and Cream Cheese

SPICY CALCIUM

SERVES 6

1 cup nonfat cream cheese
1 8-ounce can chopped jalapeños
4 scallions, chopped
1 clove garlic, minced
1 teaspoon sea salt
1 teaspoon chili powder
1 teaspoon paprika
6 whole wheat flour tortillas

Cheese—like the cream cheese found in this recipe—yogurt, and other dairy products are good sources of calcium, protein, and many other vitamins and minerals. Read the labels, though, to make sure you're not eating added sugars.

1. Cream the nonfat cream cheese in a medium bowl. Mix in the jalapeños, scallions, and garlic. Add the salt, chili powder, and paprika. Evenly spread the mixture onto tortillas.

2. Roll up the tortillas and wrap individually in clear plastic wrap. Refrigerate for a few hours until cold; slice and serve.

CALORIES 208
FAT 5G
CARBOHYDRATES 31G
PROTEIN 10G

Creamy Potato Chowder

CALCIUM

SERVES 8

2 tablespoons butter
1 onion, chopped
1 cup chopped celery
2 cups sliced carrots
½ cup water
3 cups low-sodium chicken or vegetable broth
3 potatoes, peeled and diced
3 cups nonfat milk
¼ cup flour

The starches in this creamy potato soup will help increase your metabolism by giving you sustained energy for a longer period of time.

1. Melt butter in a large, deep skillet over medium heat. Add the vegetables until tender, tossing occasionally. Add the water, broth, and potatoes; boil for 15 minutes or until potatoes are tender.

2. Add the milk, stirring to combine, and turn heat down to medium high. Add the flour to thicken. If you need to thicken further, add more flour. Serve hot.

CALORIES 158
FAT 5G
CARBOHYDRATES 34G
PROTEIN 8G

Teriyaki Vegetable Kabobs

HIGH FIBER ANTIOXIDANTS SUPERFOOD

SERVES 4

3 bell peppers (1 green, 1 red, and 1 yellow)
2 cups cherry tomatoes
2 medium zucchini
1 small red onion
16 skewers
1 cup pineapple chunks
½ cup low-sodium teriyaki sauce

Grilled vegetables such as bell peppers are a delicious way to get needed nutrients such as beta-carotene, folic acid, and vitamin B6.

1. Preheat grill or grill pan. Cut all the vegetables into 2-inch chunks. Thread the vegetables onto skewers and grill about 15 minutes, turning frequently. When grill marks appear to be steaming, vegetables are done.

2. Place pineapple on end of skewer and brush with teriyaki sauce.

CALORIES 128
FAT 1G
CARBOHYDRATES 29G
PROTEIN 5G

Baked Artichokes with Black Olives, Red Bell Peppers, and Parmesan

SPICY ANTIOXIDANTS

4 large artichokes, trimmed and split lengthwise
4 quarts water
½ fresh lemon
¾ cup Parmesan cheese, grated
10 pitted black olives, chopped
1 red bell pepper, seeded and chopped
1 clove garlic, finely chopped
1 teaspoon fresh thyme, leaves chopped
1 yellow squash, finely chopped
1 tablespoon olive oil
Sea salt and lemon pepper to taste

The spicy lemon pepper used here is an instant metabolism booster. You can use it as a seasoning in almost any recipe, including those with chicken, fish, or beef.

1. Boil the artichokes in 4 quarts of water squeezing in lemon juice, then adding in lemon half. Boil for 20–25 minutes. Drain and place on a parchment-lined baking sheet, cut-side up.
2. Preheat oven to 350°F. Scoop out artichoke, using any heart pieces in vegetable mixture. In a large mixing bowl, combine remaining ingredients, tossing with the olive oil.
3. Divide filling into artichokes, pressing between the leaves where needed.
4. Bake for 15 minutes or until hot.

CALORIES 153
FAT 9G
CARBOHYDRATES 12G
PROTEIN 3G

BURN IT UP

To maintain optimum health and boost your metabolism, include plenty of antioxidants in your diet. Foods particularly high in antioxidants include:

- Berries: wild blueberries, cranberries, blackberries, raspberries, strawberries
- Beans: small red beans, red kidney beans, pinto beans, dried black beans
- Apples: Red Delicious, Granny Smith, Gala
- Other fruits: dried prunes, sweet cherries, black plums, plums
- Other foods: artichokes, almonds, russet potatoes, tea

Three-Cheese Lasagna Rolls with Spinach

ANTIOXIDANTS SUPERFOOD

SERVES 6

1 clove fresh garlic, minced
½ teaspoon all-purpose seasoning
½ cup reduced-fat Parmesan cheese
1 cup shredded fat-free mozzarella
1 cup frozen spinach, thawed and drained
1 cup tomatoes, diced
1 teaspoon chopped fresh oregano leaves
1 teaspoon chopped fresh basil leaves
¼ teaspoon nutmeg
1 tablespoon sugar or ½ tablespoon sugar substitute such as Splenda
Nonstick cooking spray
6 whole wheat lasagna noodles, cooked
1 cup marinara sauce

Sugar substitutes are food additives with a sweet taste that contain fewer calories than traditional sugars. However, because they are a food additive and not a natural food product, use in moderation or stick to the natural sugars such as granulated sugar, raw sugar, or even honey, and discipline yourself on cutting back a little at a time.

1. Mix garlic, all-purpose seasoning, Parmesan cheese, ½ cup mozzarella cheese, spinach, tomatoes, oregano, basil, nutmeg, and sugar. Set aside.
2. Coat a 9" × 13" baking dish with nonstick spray.
3. Cut each lasagna noodle in half lengthwise. Place 2 tablespoons of spinach mixture on one end of lasagna noodle. Roll noodle around spinach mixture and place in dish.

Repeat for all noodles. Top with marinara sauce and remaining mozzarella cheese.
4. Cover with foil and bake at 375°F for 25 minutes.

CALORIES 382
FAT 28G
CARBOHYDRATES 71G
PROTEIN 21G

Marinara Sauce

ANTIOXIDANTS SUPERFOOD

MAKES ABOUT 1 QUART; SERVING SIZE: ¼ CUP

1 28-ounce can plum tomatoes, drained
Nonstick cooking spray
4 cloves garlic, minced
1 6-ounce can tomato paste
2 teaspoons chopped fresh oregano leaves
Black pepper to taste
¼ cup fresh basil leaves, minced

This low-cal, antioxidant- and mineral-rich sauce is perfect for more than just pasta. Use over lean proteins such as chicken, turkey, and even fish!

1. Place the tomatoes in a food processor and blend until smooth. Spray pan with nonstick cooking spray and place over low heat. Add the garlic and sauté until just fragrant, about 1 minute. Add the tomatoes, tomato paste, oregano, and pepper. Bring to a boil, then reduce heat to low and simmer, uncovered, to blend the flavors.
2. Allow mixture to thicken slightly, about 10 minutes. Remove from heat and stir in fresh basil.
3. Toss with pasta to serve.

CALORIES 22
FAT <1G
CARBOHYDRATES 5G
PROTEIN <1G

Whole Wheat Black Bean Burritos

PROTEIN | HIGH FIBER

SERVES 6

3 cups black beans, drained
1 cup frozen corn
½ teaspoon all-purpose seasoning
1 clove fresh garlic, minced
1 teaspoon chipotle sauce
½ cup fat-free sour cream
½ cup white onions, chopped
1 tablespoon cilantro, chopped
Nonstick cooking spray
6 whole wheat tortillas
½ cup shredded low-fat Cheddar cheese

Black beans are high in protein and fiber and contain minerals such as magnesium and phosphorus.

1. Mix all ingredients except tortillas and cheese. Coat a 9" × 13" baking dish with nonstick spray.
2. Divide mixture equally among 6 tortillas and fold each tortilla into a burrito.
3. Place each burrito in dish and top with Cheddar cheese.
4. Cover with foil and bake at 375°F for 20 minutes or until cheese melts.

CALORIES 313
FAT 4G
CARBOHYDRATES 56G
PROTEIN 16G

Enchilada Verde

SPICY | ANTIOXIDANTS

SERVES 8

1 cup tomatoes, diced
2 cups canned white beans, drained
2 cups canned pinto beans, drained
2 cups canned black beans, drained
½ teaspoon all-purpose seasoning
1 clove fresh garlic, minced
1 cup white onions, chopped
¼ cup cilantro, chopped
½ cup low-sodium chicken broth
½ cup green enchilada sauce, divided
Nonstick cooking spray
12 whole wheat tortillas
¼ cup shredded fat-free mozzarella cheese

Enchilada sauce is rich in the spices that include antioxidants and capsaicin—instant metabolism boosters.

1. Mix first 9 ingredients and ¼ cup green enchilada sauce.
2. Coat a 9" × 13" baking dish with nonstick spray. Lay 4 tortillas in the dish. Cover with half of bean mixture.
3. Place 4 tortillas over bean mixture, followed by the remaining bean mixture.
4. Top with last 4 tortillas, ¼ cup enchilada sauce, and mozzarella cheese.
5. Cover with foil and bake at 400°F for 25–30 minutes.

CALORIES 419
FAT 5G
CARBOHYDRATES 76G
PROTEIN 20G

Spinach Polenta with Tomato

SUPERFOOD

5 teaspoons olive oil
1 onion, finely chopped
2 10-ounce packages chopped
  spinach
4 cloves garlic, crushed
Sea salt to taste
Black pepper to taste
3 cups water
3 cups low-sodium vegetable broth
2 cups coarse-ground yellow
  cornmeal
2 cups tomato sauce

Whether it's fresh or frozen, superfood spinach is amazingly good for your metabolism. It's super-rich in vitamins A, C, K, and folate.

1. Preheat oven to 375°F. Lightly oil a ceramic quiche dish, set aside.
2. Heat 2 tablespoons of oil in a large skillet. Add the onion and sauté for about 2 minutes. Add the thawed spinach; sauté until soft. Add the garlic, salt, and pepper; continue to stir for 5 minutes, then set aside.
3. Combine the water, broth, and cornmeal in a medium bowl. Spoon half of the polenta into the quiche dish, pressing it down with your fingers or the back of a spoon to make a smooth surface. Spoon in the spinach filling, spreading evenly. Spoon in remaining polenta over the spinach, spreading evenly. Brush top of polenta layer with remaining oil.
4. Cover with foil and bake for 30 minutes, then remove the foil and bake for another 15 minutes or until top is browned. Remove from oven, top each wedge with tomato sauce, and serve while hot.

CALORIES 200
FAT 4G
CARBOHYDRATES 39G
PROTEIN 6G

BURN IT UP

Base your diet on the color wheel. Food that is brightly colored automatically has less fat and will help boost your metabolic rate. Try eating brightly colored foods, like red bell peppers, strawberries, melons, tomatoes, blueberries, grapes, carrots, and legumes.

CHAPTER 12

Side Dishes

In this chapter, we'll show you how to transform ordinary boring side dishes into deliciously metabolically charged entrée accompaniments. You'll learn how easy it is to incorporate nutrient-rich herbs, citrus, spices, and other healthy foods into your side dishes for an energy-boosting, fat-burning experience.

Sautéed Green Beans with Tomatoes and Garlic

SERVES: 6

I pound green beans, trimmed
½ tablespoon olive oil
1 small onion, chopped
1 tablespoon chopped garlic
1 tablespoon all-purpose flour
1 16-ounce can tomatoes, drained, liquid reserved, and chopped

The tomatoes found in this recipe are rich in copper, a necessity for metabolizing cholesterol and glucose. Copper also helps convert other nutrients into energy sources for the body.

1. Steam the green beans until tender, about 5 minutes, then plunge them into cold water to cool. Drain and set aside.

2. In a medium nonstick saucepan, heat the oil over medium heat. Add the onion and garlic and sauté for a few minutes. Stir in the flour and cook for 1 minute. Stir in the liquid from the tomatoes. Cook the mixture, stirring, until slightly thickened.

3. Add the tomatoes and green beans, mixing well. Cook, stirring, over medium heat for a couple of minutes until the beans are done but still crisp and the flavors are blended.

CALORIES 63

FAT 1G

CARBOHYDRATES 12G

PROTEIN 3G

BURN IT UP

Studies have shown that consuming 20–30 grams of fiber a day can dramatically reduce your risk of many cancers. Keep your fiber intake high by eating vegetables like garlic, green beans, tomatoes, and onions.

Parmesan Risotto with Fresh Vegetables

SERVES: 4

2 tablespoons butter
1 onion, chopped
1 cup Arborio rice
4 cups reduced-sodium, fat-free chicken broth, heated
1 cup green beans, cut in ½-inch lengths
1 cup chopped zucchini
⅓ cup minced fresh parsley
¼ cup grated Parmesan cheese
Sea salt to taste
Black pepper to taste

The carbohydrate-rich rice in this recipe gives your body the energy it needs to function throughout the day. Rice is best eaten as a side dish with foods that contain lean protein such as chicken or fish.

1. Melt 1 tablespoon of the butter in a large skillet over medium heat. Add the onion and sauté until softened. Add the rice and stir to coat with the butter. Reduce the heat to low and add ½ cup of the broth. Cook, stirring, until it is absorbed. Add 1½ cups more broth, ½ cup at a time, cooking and stirring until each addition is absorbed. Add the green beans and zucchini and cook for 2 minutes. Add the remaining broth, again ½ cup at a time. Simmer for about 15 minutes more. The risotto is done when the kernels are still slightly firm at the center and mixture is creamy.
2. Add the parsley, Parmesan, the remaining butter, salt, and pepper.

CALORIES 269
FAT 8G
CARBOHYDRATES 40G
PROTEIN 10G

Sweet Potato Bake with Apples

SERVES: 4

3 Red Delicious apples, peeled, cored, and sliced
1 tablespoon lemon juice
2 pounds sweet potatoes, peeled and sliced
⅓ cup apple juice
1 tablespoon butter, melted

Sweet potatoes are rich in vitamin A, a compound that aids in healthy skin and hair.

1. Preheat oven to 350°F. In a bowl, toss the apple slices with the lemon juice. In a 1½-quart flameproof baking dish, alternate layers of the sweet potatoes and apples. Pour the apple juice and the melted butter over the layers. Cover and bake until tender and juice is bubbling, about 1¼ hours.
2. Remove from the oven. Turn the oven to broil. Uncover the baking dish and slip in under the broiler until top is lightly browned, about 5 minutes.

CALORIES 262
FAT 4G
CARBOHYDRATES 56G
PROTEIN 3G

Asian Stir-Fry with Rice and Vegetables

SERVES: 6

1 tablespoon peanut oil
2 cups sliced zucchini
1 cup minced celery
4 cups cold cooked rice
1 red bell pepper, diced
2 eggs, lightly beaten
2 cups bean sprouts
⅓ cup oyster sauce
1 onion, chopped

Peanut oil is low in saturated fat, super flavorful, and widely used in Asian cooking.

1. In a large, deep skillet, heat the oil over medium-high heat. Add the zucchini and celery and stir-fry for 2 minutes.
2. Add the rice and stir-fry for another minute.
3. Add the bell pepper and stir-fry for another minute.
4. Add the eggs and cook, stirring, for 30 seconds.
5. Add the bean sprouts and stir-fry for 1 minute longer, or until the eggs are set.
6. Add the oyster sauce and stir until evenly distributed.
7. Sprinkle with chopped onion and serve.

CALORIES 221
FAT 4G
CARBOHYDRATES 37G
PROTEIN 8G

Wild Rice with Fresh Herbs

SERVES: 6

1 tablespoon olive oil
1 onion, diced
3 cups reduced-sodium, fat-free chicken broth
½ cup wild rice
1 cup white rice
¼ cup chopped fresh Italian flat-leaf parsley leaves
1 teaspoon chopped fresh basil leaves
Sea salt to taste
Black pepper to taste

True wild rice is actually long-grain marsh grass seed that is particularly high in folate, zinc, and other metabolism-boosting natural minerals.

1. In a large skillet, heat the oil over medium heat for 1 minute. Add the onion and sauté until tender, about 5 minutes. Add the chicken broth, stir in wild rice, and bring to a boil. Add the white rice.
2. Reduce the heat to low, cover, and cook until the rices are done, about 20 minutes.
3. Mix in the parsley, basil, salt, and pepper and serve.

CALORIES 199
FAT 2G
CARBOHYDRATES 37G
PROTEIN 6G

Long-Grain Rice with Lentils, Mushrooms, and Fresh Ginger

`PROTEIN` `HIGH FIBER`

SERVES: 8

1 tablespoon butter
2 large onions, sliced
4 cups reduced-sodium, fat-free chicken broth
2 cups sliced cremini mushrooms
1½ cups white rice
1 cup lentils
1 tablespoon peeled and minced fresh ginger
1 teaspoon curry powder
¼ teaspoon ground cinnamon
2 cloves garlic, minced
½ cup chopped fresh Italian flat-leaf parsley
Sea salt to taste
Black pepper to taste

Lentils, part of the legume family, are related to beans and peanuts. Unlike dried beans though, lentils do not require pre-soaking. They are full of both protein and fiber and are rich in iron and low in fat.

1. In a heavy skillet, melt the butter over low heat. Add the onions and cook, stirring occasionally, until tender, about 20 minutes.
2. Meanwhile, in a saucepan, combine the broth, mushrooms, rice, lentils, ginger, curry powder, cinnamon, and garlic. Bring to a boil, add in the cooked onions, reduce the heat to low, cover, and cook until the rice and lentils are tender and the liquid is absorbed, about 30 minutes.
3. Uncover and mix in the parsley, salt, and pepper. Serve at once.

`CALORIES` 258
`FAT` 2G
`CARBOHYDRATES` 48G
`PROTEIN` 12G

Creamy Cucumbers with Dill

`HIGH FIBER`

SERVES: 10

2 cups plain fat-free yogurt
2 medium cucumbers, chopped
1 clove garlic, minced
2 teaspoons minced fresh dill
1 tablespoon olive oil
2 teaspoons distilled white vinegar

Cucumbers have a high water content, which helps you feel full, keeps you hydrated, and helps prevent kidney stones. Cucumbers also contain the enzyme erepsin, which helps digest protein.

1. In a bowl, combine all the ingredients.
2. Cover and chill for at least 1 hour before serving.
3. Serve as a side dish with a dash of curry, if desired.

`CALORIES` 55
`FAT` 2G
`CARBOHYDRATES` 6G
`PROTEIN` 3G

Western Barbeque Rice with Beef

SPICY PROTEIN

SERVES: 6

½ pound lean ground beef
1 medium onion, chopped
2 cups hot cooked white rice
1 10-ounce can corn kernels, drained and heated
½ cup barbeque sauce (see following recipe)

Barbeque sauce, like the one below, instantly increases your metabolism with spice, spice, spice, and more spice from mustard, pepper, and pungent, fiber-rich onion.

1. In a large nonstick skillet, cook the beef until browned, about 5 minutes. Drain off any fat. Add the onion and continue to cook until the onion is soft, about 8 minutes longer. Drain again.
2. Place the beef-onion mixture in a serving bowl. Add the rice, corn, and barbecue sauce and mix well.

CALORIES 195
FAT 6G
CARBOHYDRATES 26G
PROTEIN 9G

Easy Barbeque Sauce

SUPERFOOD

MAKES 2 CUPS; SERVING SIZE: ⅛ CUP

⅔ cup cider vinegar
1 cup water
2 tablespoons Dijon mustard
2 tablespoons firmly packed brown sugar
1 teaspoon black pepper
½ cup lemon juice
2 white or yellow onions, minced
½ cup Worcestershire sauce
⅔ cup ketchup

Barbeque sauce can be metabolic friendly when not laden with sugar. This recipe focuses on spice, citric acid, and lots of metabolism-boosting onion.

1. In a saucepan, mix together all ingredients except ketchup.
2. Bring to a boil, then reduce heat to low and simmer for 20 minutes, stirring occasionally.
3. Remove from heat and stir in the ketchup.

CALORIES 94
FAT <1G
CARBOHYDRATES 23G
PROTEIN 2G

Spiced Black Beans and Rice with Sour Cream

SPICY HIGH FIBER ANTIOXIDANTS

SERVES: 8

> 2 19-ounce cans black beans, drained
> 2 teaspoons ground cumin
> 4 cloves garlic, minced
> 2 bay leaves
> 2 teaspoons chopped fresh oregano leaves
> 1 teaspoon sea salt
> 1 medium onion, chopped
> 1 green bell pepper, chopped
> 2 tablespoons lemon juice
> 1 16-ounce can tomatoes, drained and cut up
> 4 cups hot cooked white rice
> 1 cup shelled green peas, blanched
> 1 cup chopped fresh tomatoes
> 2 scallions, thinly sliced
> 2 tablespoons low-fat sour cream

Bell peppers, no matter the color, are rich in vitamins A, B6, and C. They are great sautéed, grilled, roasted, or baked.

1. In a large saucepan, combine the beans, cumin, garlic, bay leaves, oregano, salt, onion, bell pepper, lemon juice, and canned tomatoes. Bring to a boil, reduce the heat to medium, cover, and cook until the vegetables are done, about 30 minutes.
2. Discard the bay leaves. Mix the beans with the hot rice and stir in the green peas, chopped fresh tomatoes, scallions, and sour cream and serve.

CALORIES 259
FAT 2G
CARBOHYDRATES 50G
PROTEIN 12G

Simple Baked Acorn Squash

HIGH FIBER ANTIOXIDANTS

SERVES: 4

> 1 acorn squash
> 1 tablespoon butter
> 1 teaspoon brown sugar (optional)

Also known as a winter squash, acorn squash is high in vitamins A and C, iron, and magnesium. It tastes great baked or pureed as a soup.

1. Preheat oven to 400°F. Cut the squash in half and scoop out the seeds.
2. Bake the squash on parchment paper–lined baking sheet for about 30 minutes, or until tender. Scoop out the pulp and mix with butter and the brown sugar.
3. Return the mixture to the shells or place in a baking dish and heat thoroughly, about 15 minutes.

CALORIES 78
FAT <1G
CARBOHYDRATES 17G
PROTEIN 1G

Potatoes Au Gratin

SERVES: 6

PROTEIN CALCIUM

6 russet potatoes

2 cups 1% low-fat cottage cheese

2 tablespoons olive oil

1 onion, chopped

2 tablespoons all-purpose flour

1 teaspoon chopped fresh Italian flat-leaf parsley leaves

1 teaspoon chopped fresh thyme leaves

⅛ teaspoon sea salt

Black pepper to taste

⅓ cup nonfat milk

½ cup fine dried bread crumbs

2 tablespoons grated Parmesan cheese

2 tablespoons butter

These lean potatoes au gratin use cottage cheese and nonfat milk to keep the protein high, the fat low, and to give you energy-boosting carbs.

1. Place the potatoes in a saucepan with water to cover. Bring to a boil, reduce the heat to medium, and simmer until tender, about 25 minutes. Drain and, when cool enough to handle, peel and slice.

2. Preheat oven to 350°F. Grease a 1½-quart baking dish. In a bowl, beat together the cottage cheese and oil with a rotary beater until fluffy. Mix in the onion. In a small bowl, stir together the flour, parsley, thyme, salt, and pepper. Make a layer of ⅓ of the sliced potatoes in the prepared baking dish. Cover with a layer of half of the cottage cheese. Sprinkle with half of the seasoned flour. Repeat the layers, then end with a layer of potatoes. Pour the milk evenly over the potato-cheese layers. Mix the bread crumbs with the Parmesan cheese and sprinkle over the potatoes. Dot with margarine.

3. Bake until cheese is lightly browned, about 30 minutes. Serve hot directly from the dish.

CALORIES 327

FAT 11G

CARBOHYDRATES 41G

PROTEIN 15G

BURN IT UP

From dark leafy greens rich in calcium, iron, and magnesium, to the cruciferous vegetables like bok choy, broccoli, cabbage, turnips, and watercress that have cancer-preventing antioxidants, to nutrient-rich vegetables like carrots, potatoes (like the russet found in this recipe), yams, and tomatoes, vegetables are always a good thing to snack on and include with each meal.

Baked Citrus Sweet Potatoes with Almonds

SERVES: 6

3 large sweet potatoes
¼ cup orange juice
1 tablespoon butter
⅛ teaspoon sea salt
¼ teaspoon pepper
¼ teaspoon ground ginger
3 oranges, peeled and cut into small pieces
¼ cup toasted almonds, slivered (optional)

Almonds are a great source of vitamin E, one of the richest antioxidants available.

1. Preheat oven to 400°F. Pierce potatoes with fork and bake until tender, about 1 hour. Remove from the oven and leave the oven set at 400°F. Halve the sweet potatoes lengthwise and scoop out the pulp into a bowl, being careful to keep the skins intact. Set the skins aside. Mash the pulp, then add the orange juice, butter, salt, pepper, and ginger. Stir the orange pieces into the mixture. Spoon into the skins and place on a baking sheet. Top with the almonds, if desired.
2. Bake until heated through, about 15 minutes. Serve hot.

CALORIES 171
FAT 2G
CARBOHYDRATES 36G
PROTEIN 2G

Creamy Buttermilk Potatoes

SERVES: 12

3 pounds potatoes, peeled and quartered
1¼ cups low-fat buttermilk, heated
2 tablespoons butter
1 onion, chopped
Pinch ground nutmeg
Sea salt to taste
Black pepper to taste

Buttermilk is high in calcium and full of protein, phosphorus, and riboflavin.

1. Place the potatoes in a large saucepan with enough water to cover them. Bring to a boil, cover, reduce the heat to medium, and cook until tender, about 20 minutes.
2. Drain, return to the pan, and mash until smooth. Gradually add the buttermilk, stirring constantly. Stir in the butter, then add the onion, nutmeg, salt, and pepper.
3. Serve immediately.

CALORIES 105
FAT 2G
CARBOHYDRATES 18G
PROTEIN 3G

Chili Pepper Potatoes

SERVES: 6

4 large potatoes, cut into fries
1 tablespoon olive oil
½ teaspoon paprika
½ teaspoon chili powder

Baking these fries gives you the crunchy carbohydrates you need without the heavy, oily fat that you don't.

1. Preheat oven to 475°F.
2. In a medium bowl, toss together the potatoes, oil, paprika, and chili powder.
3. Spread out on a baking sheet.
4. Bake until golden, turning occasionally, about 30 minutes. Serve hot.

CALORIES 132
FAT 2G
CARBOHYDRATES 25G
PROTEIN 3G

Herb-Stuffed Potatoes

SERVES: 8

4 baking potatoes
¾ cup low-fat cottage cheese
¼ cup nonfat milk
2 tablespoons butter
1 teaspoon chopped fresh dill
¾ teaspoon herb seasoning
4–6 drops Tabasco sauce
2 teaspoons grated Parmesan cheese

The capsaicin found in the spicy Tabasco sauce used in this recipe gives your metabolism the kick it needs to start burning carbs and fats.

1. Preheat oven to 425°F. Prick the potatoes with a fork. Bake until easily pierced with a fork, about 1 hour. Remove from the oven and leave the oven set at 425°F.
2. Halve the potatoes lengthwise and scoop out the pulp into a bowl, leaving shells about ½ inch thick. Mash the pulp, then mix in all the remaining ingredients except the Parmesan cheese. Spoon into the potato shells. Place on a baking sheet, and sprinkle the top of each with ¼ teaspoon Parmesan cheese. Bake until tops are golden brown, 15–20 minutes.

CALORIES 145
FAT 5G
CARBOHYDRATES 22G
PROTEIN 3G

Three-Cheese Mac and Cheese

CALCIUM PROTEIN

SERVES: 8

2 cups macaroni
1 onion, chopped
2 cups nonfat milk
2 tablespoons cornstarch
1 teaspoon dry mustard
1 cup shredded fat-free Cheddar cheese
1 cup shredded low-fat mozzarella cheese
Sea salt to taste
Black pepper to taste
½ cup seasoned dried bread crumbs
2 tablespoons grated Parmesan cheese
1 tablespoon butter, melted

Using low-fat or fat-free cheeses gives you the calcium your body craves without the extra unwanted fat.

1. In a large pot, bring water to a boil. Add the macaroni and cook for 5 minutes. Add the onion and cook for another 5 minutes, or until the macaroni is nearly al dente. Drain and set aside.
2. Preheat oven to 350°F. In a large saucepan, combine the milk, cornstarch, and mustard, stirring to dissolve the cornstarch and mustard. Place over medium heat and cook, stirring, until thickened. Add the Cheddar and mozzarella cheeses and cook, stirring, until the cheeses melt. Add the cooked macaroni, and season with salt and pepper. Pour into a 9" × 13" baking dish. In a small bowl, stir together the bread crumbs, Parmesan cheese, and butter. Scatter over the macaroni.

3. Bake until bubbly, about 20 minutes. Serve hot.

CALORIES 244
FAT 5G
CARBOHYDRATES 33G
PROTEIN 16G

Tuscan Baked Potatoes

HIGH FIBER

SERVES: 8

Nonstick cooking spray
1 tablespoon olive oil
1 teaspoon butter
2 onions, chopped
6 cloves garlic, minced
1 35-ounce can tomatoes, well drained and diced
Sea salt to taste
Black pepper to taste
2 tablespoons minced fresh Italian flat-leaf parsley leaves
1 teaspoon chopped fresh basil leaves
1 teaspoon chopped fresh oregano leaves
2½ pounds russet potatoes, thinly sliced
½ cup grated Parmesan cheese

This recipe is full of fibrous, nutrient-rich herbs such as parsley, basil, and oregano. These herbs not only add taste to this dish, but the nutrients they contain also help metabolize the natural carbs in the potatoes.

1. Preheat oven to 325°F. Spray a 3-quart baking dish with nonstick cooking spray. In a skillet, heat the oil and the butter over medium heat. Add the onions and garlic and sauté for 1 minute. Cover, reduce the heat to low, and cook until the onions are

translucent, about 5 minutes. Remove from the heat and add the tomatoes, salt, pepper, parsley, basil, and oregano. Mix well.

2. Spread ⅓ of the onion mixture in the prepared dish. Spread half of the sliced potatoes on top. Sprinkle salt and pepper and ¼ cup of the Parmesan over the potatoes. Repeat the layers. Top with the remaining onion mixture. Cover with foil. Bake for 1¼ hours. Uncover and continue to bake until the potatoes are tender, about 30 minutes longer. Serve hot.

CALORIES 205
FAT 4G
CARBOHYDRATES 35G
PROTEIN 6G

Tabbouleh with Raisins and Lime

HIGH FIBER ANTIOXIDANTS

SERVES: 8

1 cup bulgur
2 cups boiling water
½ cup chopped fresh Italian flat-leaf parsley
  leaves
⅔ cup raisins
1 cup chopped scallions
⅓ cup lime juice
2 tablespoons olive oil
Sea salt to taste
Black pepper to taste

Bulgur wheat is often used to "bulk" up foods because of its high fiber content. Having a diet rich in fiber helps cleanse your body of toxins from sodas, alcoholic beverages, and sugary foods while at the same time lowering the risk of diabetes, cardiovascular disease, and colorectal cancer.

1. In a medium bowl, mix together the bulgur and boiling water. Allow to stand for up to 1 hour, or until tender.

2. Drain the bulgur in a colander to remove excess moisture, then transfer to a serving bowl. Add the parsley, raisins, and scallions. Toss to mix well.

3. In a small bowl, stir together the lime juice, oil, salt, and pepper.

4. Add to the bulgur mixture, toss well, and serve.

CALORIES 133
FAT 3G
CARBOHYDRATES 24G
PROTEIN 3G

Sweet Potato with Soy Dressing

SPICY ANTIOXIDANTS

2 pounds sweet potatoes
1 small onion, chopped
2 celery stalks, minced
½ cup chopped fresh Italian flat-leaf parsley leaves
1 tablespoon olive oil
2 tablespoons lemon juice
1 teaspoon low-sodium soy sauce
Black pepper to taste

This dish is packed with metabolism-boosting ingredients such as the nutrient-rich and mineral-filled sweet potatoes, onion, parsley, acidic lemon, and spicy pepper.

1. In a saucepan, combine the sweet potatoes with enough water to cover. Cover the pan, bring to a boil, reduce the heat to medium, and cook until tender, 30–40 minutes. Drain and let cool.
2. Peel and dice the sweet potatoes and place in a large bowl. Add the onion, celery, and parsley and stir to mix.
3. In a small bowl, whisk together the olive oil, lemon juice, soy sauce, and pepper to form a dressing.
4. Add the dressing to the potato mixture, toss gently, and serve warm.

CALORIES 110
FAT 2G
CARBOHYDRATES 22G
PROTEIN 2G

BURN IT UP

Sweet potatoes are filled with vitamins and minerals and have high amounts of beta-carotene, equal to that of carrots; for only 90 calories per sweet potato, you get a huge amount of health-building nutrients. Beta-carotene may help fight cancer, heart disease, asthma, and rheumatoid arthritis. The bright orange flesh contains carotenoids that help boost your metabolism, stabilize your blood sugar, and lower insulin resistance, which makes your cells more responsive to insulin.

Crispy Green Beans with Spicy Cider Vinaigrette

SUPERFOOD

SERVES: 6

1 pound green beans, trimmed
3 cloves garlic, minced
12 fresh dill sprigs, chopped
1 teaspoon red pepper flakes
½ teaspoon dry mustard
1 cup cider vinegar
1 cup water
2 tablespoons sugar
½ teaspoon sea salt

The spicy red pepper flakes found in this recipe can increase your metabolism after eating, sometimes for up to several hours.

1. Steam the beans until tender, about 5 minutes, then immediately plunge in cold water to cool. Drain.
2. Place beans in a bowl. Add the garlic, dill, red pepper flakes, and mustard.
3. Combine the vinegar, water, sugar, and salt in a small saucepan and bring to a boil. Pour the hot marinade over the beans and let cool.
4. Cover and chill overnight before serving.

CALORIES 44
FAT 1G
CARBOHYDRATES 10G
PROTEIN 2G

Long-Grain Rice with Sage, Water Chestnuts, and Pecans

SUPERFOOD

SERVES: 10

1½ cups water
1 cup reduced-sodium, fat-free chicken broth
1⅓ cups long-grain white rice
1 tablespoon butter
2 tablespoons finely chopped onion
1 cup finely chopped celery
2 tablespoons finely chopped green bell pepper
½ cup chopped pecans
½ cup sliced water chestnuts
¼ teaspoon ground sage
⅛ teaspoon black pepper

Long-grain rice is rich in iron, manganese, and zinc, and surprisingly contains protein.

1. In a medium saucepan, bring the water and broth to a boil. Add the rice, stir, cover, reduce the heat to low, and simmer for 20 minutes. Remove from the heat. Let stand, covered, until all the liquid is absorbed, about 5 minutes.
2. Meanwhile, melt the butter in a large nonstick skillet over medium heat. Add the onion, celery, and peppers and sauté until tender, about 3 minutes. Stir in the pecans, water chestnuts, sage, and pepper and heat through. Add the rice and fluff with a fork to distribute all the ingredients evenly, then serve.

CALORIES 110
FAT 2G
CARBOHYDRATES 22G
PROTEIN 2G

Sweet Potato Purée with Sunflower Seeds

SERVES: 12

ANTIOXIDANTS

3 pounds sweet potatoes, peeled and cubed
2 large apples, cored, peeled, and chopped
½ cup water
1 tablespoon butter
Ground nutmeg to taste
Sea salt to taste
Black pepper to taste
2 tablespoons sunflower seeds, toasted

Use this fiber- and mineral-rich and low-fat purée as a side dish or as a spread on vegetables such as celery.

1. In a medium saucepan, combine the potatoes with enough water to cover. Cover, bring to a boil, reduce the heat to medium, and cook until tender, about 15 minutes. Drain.
2. Meanwhile, in a small saucepan, combine the apples with the ½ cup water. Bring to a simmer over medium heat and cook until tender, about 5 minutes.
3. Transfer the potatoes and undrained apples to a food processor and purée until smooth. Transfer to a warmed serving bowl. Add the butter, nutmeg, salt, and pepper and stir to mix and melt the butter.
4. Sprinkle with the sunflower seeds and serve.

CALORIES 114
FAT 2G
CARBOHYDRATES 23G
PROTEIN 2G

BURN IT UP

Sunflower seeds are particularly high in vitamin E, a fat-soluble antioxidant vitamin that helps reduce inflammation and symptoms associated with arthritis. They also have high levels of niacin, also know as vitamin B3, which is instrumental in the metabolism of carbohydrates, fatty acids, and amino acids. These seeds help release energy from food, aid in the repair of DNA, help lower blood levels of cholesterol and triglycerides, and boost the metabolism.

Baby Carrots and Asparagus with Lemon

SERVES: 6

HIGH FIBER | ANTIOXIDANTS | SUPERFOOD

2 pinches salt
2 cups fresh asparagus, trimmed and
   cut into ½-inch pieces
½ pound baby carrots
2 tablespoons lemon juice
1 teaspoon lemon pepper

Spicy peppers and high-fiber vegetables—like the nutrient-rich carrots and asparagus found in this recipe—have natural compounds that immediately boost your metabolism. They are the perfect side dish to a hearty, protein-filled entrée because they continually increase your metabolism and won't slow you down.

1. Fill large quart boiler ¾ full with water. Bring to a boil. Add 2 pinches of salt and all of the asparagus. Remove asparagus after 30 seconds. Transfer to bowl filled with ice water.

2. Add carrots to boiling water and remove after 1 minute. Transfer to ice water. Drain well and chill for 30 minutes.

3. To serve, toss asparagus and carrots with lemon juice and pepper.

CALORIES 131
FAT 3G
CARBOHYDRATES 20G
PROTEIN 5G

BURN IT UP

Asparagus is high in vitamins A, C, and K, as well as folate. This vegetable is easy to cook and also contains the carbohydrate inulin, which promotes the growth and activity of good bacteria in your intestines. Pregnant women can especially benefit from its high folate levels, as this compound helps prevent birth defects

CHAPTER 13
Smoothies and Snacks

It's natural to crave snacks throughout the day, but why blow a healthy diet with fat-laden, sugary foods when healthy, metabolism-boosting snacks are right at your fingertips? For example, antioxidant-rich fruits and superfoods like blueberries and blackberries give you instant energy boosts and kick-start your metabolism. Healthy snacks also help keep your energy up and your metabolism running at full speed throughout the day.

Lemon Citrus Smoothie with Fresh Blueberries

SUPERFOOD CALCIUM PROTEIN

½ banana
1 cup fresh frozen blueberries
1 cup nonfat lemon yogurt
¾ cup white grape juice
1 teaspoon honey

Bananas are rich in potassium, a key component to boosting your metabolism. The body needs potassium to make muscles contract, and this valuable mineral also helps convert blood sugar into glycogen.

1. Place all ingredients in a blender or food processor and blend until smooth.
2. Pour into two glasses and serve.

CALORIES 219
FAT 5G
CARBOHYDRATES 41G
PROTEIN 7G

BURN IT UP

Blueberries are filled with antioxidants, which purify your body, help improve your immune system, and help fight against cancer. By eating only half a cup of fresh or frozen blueberries a day, you can receive their antioxidant protection and benefit from their antiaging and metabolism-boosting properties. When out of season, use frozen blueberries in a smoothie or mixed with yogurt and walnuts as a delicious snack.

Pineapple Coconut Smoothie

SERVES 1

1 cup canned, unsweetened pineapple chunks
1 cup coconut water
½ cup nonfat yogurt
½ cup skim milk

The coconut water in this smoothie provides the vitamin C, fiber, and minerals like calcium needed to keep your metabolism running smoothly.

Puree all ingredients in a blender until smooth. Pour into a tall glass and enjoy!

CALORIES   307
FAT   1G
CARBOHYDRATES   63G
PROTEIN   14G

Fresh Blackberry Smoothie with Mango

SERVES 2

½ banana
1 cup fresh frozen mango cubes
1 cup fresh blackberries
½ cup nonfat vanilla frozen yogurt
¾ cup fresh orange juice
1 teaspoon honey

Bananas are high in fiber and are filled with vitamins B6 and C, potassium, and manganese, which have antioxidant properties and are important for the metabolism of carbohydrates and fats.

Place all ingredients in a blender or food processor and blend until smooth. Pour into two tall glasses or parfait glasses and serve.

CALORIES   195
FAT   1G
CARBOHYDRATES   46G
PROTEIN   4G

Banana Smoothie with Fresh Raspberries

SERVES 1

1 banana
1 cup raspberries
1 cup nonfat plain or vanilla yogurt
½ cup skim milk

Raspberries are antioxidant rich, high in fiber, and filled with vitamin C.

Combine all ingredients in a blender until smooth. Pour into a tall glass.

CALORIES   365
FAT   2G
CARBOHYDRATES   71G
PROTEIN   21G

Peach Yogurt Smoothie

ANTIOXIDANTS

SERVES 2

½ banana
1½ cups fresh peaches, cubed
1 cup low-fat vanilla yogurt
¾ cup orange juice
1 teaspoon honey

The natural sugars found in these recipe ingredients give you much-needed energy that your body can metabolize right away. Enjoy this as a morning pick-me-up or before a workout.

Place all ingredients in a food processor or blender and blend until smooth. Pour into two glasses and serve for a quick, healthy, tasty breakfast.

CALORIES 309
FAT 2G
CARBOHYDRATES 69G
PROTEIN 8G

Blueberry Smoothie with Lemon

SUPERFOOD ANTIOXIDANTS

SERVES 1

1 cup blueberries
1 cup nonfat vanilla yogurt
½ cup skim milk

The nonfat vanilla yogurt in this recipe would give any smoothie a rich, vanilla undertone while also adding needed protein and cancer- and infection-fighting bacteria cultures.

Combine all ingredients in a blender until smooth. Pour into a tall glass.

CALORIES 261
FAT 1G
CARBOHYDRATES 45G
PROTEIN 19G

Peach Smoothie with Banana

CALCIUM ANTIOXIDANTS

SERVES 1

1 banana
1 peach, sliced
1 cup nonfat yogurt
½ cup skim milk

Enhance your metabolism even more and make a complete meal out of your smoothie by adding other natural ingredients such as wheat germ, flaxseed, or even something as simple as a little fresh gingerroot, which boosts thermogenesis and your body's ability to metabolize food.

Combine all ingredients in a blender until smooth. Pour into a tall glass.

CALORIES 347
FAT 1G
CARBOHYDRATES 67G
PROTEIN 20G

Green Tea Smoothie

CALCIUM ANTIOXIDANTS

1 cup brewed green tea, chilled
½ cup skim milk
½ cup fat-free vanilla ice cream

If you are not a tea drinker but want the health benefits of drinking tea, enjoy this green tea smoothie. You'll get all of the qualities that may help prevent cancer, reduce cardiovascular disease, and improve immune function without having to drink something you don't enjoy. The skim milk and ice cream in this smoothie also give your body and bones much-needed calcium.

1. Brew 1 cup of green tea, then chill.
2. Combine all ingredients in a blender until smooth.
3. Pour into a tall glass and enjoy.

CALORIES 67
FAT 0G
CARBOHYDRATES 13G
PROTEIN 4G

BURN IT UP

Green tea and oolong tea contain caffeine and catechins, which have been shown to boost the metabolism for approximately 2 hours. Researchers say drinking 2–4 cups of green or oolong tea throughout the day may help you burn an extra 50 calories, which can lead to a 5-pound loss over a year—without any other change in your diet. Obviously, adding sugar or cream would counteract the positive effects. Also, avoid green tea beverages that have high-fructose corn syrup, as they are loaded with sugar and not good for your metabolism.

Blackberry Smoothie with Apples

SUPERFOOD ANTIOXIDANTS

SERVES 1

1 cup blackberries
1 apple, sliced
1 cup nonfat yogurt
½ cup skim milk

Blackberries, like blueberries, are some of the best foods you can eat. They are filled with fiber, vitamin C, and cancer-fighting antioxidants. In addition to providing you with the benefits of blackberries, this smoothie also has tons of fiber and protein, making it optimum for instant metabolism increase. For more protein, add a little protein powder.

Combine all ingredients in a blender until smooth. Pour into a tall glass.

CALORIES 380
FAT 2G
CARBOHYDRATES 75G
PROTEIN 20G

Blackberry Peach Smoothie

ANTIOXIDANTS SUPERFOOD

SERVES 1

1 cup blackberries
1 large peach, sliced
1 cup nonfat yogurt
½ cup skim milk

Antioxidant-rich blackberries have properties that may help protect the skin from ultraviolet damage. You can get similar metabolic stimulus from blueberries, oranges, and nectarines.

Combine all ingredients in a blender until smooth. Pour into a tall glass.

CALORIES 322
FAT 1G
CARBOHYDRATES 61G
PROTEIN 20G

Creamy Strawberry Smoothie

HIGH FIBER SUPERFOOD

SERVES 1

½ cup fat-free vanilla ice cream
1 cup fresh strawberries
½ cup nonfat yogurt
½ cup skim milk

Adding fresh superfood strawberries adds vitamin C, manganese, and fiber. Strawberries are also a natural source of iodine, which is necessary for proper thyroid function. Strawberries are also low in calories!

Combine all ingredients in a blender until smooth. Pour into a tall glass.

CALORIES 251
FAT 1G
CARBOHYDRATES 46G
PROTEIN 15G

Fresh Orange Smoothie

SERVES 1

1 cup fresh orange juice, not from
   concentrate
½ cup nonfat yogurt
½ cup skim milk

Orange juice is a source of calcium, vitamin C, protein, and important metabolism-boosting minerals such as phosphorus and potassium. This recipe helps you reap all of its benefits.

Combine all ingredients in a blender until smooth. Pour into a tall glass.

CALORIES 221
FAT 0G
CARBOHYDRATES 41G
PROTEIN 12G

BURN IT UP

For an instant metabolism boost, keep sliced frozen fruits such as pineapple, berries, and bananas on hand to add to any smoothie for extra nutrients and flavor. You can also munch on these fruit bites if you need a quick snack on a busy day.

Wild Berry Smoothie with Peaches

ANTIOXIDANTS SUPERFOOD

SERVES 1

¼ cup fresh or frozen blueberries
¼ cup fresh strawberries
1 large peach, sliced
1 cup raspberries
½ cup nonfat yogurt
½ cup skim milk

The blueberries, strawberries, and raspberries found in this recipe are all rich in antioxidants, making this superfood smoothie an excellent metabolism booster.

Combine all ingredients in a blender until smooth. Pour into a tall glass.

CALORIES 272
FAT 2G
CARBOHYDRATES 55G
PROTEIN 14G

Refreshing Carrot Smoothie with Citrus Lemon and Orange

CALCIUM

SERVES 1

½ cup finely grated carrots
¼ cup carrot juice
1 tablespoon lemon juice
¼ cup orange juice
½ cup nonfat yogurt
½ cup skim milk

Carrots are high in beta-carotene, which is essential for healthy eyes and skin. They may also help decrease your risk of developing lung and prostate cancer.

1. Blend grated carrot, lemon juice, orange juice, yogurt, and skim milk until smooth.
2. Then blend in the carrot juice. Pour into a tall glass.

CALORIES 190
FAT 1G
CARBOHYDRATES 34G
PROTEIN 13G

Smoothie with Fresh Blueberries and Peaches

PROTEIN ANTIOXIDANTS

SERVES 1

½ cup fresh or frozen blueberries
1 large peach, sliced
½ cup nonfat yogurt
½ cup skim milk

Peaches are rich in vitamin A and potassium, and are naturally low in fat and calories. They are seasonal, however, and available primarily May through October. Substitute potassium-rich bananas for them during the off-season.

Combine all ingredients in a blender until smooth. Pour into a tall glass.

CALORIES 220
FAT 1G
CARBOHYDRATES 43G
PROTEIN 13G

Peanut Butter Pops

ANTIOXIDANTS SUPERFOOD

3 large bananas
6 pop sticks
6 tablespoons crunchy peanut butter

If you are not a fan of peanut butter, use healthy Nutella instead. Nutella is a hazelnut-based food product with a consistency similar to that of smooth peanut butter.

1. Peel and cut bananas in half lengthwise.
2. Press popsicle sticks gently onto flat side of each banana slice.
3. Freeze bananas on wax paper for 30 minutes.
4. Remove from freezer and spread one tablespoon of peanut butter on each banana. Serve immediately or refreeze.

CALORIES 149
FAT 8G
CARBOHYDRATES 17G
PROTEIN 4G

BURN IT UP

Because of its nutrient-rich nature, peanut butter is effective in boosting your metabolism. Peanuts are also a great source of energy, since they contain 25 grams of protein per 100-gram serving, and most of the fat is mono and polyunsaturated fat. They are also packed with niacin, which is one of the most effective vitamins for increasing your good cholesterol. Peanuts also have the flavonoid resveratrol—also found in red wine—that may contribute to cardiovascular health. But, as we also know, peanuts and peanut butter are high in calories, so consume them in moderation.

Quick Pick-Me-Up Trail Mix

`HIGH FIBER` `PROTEIN` `SUPERFOOD`

SERVES 2

4 cups air-popped popcorn
4 tablespoons raisins
4 tablespoons unsalted peanuts

On its own, popcorn doesn't add much to your metabolism but, when combined, with nutrient-rich raisins and peanuts, as it is here, the fiber helps move carbohydrates and fats through your digestive system. Other great trail mix combinations are almonds, pistachios, sunflower seeds, and dried fruits such as apricots, bananas, and cranberries.

1. Pop popcorn with an air popper.
2. Combine popcorn with raisins and nuts.

CALORIES 220
FAT 10G
CARBOHYDRATES 30G
PROTEIN 7G

Sugar-Free Lemonade Bars

`ANTIOXIDANTS`

MAKES 8 8-OUNCE SERVINGS

Crystal Light lemonade drink mix
¼ cup minced fresh mint leaves
Water
Popsicle sticks

Although these lemonade bars don't provide tons of nutrients, they are naturally sugar-free and very low calorie. Keep them on hand for a quick snack in between meals to help prevent the overeating that leads to a slower metabolism. They are also perfect for a late-night snack as they are caffeine free.

1. Make your favorite Crystal Light drink as directed and mix in fresh mint leaves.
2. Pour beverage into ice cube trays or other bar molds. Add popsicle sticks.
3. Freeze for 1 hour or more.

CALORIES 5
FAT 0G
CARBOHYDRATES 0G
PROTEIN 0G

CHAPTER 14
Desserts

Desserts can actually play a key role in boosting your metabolism by helping to stave off sugar cravings and keeping your body fueled with energy. The key is to enjoy healthier desserts such as those made with foods naturally high in fiber like apples, bananas, and nuts, as well as metabolism-boosting spices. You'll be pleasantly surprised at how you can enjoy your favorite desserts while still boosting or maintaining your high metabolic rate.

Double Chocolate Cake

SERVES 12

Nonstick cooking spray
2 cups all-purpose flour
⅓ cup unsweetened cocoa powder
1 teaspoon baking soda
½ teaspoon sea salt
1 cup sugar
2 tablespoons canola oil
1 egg white
1 cup nonfat vanilla yogurt
2 teaspoons vanilla extract
¼ cup fat-free fudge topping or chocolate syrup

Spicy cocoa, nutrient-rich yogurt, and naturally low-fat egg white make this dessert more easily digestible. Feel free to add a few fresh raspberries, strawberries, or even mandarin oranges for added nutrition and fruity texture.

1. Preheat oven to 350°F. Spray 8-inch-square pan with light cooking spray. Set aside.
2. In a large bowl, mix the flour, cocoa, baking soda, salt, and sugar well.
3. In a medium bowl, thoroughly mix the oil, egg white, yogurt, vanilla, and fudge topping. Add the wet mixture to the dry mixture and mix thoroughly.
4. Pour the batter into the prepared baking dish and bake for 35 minutes.

CALORIES 203
FAT 3G
CARBOHYDRATES 42G
PROTEIN 4G

New York Cheesecake with Wild Berries

SERVES 8

1 cup reduced-fat graham crackers, finely crushed
¼ cup butter, melted
16 ounces fat-free cream cheese
¼ cup sugar substitute such as Splenda
1 teaspoon vanilla extract
2 egg whites
3 tablespoons cake flour
¼ teaspoon sea salt
½ cup fat-free milk
1 cup fresh wild berries such as blackberries, raspberries, or blueberries, for garnish

Sugar substitutes save on calories and don't cause fluctuations in your blood glucose as regular sugar does.

1. Preheat oven to 350°F. Stir the graham cracker crumbs and butter together until they are evenly mixed. Press crumb mixture into the bottom of a baking dish.
2. Mix cream cheese, sugar substitute, vanilla, and egg whites in a standing mixer or medium bowl with hand mixer. Add the cake flour, salt, and milk. Mix thoroughly. Pour batter into the crust. Bake for 1 hour. Cool about 10 minutes before placing in fridge. Refrigerate at least 3 hours before serving. Serve with fresh wild berries.

CALORIES 246
FAT 8G
CARBOHYDRATES 31G
PROTEIN 12G

Chocolate Cupcakes

PROTEIN CALCIUM

1 cup self-rising flour

½ cup nonfat dried milk powder

1 3.4-ounce box sugar-free chocolate Jell-O pudding mix

1 tablespoon unsweetened cocoa powder

¼ cup sugar substitute such as Splenda

1 teaspoon vanilla extract

½ cup applesauce

¼ teaspoon baking soda

4 egg whites

Pinch sea salt

Nonfat milk powder is as high in protein and calcium as liquid milk and is naturally fat free. It's a natural milk substitute and can be used in many recipes.

1. Preheat oven to 350°F. Mix flour, milk powder, Jell-O mix, cocoa, and sugar substitute in a medium bowl. In a separate bowl, blend the vanilla, applesauce, and baking soda.

2. In a small bowl, beat the egg whites and salt until stiff. Add the flour mixture to the egg whites, beating with an electric mixer. Add the applesauce and beat until blended.

3. Line a muffin tin with paper cupcake wrappers and fill each ¾ of the way with batter. Bake for 20 minutes or until toothpick inserted comes out clean.

CALORIES 121

FAT <1 GRAM

CARBOHYDRATES 23G

PROTEIN 6 GRAMS

BURN IT UP

Chocolate is good for you. Well, sort of. It's still high in calories, but an ounce of dark chocolate will provide you with antioxidants and may help lower your blood pressure. Just keep in mind that the darker the chocolate, the better off you are because dark chocolate contains the highest amount of flavonoids.

Sour Cream Pound Cake

CALCIUM

SERVES 16

Unsalted butter for greasing pan
1 cup nonfat sour cream
½ cup sugar
½ cup brown sugar
2 eggs
2 teaspoons vanilla extract
1¾ cups flour
1 teaspoon baking powder
1 teaspoon baking soda
¼ teaspoon sea salt
¼ teaspoon ground nutmeg

Nutmeg possesses antioxidant and immu-nomodulatory properties, making it a wel-come addition to many desserts.

1. Preheat oven to 350°F. Grease 9" × 13" pan with unsalted butter and set aside.
2. In a large bowl, combine sour cream and sugar; beat well. Add brown sugar and beat. Add eggs, one at a time, beating well after each addition. Stir in vanilla.
3. Sift flour with baking powder, baking soda, salt, and nutmeg. Stir into sour cream mixture and beat at medium speed for 1 minute. Pour into prepared pan.
4. Bake for 25–35 minutes or until cake pulls away from sides of pan and top springs back when touched lightly in center. Cool completely on wire rack; store covered at room temperature.

CALORIES 140
FAT 4G
CARBOHYDRATES 24G
PROTEIN 3G

Citrus-Glazed Grilled Pineapple

ANTIOXIDANTS

SERVES 4

4 thick slices pineapple, about 1-inch each
Juice of ½ lime
Juice of ½ orange
4 teaspoons brown sugar

The nutrients in grilled pineapple are accented by the citric acid, found in the lime and orange, which works to metabolize the natural brown sugar.

1. Preheat grill. In small bowl, combine lime and orange juices. Brush both sides of the pineapple slices with juice and sprinkle with brown sugar. Place pineapple slices on a hot grill; turn after 3 minutes. Grill another 3 minutes.
2. When the pineapples are done, you should have a nice brown caramel color.

CALORIES 29
FAT 0G
CARBOHYDRATES 13G
PROTEIN 1G

Honey-Glazed Nectarines with Citrus Mascarpone

HIGH FIBER ANTIOXIDANTS

SERVES 2

2 nectarines, cut in halves, pits discarded
4 teaspoons mascarpone cheese
½ teaspoon finely grated lemon zest
½ teaspoon finely grated orange zest
2 tablespoons honey

Nectarines have natural sugars and potassium and are a good source of lycopene.

1. Place the nectarines, cut side down on a hot grill for 5 minutes.
2. In small mixing bowl, mix mascarpone with lemon and orange zest. Spoon mixture into the center of nectarines. Drizzle with honey and serve.

CALORIES 108
FAT 5G
CARBOHYDRATES 16G
PROTEIN 2G

Sour Cream Coffee Cake

CALCIUM

SERVES 20

Nonstick cooking spray
1½ cups flour
¾ cup packed light brown sugar
½ teaspoon baking powder
1 teaspoon baking soda
1 teaspoon ground cinnamon
1 teaspoon sea salt
¾ cup fat-free sour cream
2 tablespoons canola oil
1 cup unsweetened applesauce

Because of its natural sweetness, high fiber content, and good amount of vitamin C, applesauce is one of the best substitutes for sugar in dessert recipes. It helps keep carbs down, while bringing flavor and food-digesting fiber up.

1. Preheat oven to 350°F. Coat a square baking pan with light cooking spray.
2. Mix the flour, brown sugar, baking powder, baking soda, cinnamon, and salt in a large bowl.
3. Separately, mix the sour cream, oil, and applesauce in a small bowl. Add sour cream mixture to flour mixture. Mix well but do not beat.
4. Pour batter into cake pan and bake until done, about 40 minutes, or until toothpick inserted comes out clean.

CALORIES 92
FAT 2G
CARBOHYDRATES 18G
PROTEIN 1G

Baked Peach Apple Crumble

SERVES 4

Nonstick cooking spray
2 tart apples, peeled, cored, and
   sliced
4 medium peaches, blanched, skins
   and pits removed, sliced
Juice of ½ lemon
½ cup flour
¼ cup dark brown sugar
½ teaspoon cinnamon
½ teaspoon coriander seed, ground
½ teaspoon cardamom seed, ground
½ teaspoon sea salt
1 cup oatmeal
½ stick butter, softened

You should use spices whenever you can. The cinnamon, coriander, and cardamom in this recipe boost your metabolism instantaneously.

1. Preheat the oven to 350ºF. Prepare a gratin dish or baking dish with nonstick spray.
2. Distribute the apple and peach slices in the dish and sprinkle with lemon juice.
3. Using your hands, thoroughly mix together the flour, brown sugar, spices, salt, oatmeal, and butter. Spread over the crisp and bake for 45 minutes, or until the fruit is bubbling and the top is brown.
4. Serve with vanilla ice cream or whipped cream.

CALORIES 360
FAT 14G
CARBOHYDRATES 60G
PROTEIN 6G

BURN IT UP

Oatmeal is a marvelous choice for healthy fiber, both soluble and insoluble. The insoluble fiber found in oatmeal is good for people with diabetes because it slows down the digestion of starch, preventing a sharp rise in blood glucose levels after a meal. Soluble fiber aids in the processing and elimination of food, moving it quickly and efficiently through your body. The fiber in oatmeal also has cancer-fighting qualities and may reduce LDL cholesterol levels.

Baked Stuffed Apples

SERVES 2

HIGH FIBER | ANTIOXIDANTS

2 large apples, such as Macintosh, Rome, or Granny Smith
2 teaspoons brown sugar
½ teaspoon cinnamon
2 teaspoons chopped walnuts
2 teaspoons raisins
2 teaspoons butter

Baked apples are high in fiber and vitamin C. They are a great way to enjoy a lower-fat, lower-calorie dessert that still has plenty of flavor.

1. Preheat the oven to 350°F. Using a corer, remove the center portions of the apples, being careful not to cut through the bottom of the apple.
2. Form a cup with a double layer of aluminum foil, going ⅓ of the way up the apple. This will stabilize the apple when baking.
3. Mix together the brown sugar, cinnamon, walnuts, and raisins and stuff the mixture into the apples. Top each apple with 1 teaspoon of butter. Put 1 tablespoon of water into the aluminum foil cups.
4. Bake for 25 minutes, or until the apples are soft when pricked with a fork.

CALORIES 181
FAT 8G
CARBOHYDRATES 28G
PROTEIN 1G

BURN IT UP

Apples are fabulous for you—and your metabolism. The active ingredient in apple pulp is pectin, a soluble form of fiber that helps reduce LDL ("bad") cholesterol by keeping it in the intestinal tract until it is eliminated. Pectin also creates a sensation of fullness and suppresses appetite. A study published in the *Journal of the National Cancer Institute* shows that pectin binds certain cancer-causing compounds in the colon, accelerating their removal from the body.

Ricotta Tort with Candied Orange

SERVES 6-8

5 eggs
1 pound skim milk ricotta cheese
4 ounces nonfat cream cheese
1 teaspoon vanilla extract
1 teaspoon salt
¾ cup candied orange peel, chopped
1 cup chocolate chips or chopped chocolate
    pieces
Nonstick cooking spray

Ricotta cheese is rich in calcium, vitamin A, and iron, and is a great source of protein.

1. Preheat oven to 350°F. Separate the eggs and beat the whites until stiff. Set aside.
2. Put the yolks, cheeses, vanilla, and salt in the food processor and whirl until smooth.
3. Place in a bowl and fold in the egg whites, the orange peel, and the chocolate bits. Prepare a pie dish with nonstick spray. Pour in the egg mixture and bake for 45 minutes or until set and golden on top.

CALORIES 122
FAT 4G
CARBOHYDRATES 12G
PROTEIN 10G

Carrot Cake with Ginger

HIGH FIBER SPICY

SERVES 8-10

4 eggs, separated
½ cup brown sugar
1½ cups grated carrots
1 tablespoon lemon juice
Fine zest of ½ fresh orange
½ cup corn flour
1 inch fresh gingerroot, peeled and minced
1½ teaspoons baking soda
½ teaspoon sea salt

This cake is a triple threat: carrots are great for your eyesight, ginger root is great for boosting your metabolic rate, and corn flour is higher in fiber and potassium than traditional flour. Add all that up and you've got a more body-efficient—and metabolism-boosting—carrot cake than found in other recipes.

1. Butter a springform pan and preheat oven to 325°F. Beat the egg whites until stiff and set aside.
2. Beat the egg yolks, brown sugar, and carrots together. Add lemon juice, orange zest, and corn flour. When smooth, add the gingerroot, baking soda, and salt. Gently fold in the egg whites.
3. Pour the cake batter into the springform pan and bake for 1 hour or until done, when toothpick inserted comes out clean.

CALORIES 326
FAT 16G
CARBOHYDRATES 42G
PROTEIN 3G

Chocolate Meringue with Hazelnuts

MAKES ABOUT 40 COOKIES

½ cup sugar, divided
¼ cup unsweetened cocoa powder
⅛ teaspoon sea salt
3 egg whites (from extra-large eggs)
⅛ teaspoon cream of tartar
½ cup hazelnuts, lightly toasted,
  skinned, and coarsely chopped

Most of the fat in this recipe comes from the nuts. If you're not a fan of hazelnuts, you can sub in alternatives like pistachios or walnuts.

1. Preheat oven to 275°F. Line two cookie sheets with parchment paper. Sift ¼ cup of sugar and ¼ cup of cocoa powder together in a bowl. Add salt.
2. Beat egg whites with cream of tartar. When peaks begin to form, add the remaining ¼ cup sugar, a teaspoon at a time. Slowly beat in the cocoa mixture. The meringue should be stiff and shiny.
3. Add chopped nuts. Drop by the teaspoonful on the parchment paper. Bake for 45–50 minutes. Cool on baking sheets. Serve or place in an airtight container for later use.

CALORIES 21
FAT <1G
CARBOHYDRATES 2G
PROTEIN: 2G

BURN IT UP

Because the hours between lunch and dinner can create a mini-fast, many crave sweets in the late afternoon. Before you reach for a candy bar, a piece of chocolate, or a brownie, seek out snacks that contain all three macronutrients—like carbohydrates, protein, and fat. Hazelnuts will provide you with all three!

Chocolate Soufflé with Fresh Raspberries

SERVES 4

2 squares bittersweet chocolate
½ cup sugar
1 tablespoon butter plus 1 tablespoon for soufflé dish
2 tablespoons raspberry liqueur like Chambord
3 tablespoons rice flour or cornstarch
3 tablespoons cold reduced-fat milk
4 egg yolks
5 egg whites
Pinch cream of tartar
½ pint fresh raspberries

Berries in general are fiber and antioxidant rich, so add a few blackberries to this recipe, if desired, for extra flavor, color, and texture.

1. Preheat the oven to 375°F. In a medium-sized, heavy saucepan, melt the chocolate with the sugar, butter, and liqueur. Remove from heat. Whisk the flour and milk together and add to the chocolate mixture.
2. Beat the egg yolks, one at a time, into the chocolate mixture. Whip the egg whites and cream of tartar together until stiff. Fold the egg whites into the chocolate mixture and pour into a buttered 1½-quart soufflé dish.
3. Bake for 35–40 minutes or until puffed and brown. Pour fresh raspberries over each portion and garnish with whipped cream if desired.

CALORIES 160
FAT 9G
CARBOHYDRATES 17G
PROTEIN 8G

Baked Espresso Crème

SERVES 4

3 tablespoons instant espresso powder
2 tablespoons boiling water
1½ cups whipping cream
3 whole eggs
4 teaspoons cornstarch
4 teaspoons cold water
½ cup sugar, or to taste
1 teaspoon vanilla extract

Coffee may improve brain function and has been linked to lowering the risk for diabetes and certain cancers. Caffeine also naturally stimulates your metabolism.

1. Preheat oven to 325°F. Whisk together the espresso powder and boiling water, add the cream, and beat in the eggs. Whisk the cornstarch and water together until smooth and beat into the mixture.
2. Add the rest of the ingredients and stir well. Place 4 buttered 6-ounce custard cups in a roasting pan of hot water in the middle of the oven. Add the custard.
3. Bake for 50–60 minutes. Serve warm, at room temperature, or chilled with whipped cream.

CALORIES 460
FAT 36G
CARBOHYDRATES 27G
PROTEIN 26G

Zesty Lime Pie

SERVES: 8

CALCIUM

Crust:
15 graham crackers, crushed
2 tablespoons butter, melted

Filling:
⅓ cup frozen apple juice concentrate, thawed
1 envelope unflavored gelatin
½ cup sugar
1 tablespoon grated lime zest
⅓ cup lime juice
1 teaspoon pure vanilla extract
1½ cups plain low-fat yogurt

Lime juice is well known as a cure for scurvy, a disease caused by lack of vitamin C. The flavonoids found in limes have antioxidant and anticancer properties as well.

1. To make the crust, mix together the graham cracker crumbs and butter in a bowl. Grease a 9-inch pie pan. Transfer the crumb mixture to the prepared pan and pat onto the bottom and sides, forming an even layer. Place in the freezer.
2. To make the filling, pour the apple juice concentrate into a saucepan, add the gelatin, and let the mixture stand for a few minutes to allow the gelatin to soften. Stir in the sugar and heat the mixture over low heat until the gelatin and sugar dissolve. Pour into a bowl and add 2 teaspoons of the lime zest, the lime juice, and the vanilla. Place the mixture in the refrigerator until partially set (the consistency of unbeaten egg whites), about 30 minutes.
3. In standing mixer or with hand mixer, whip the lime mixture until fluffy. Add the yogurt and whip again. Remove the crust from the freezer and pour the lime mixture into it. Sprinkle the remaining 1 teaspoon lime zest over the top. Chill the pie until firm before serving.

CALORIES 182
FAT 5G
CARBOHYDRATES 31G
PROTEIN 4G

BURN IT UP
Yogurt is an excellent source of calcium that also provides about 9 grams of animal protein per 6-ounce serving. It also has a good supply of riboflavin, vitamin B12, potassium, and magnesium. One of the most beneficial aspects of yogurt comes from the use of active, good bacteria, known as probiotics, that adjust the natural balance of organisms, known as microflora, in the intestines to aid digestion.

Citrus-Poached Pears

SERVES: 4

4 pears, peeled, cored, and halved lengthwise
2 cups cranberry juice
2 tablespoons sugar
½ teaspoon ground cinnamon
½ teaspoon ground cloves
1 teaspoon grated orange zest
1 teaspoon grated lemon zest

Pears are a nutritious fruit that are naturally high in fiber and antioxidants. The high amounts of pectin found in pears aids in digestion and promotes healthy cholesterol levels. They have a low glycemic index, meaning they produce a more gradual rise in blood sugar and insulin levels.

1. Combine all the ingredients in a saucepan.
2. Bring to a boil, cover, reduce the heat to low, and simmer until tender, about 15 minutes. Serve the pears warm or chilled.

CALORIES 196
FAT 1G
CARBOHYDRATES 50G
PROTEIN 1G

Vanilla Custard with Spiced Cherries

SERVES: 4

2 tablespoons sugar
⅛ teaspoon sea salt
1⅓ cups nonfat milk
¼ teaspoon pure vanilla extract
2–3 teaspoons sherry
3 egg whites, lightly beaten

Spiced Cherry Sauce:
1 8-ounce can cherries, unsweetened or fresh, pitted
3 drops of red food coloring
1 teaspoon cornstarch
2 teaspoons water or lemon juice
Pinch ground cloves
Pinch ground cinnamon
Pinch ground ginger

Fresh cherries are a fiber-filled, natural source of vitamin A, and studies have shown that they may reduce the risk for heart disease, diabetes, and certain cancers.

1. Preheat oven to 325°F. In a saucepan, combine the sugar, salt, and milk. Place over medium heat and stir until the sugar dissolves. Cool. Add the vanilla, sherry, and egg whites. Stir well and pour through a sieve into a 2-cup baking dish. Place in a baking pan, and pour hot water into the pan to reach halfway up the sides of the dish. Bake until a knife comes out clean, about 1 hour.
2. Meanwhile, make the sauce: in a saucepan, combine the cherries and food coloring. Place over medium heat and bring to a simmer. In a small bowl, stir together the

cornstarch and water or lemon juice. Add to the pan and cook, stirring, until the sauce is clear, about 5 minutes. Stir in the spices.

3. Remove the custard from the oven. Serve warm with the warm cherry sauce drizzled over the top.

CALORIES 121
FAT 3G
CARBOHYDRATES 16G
PROTEIN 6G

Chocolate Banana Cake

HIGH FIBER SUPERFOOD ANTIOXIDANTS
SERVES 9

¾ cup whole wheat flour
¾ cup all-purpose flour
1 teaspoon baking powder
¼ teaspoon baking soda
¾ cup sugar substitute such as Splenda
⅛ teaspoon salt
⅔ cup dark chocolate chips
⅔ cup mashed ripe bananas
⅓ cup unsweetened applesauce
⅓ cup fat-free plain yogurt
½ cup Egg Beaters
1 teaspoon banana extract

This dessert is remarkably high in nutritional value thanks to the high fiber from the wheat flour, the protein from the yogurt and Egg Beaters, and the antioxidant-rich dark chocolate.

1. Preheat oven to 350°F.
2. Combine flours, baking powder, baking soda, Splenda, salt, and chocolate chips in a large bowl and stir well. Add remaining ingredients; stir until smooth.

3. Pour batter into an 8-inch-square pan. Bake for 30 minutes. Cool and cut into nine squares.

CALORIES 163
FAT 4G
CARBOHYDRATES 33G
PROTEIN 5G

Chocolate Chunk Brownies

ANTIOXIDANTS

SERVES 12

Nonstick cooking spray
1 box Betty Crocker Hershey's Triple Chunk Supreme Brownie Mix
2 ounces dark chocolate chips
½ cup Egg Beaters
½ cup sugar-free chocolate syrup
3 tablespoons water

Often enhanced with additional nutrients, Egg Beaters is a reputable egg substitute that consists mainly of egg whites. Egg Beaters is also cholesterol free.

1. Coat a 9" × 13" baking dish with nonstick spray.
2. Stir brownie mix, dark chocolate chips, Egg Beaters, syrup, and water together in a bowl. Blend well. Pour mix into baking dish.
3. Bake in oven at 350°F for 26–28 minutes.

CALORIES 48
FAT 0G
CARBOHYDRATES 10G
PROTEIN 1G

Honey Bread Pudding with Pecans

SERVES: 8

PROTEIN CALCIUM SUPERFOOD

4 cups coarsely crumbled stale bread
3–4 apples, peeled and grated
½ cup raisins
½ cup chopped pecans
3 cups nonfat milk
3 eggs
2 teaspoons pure vanilla extract
6 tablespoons honey
1 teaspoon ground cinnamon
½ teaspoon ground nutmeg
Juice of ½ lemon

The nonfat milk and natural honey in this recipe make this bread pudding low in fat and calories without sacrificing flavor.

1. Preheat oven to 350°F.
2. In an 8-inch-square baking pan, stir together the bread crumbs, grated apple, raisins, and nuts.
3. In a blender or food processor, combine all the remaining ingredients. Process until blended. Pour over the bread crumb mixture. Make sure the bread is saturated.
4. Bake until the bread on top starts to turn slightly brown, about 35 minutes. Serve hot.

CALORIES 273
FAT 8G
CARBOHYDRATES 44G
PROTEIN 8G

BURN IT UP

There are many ways to disguise the word *sugar* on a food label. Here's a big list of what doesn't sound like sugar, but definitely is: high-fructose corn syrup, fruit juice concentrate, sucrose, glucose, dextrose, honey, molasses, brown sugar, corn sweetener, corn syrup, fructose, and invert sugar. Natural sugars, like the honey found in this recipe, are among the best types of sweeteners available, but should be used in moderation due to their high calorie content.

Strawberry Pie

SERVES 8

HIGH FIBER ANTIOXIDANTS

9-inch pie shell
3 cups water
3 rounded tablespoons cornstarch
2 3-ounce boxes sugar-free strawberry gelatin
2 pounds fresh strawberries, chopped

Gelatin is high in phosphorus, a mineral that is as important as calcium to the development and formation of bones and teeth. Phosphorus is essential to bone strength and aids in glycolysis and glucose utilization needed for optimum metabolic efficiency.

1. Bake pie shell and let cool.
2. Add water, cornstarch, and boxes of gelatin to a large saucepan over medium-low heat. Stir constantly until it boils and cook for 1 minute. Cool to room temperature.
3. Add strawberries to gelatin, then mix and pour into pie shell. Refrigerate 2 hours.

CALORIES 145
FAT 6G
CARBOHYDRATES 20G
PROTEIN 2G

BURN IT UP

Strawberries, like most berries, are packed with antioxidants and fiber, and they may lower the risk of heart disease. Use them to enhance a dessert, enjoy them on their own as a perfect metabolism-boosting snack or, better yet, eat fresh strawberries with your breakfast to kick off your day!

Additional Metabolism-Boosting Foods

Throughout this book, you've learned about many foods that will send your metabolism through the roof. As you probably suspect, there are many more that we didn't cover that we'd like you to know more about. Read about them here!

Broccoli Sprouts

Broccoli sprouts boost enzymes in the body while detoxifying potential carcinogens. Researchers estimate that broccoli sprouts provide 10–100 times the power of mature broccoli to neutralize carcinogens. Dr. Paul Talalay, a researcher at the Johns Hopkins School of Medicine, found that three-day-old broccoli sprouts consistently contained 20–50 times the amount of chemo-protective compounds as found in mature broccoli heads, offering a simple, dietary means of chemically reducing cancer risk. The antioxidants found in broccoli sprouts may help boost the metabolism as well as prevent, heart disease, macular degeneration, and stomach ulcers. They may also help reduce cholesterol levels.

Chives

Chives and chive flowers are high in vitamin C, folic acid, potassium, calcium, and blood-building iron. They promote good digestion, reduce flatulence, prevent bad breath, and help stimulate your metabolism. Chives, when eaten regularly, may help to lower blood cholesterol levels. Because of their high vitamin C content, they may help speed recovery from a cold; the sulfurous compounds contained in chives are natural expectorants. Best used fresh, chives are easy to grow in pots at home.

Cumin Seeds

Cumin seeds stimulate the metabolism by turning up the body's internal heat, but they are also rich in iron and may help promote the secretion of pancreatic enzymes that help with digestion and the absorption of nutrients. Cumin has also been thought to be able to improve the functioning of our immune systems and help the liver process the body's toxins. In fact, recent studies have indicated that this powerful little seed may reduce the risk of stomach and liver tumors in animals. However, patients with bile duct obstruction, gallstones, and gastrointestinal disorders (including stomach ulcers and hyperacidity disorders) should avoid using cumin.

Curry

Next time you're out at the grocery store or an Indian restaurant, order some curry. One of the primary ingredients in curry, turmeric, aids digestion by stimulating the flow of bile and the breakdown of dietary fats. It's also a powerful source of antioxidants, containing in a single teaspoon as many antioxidants as in ½ cup of grapes. Its antioxidant and anti-inflammatory capabilities can be traced back to curcumin, which gives turmeric its characteristic yellow color. For centuries, curcumin alone has been used to cure everything from heartburn to arthritis and, according to *Earl Mindell's Herb Bible*, "The herbs that are combined to make curry help prevent heart disease and stroke by reducing cholesterol and preventing clots."

Flax

Loaded with omega-3 fatty acids, flax bolsters cell membranes and helps your body respond more efficiently to insulin, thereby improving glucose absorption which in turn helps stabilize blood sugar levels. In other words, flax is one superfood you can easily incorporate in your diet and reap major metabolic benefits. You can buy flaxseed oil at most supermarkets or health food stores, or toss ground flaxseeds (if they aren't ground, they don't provide the same benefits) on your granola or oatmeal. Flax is also readily available in many types of bread; just check the ingredients!

Grapes (Frozen)

If you're craving a sweet treat but don't want to blow your healthy eating habits, throw some grapes in the freezer and munch on them a few hours later. They taste like sorbet and they contain manganese, flavonoids, and B6—an excellent metabolism booster—which may lower your risk for heart disease. Frozen grapes are a treat that's both healthy and sweet!

Hummus

It's hard to complain about hummus. All of the ingredients used to produce it—chickpeas, olive or canola oil, pureed sesame seeds (also known as tahini), lemon juice, spices, and garlic—are extremely good for you and most are known to boost the metabolism. Chickpeas themselves are an excellent source of energy since they're made of complex carbohydrates and protein, and tahini is rich in minerals, fatty acids, and amino acids. So, enjoy hummus, but keep your intake in check because hummus is high in calories and it's easy to eat a lot of it if you're using it as a dip. We recommend spreading 2 tablespoons of hummus on a slice of whole-grain bread or eating a ¼ cup of hummus with carrots or broccoli.

Kale and Other *Brassica* Vegetables

Loaded with cancer-fighting antioxidants and rich in calcium, kale is one of the healthiest foods in the vegetable kingdom; together with its cousin broccoli, kale offers strong protection against cancer and other disease. Kale and other vegetables in the *Brassica* family contain a potent glucosinolate phytonutrient that actually boosts your body's detoxification enzymes, clearing potentially carcinogenic substances more quickly from your body. More common members of the prestigious *Brassica* genus of vegetables include cabbage, broccoli, Brussels sprouts, cauliflower, collard and mustard greens, bok choy, and broccoli rabe or rapini. With so many choices, you should be able to take advantage of this diverse group and have at least one each day of the week.

Mackerel

Mackerel and salmon are great sources of vitamin D because you'll obtain 90 percent of your dietary allowance simply by eating just 3.5 ounces of either fish. As an added bonus, you'll take in some heart-healthy, metabolism-boosting omega-3s. Other healthy sources of vitamin D include milk, fortified cereal, and eggs.

Mango Smoothies

Mangos are packed with vitamins, minerals, and antioxidants. They are especially high in many carotenoids, including beta-carotene, and also come loaded with magnesium, potassium; phosphorous; selenium; folic acid; zinc; and A, B, and E vitamins. And, on top of all that, they contain an enzyme that has stomach-soothing properties to help with digestion. Add some whey protein and water or low-fat yogurt to thicken up your drink and you've got a super-healthy, immune-boosting, metabolism-blasting snack!

Micro-plants

Micro-plants, including blue-green algae, chlorella, spirulina, wheat grass, and barley grass, contain more vitamins and minerals than kale and broccoli. They are an excellent source of two important phytochemicals: chlorophyll and lycopene. Micro-plants, commercially known as "green foods," contain a concentrated combination of phytochemicals, vitamins, minerals, bioflavonoids, proteins, amino acids, essential fatty acids, enzymes, coenzymes, and fiber. They support your body's ability to detoxify heavy metals, pesticides, and other toxins, plus boost your immunity to disease.

Olives

Long an essential part of the Mediterranean diet, olives are a delicious addition to any dieter's eating habits. Olive oil, high in monounsaturated fats, has been in the news because of its ability to reduce "bad" cholesterol in the blood. Researchers also suspect that olive oil may protect against gastrointestinal cancer by influencing the metabolism of the gut. In fact, Dr. Andrew Weil recommends olive oil be substituted for fat in the diet on a permanent basis. Studies have shown that people who consume olive oil in preference to other fats have a lower incidence of heart disease.

Pumpkin Seeds

Pumpkin seeds, also known as pepitas, are nestled in the core of the pumpkin and encased in a white-yellow husk. This superseed contains a number of minerals such as zinc, magnesium, manganese, iron, copper, and phosphorus. It's also fortified with proteins, monounsaturated fat, and the omega-fatty acids 3 and 6—all of which will help boost your metabolism. These wonderful seeds have been found to help prevent prostate cancer in men, protect against heart disease, and have anti-inflammatory benefits.

Quinoa

Once known as "the gold of the Incas," this grain—a complete protein—includes all nine essential amino acids, making it an excellent choice for vegetarians, vegans, and everyone else as well! Quinoa has extra-high amounts of the amino acid lysine, which is essential for tissue growth and repair. Combine this protein with quinoa's magnesium and high amounts of potassium, and you've got a food that will help lower your blood pressure and strengthen your heart. For such a small grain, quinoa not only provides a whole lot of nutrients while boosting your metabolism, but it may also be especially valuable for people with migraine headaches, diabetes, atherosclerosis, and other debilitating health issues. It is also a very good source of manganese as well as iron, copper, phosphorus, and B-vitamins.

Sardines

Sardines are packed with nutrients, including calcium, coenzyme Q10, protein, and potassium. They are particularly good sources of calcium, providing the same amount as a glass of whole milk. Sardines also pack balanced amounts of vitamin D and phosphorus so you can effectively absorb that calcium.

Sea Vegetables

Gram for gram, sea vegetables—seaweeds and algae—are higher in essential vitamins and minerals than any other known food group. These minerals are bioavailable to the body

in chelated, colloidal forms that make them more easily absorbed. Sea vegetables that provide minerals in this colloidal form have been shown to retain their molecular identity while remaining in liquid suspension. The following is a descriptive list of what sea vegetables can add to your daily diet:

- They can contain as much as 48 percent protein.
- They are a rich source of both soluble and insoluble dietary fiber.
- The brown sea varieties—kelp, wakame, and kombu—contain alginic acid, which has been shown to remove heavy metals and radioactive isotopes from the digestive tract.
- They contain significant amounts of vitamin A, in the form of beta-carotene, as well as vitamins B, C, and E.
- They are high in potassium, calcium, sodium, iron, and chloride.
- They provide the fifty-six minerals and trace minerals that your body requires to function properly.

Sunflower Seeds

Sunflower seeds are a low-calorie option for getting your daily protein that also happen to be a good source of magnesium, copper, selenium, phosphorous, folate, manganese, vitamin B5, vitamin E, and phytosterols. Vitamin E is the body's primary fat-soluble antioxidant and stops free radicals from damaging cell membranes and brain cells. The vitamin has also been shown to reduce the risk of colon cancer and hot flashes in menopausal women. Phytosterols—cholesterol-like compounds that are found only in plants—can actually reduce your own cholesterol levels, pump up your immune system, and help prevent cancer. So toss some seeds on your salads or breakfast cereals, or munch on a handful as a snack for a healthy metabolic boost.

Tofu

Tofu is made from crushing soybeans and turning them into a curd. Unlike foods from animal sources, this marvelous source of protein is cholesterol free. It contains no saturated fat, is a great source of fiber, contains calcium, vitamin E, and B vitamins, and is rich in the two polyunsaturated fats essential to optimal health. Soy-based foods may also aid in controlling diabetes by slowing the absorption of glucose (blood sugar) into the bloodstream and keeping blood sugar levels steadier. Most soy foods are also high in iron and, compared to other plant sources, are an excellent source of protein.

Tuna

It's not a coincidence that 90 percent of all bodybuilders and fitness competitors in the world will tell you they make a habit of feasting on tuna. These people need to be lean to compete, and tuna is often their answer because they know it's an excellent source of protein that offers very few calories and almost no fat. *Caution*: eat tuna in moderation (once or twice a week) because it can be high in mercury. Alternate it with other fish, such as salmon.

Turnip Greens

Turnip greens are good sources of vitamin K. Try them in a salad for a quick, healthy metabolism boost. Other foods rich in vitamin K include green leafy vegetables like spinach or kale, broccoli, cabbage, beef liver, egg yolk, and wheat bran or wheat germ.

Wild Salmon

Salmon is one of the primary superfoods. This designation comes from the fact that it's laden with two types of omega-3 fatty acids, DHA and EPA, that can have a dramatic impact on reducing heart disease, Alzheimer's disease, Parkinson's disease, and osteoporosis. With their anti-inflammatory properties, these fatty acids also help prevent blood clots from forming unnecessarily within the circulatory system and may even prevent cardiac arrhythmia. On top of all that, salmon may help calm an overactive immune system in people with autoimmune diseases. For the healthiest, most eco-friendly and nutrient-packed salmon, check your grocery or local farmers' market for wild salmon.

Supplement Your Diet

Throughout this book, we have stressed that the first and best thing you can do to improve your metabolism is nourish your body with ideal proportions of a variety of healthy food choices. Once you have taken this step, you may want to explore other supplements that can provide your body with additional nutrients and short- and long-term health and metabolism benefits with very little effort. However, David Grotto, RD, a spokesperson for the American Dietetic Association, warns "Supplements can enhance a diet where there are shortfalls, but a handful of vitamin, mineral, or other dietary supplements can never take the place of a healthy diet."

Please note that a supplement labeled *natural* or *herbal* is not inherently safe. Be sure to consult your physician before starting, or radically changing, any physical, nutritional, or supplemental regimen. Some supplements may interact with other medications or other supplements, and some may be dangerous if you take too many.

Alpha Lipoic Acid

Alpha lipoic acid is a fatty acid found in each cell in the human body and in limited amounts in foods rich in lipoyllysine. These foods include spinach, broccoli, and organ meats. This antioxidant is both water and fat soluble and can protect against free radicals throughout the body, including those created during the synthesis of vitamin E. However, its primary function is to convert glucose into energy, thereby boosting metabolism.

Carnitine

Carnitine is a naturally occurring amino-acid derivative that helps the body convert fat into energy. After you eat, the compound takes the fatty acid molecules from your food and brings them into a cell's mitochondria so they can be broken down and used for energy. Though carnitine is usually found in the skeletal muscles, heart, brain, and sperm in adequate quantities, you can turn to red meat and dairy for an extra boost.

People with certain conditions such as peripheral vascular disease, hypertension (high blood pressure), alcohol-induced liver disease (cirrhosis), diabetes, and kidney disease should talk to their doctor before taking carnitine. Also talk to your doctor if you are taking AZT, doxorubicin, isotretinoin, or valproic acid.

Fish Oil Capsules

Over the years, fish oil has been touted to help with myriad medical problems—including protecting the body from the onset of Parkinson's disease and schizophrenia—but what is very exciting is its ability (because of the high levels of omega-3 it contains) to lower the body's cholesterol levels, reduce overall blood pressure, and keep you fuller longer. There is also recent evidence from the *International Journal of Obesity* that suggests fish oil helps the body burn fat and that those who supplement with fish oil will metabolize more fat as they exercise. When you're looking for a fish oil supplement, reach for those containing 300 milligrams of the fatty acid EPA and 200 milligrams of the fatty acid DHA. Take two of these capsules each day. Ask your doctor before taking omega-3 supplements if you have an increased risk of bleeding.

Ginseng

Ginseng has many beneficial effects. It has been used for thousands of years by herbalists to reduce cholesterol levels, increase the absorption of nutrients through the intestinal walls, mop up free radicals in the blood, and protect against cancer. *Ginseng* may decrease muscle injury and inflammation following exercise, and some studies suggest that it may reduce oxidation of LDL ("bad") cholesterol and brain tissue. This herb can also boost your metabolism, primarily by alleviating stress and reducing the amount of carbohydrates that enter your bloodstream and cause your glucose levels to spike. People scheduled for surgeries should stop taking ginseng a week before the operation. You should also be cautious if you take anticoagulants. Patients with hormone-sensitive diseases—like certain cancers—should not consume ginseng.

Pancreatin

Pancreatin, or pancreatic acid, is a combination of the pancreatic enzymes lipase, protease, and amylase that improves digestion by signaling more digestive enzymes to take on the task. These enzymes help the body be more effective at breaking down fats, starches, and complex proteins into nutrients so they can be absorbed into the body.

Be sure to take only the recommended dose of this supplement, as high doses can cause problems such as colon damage and high levels of a dangerous substance called uric acid.

Proteolytic Enzymes

Proteolytic enzymes help regulate protein function. Your body produces these enzymes naturally, but production slows as you age. Some of the foods you eat—cooked or processed meat, for example—cause the enzymes to be diverted from their main role to help digest the food. Proteolytic enzymes also combat inflammation by neutralizing certain biochemicals. Between the body's natural slowdown in enzyme production and diversion of the enzymes for digestion, you are losing a soldier, so to speak, in the battle against inflammation caused by free-radical damage. Supplements work well in replacing those lost enzymes. You can find proteolytic enzyme supplements at any health food store.

Resveratrol

It appears that resveratrol, an antioxidant found in red wine, is the key to unlocking the maddening "French Paradox." Though, at this juncture, most of the research has been conducted on nonhuman species, studies suggest that this fat-soluble compound helps the liver process carbohydrates—thereby boosting the metabolism. Resveratrol acts as an antioxidant and may help protect against atherosclerosis and heart disease. It also activates SIRT1, a gene that helps the body process fat, improves overall aerobic activity, and may have a positive impact on longevity. Resveratrol should not be used with drugs that increase risk of bleeding, including warfarin/Coumadin, aspirin, heparin, and Lovenox. Until more is known about the estrogenic activity of resveratrol in humans, women with a history of estrogen-sensitive cancers, such as breast, ovarian, and uterine cancers, should avoid resveratrol supplements.

Schizandra

Schizandra berries, also known as the "five flavor fruit" because they stimulate all five of the types of taste buds, have been used in Chinese medicine for centuries. This herb reduces the body's response to stressful situations, but herbalists believe that it can also improve endurance, mental alertness, and aid the metabolism by regulating blood sugar levels. In addition, it is said to help detoxify the liver and improve the workings of many of the body's organ systems.

Vanadium

Mushrooms, black pepper, parsley, dill weed, and whole grains contain vanadium, a compound that boosts your body's sensitivity to insulin. You need that insulin to properly process calories and stabilize your blood sugar. You can also take supplements containing vanadium, but it can be toxic if you don't follow the product's instructions. DO NOT EXCEED 1.8 milligrams daily. People with kidney disease should not take vanadium, and the recommended doses should be adhered to, as high doses of vanadium (more than 1.8 mg per day) may cause liver or kidney damage.

Metabolic Tips and Tricks

So you now know what to eat to boost your metabolism, but what else can you do? Well, here are some tips and tricks that you can use to make your food work for you!

Laugh

Not only does laughing ratchet down your stress level instantaneously, a study by Vanderbilt University reported a 20 percent boost in the metabolism after laughing. Even if you're not feeling particularly joyful, try forcing a laugh anyway. There's a good chance that just trying to laugh will lift your mood and metabolism.

Sit in the Sunshine

Not only does it feel good, but sitting in sunlight decreases melatonin and increases serotonin, helping your body feel fully awake and your metabolic rate increase. The sun's rays are also a major source of vitamin D—a metabolism booster. If you are locked up inside all day, find 10 minutes in your day to go out into the sunshine and soak up some rays.

Listen to Relaxing Music

Listening to music that has a calming effect has been shown to reduce cortisol, one of the primary hormones that negatively affect metabolism. When you're ready to rock again, switch to music that leaves you feeling energized; it will raise your heart and breathing rates, boosting your metabolism.

Don't Skip Meals

One of the worst things you can do to your metabolism is skip meals; doing so slows your metabolism. Your body thinks it is going into starvation mode and needs to conserve energy by storing fat, even though your head knows you're trying to lose weight. Aggravating, we know. But also consider that by skipping one potentially healthy meal you may later overeat and throw off your day's calorie intake altogether. Instead of skipping meals, do the opposite—eat well-balanced meals and snack on healthy foods throughout the day. This will help boost your metabolism instead of bringing it to a standstill.

Keep Your Blood Sugar Stable

In addition to the types of fuel you put into your body, your energy can be directly linked to the type of energy you add to your "furnace" and timing of your meals. Nutrition, as you know, is all about fueling the body for optimum function. Many Americans have become so preoccupied with weight loss that they have lost sight of the main event: you need food and glucose—the energy source found in food—to live. If you don't give your body glucose through balanced meals, your metabolism will slow down and your sugar cravings will increase. When blood sugar dips too low, your brain thinks it's starving. As a result, you end up craving high-sugar foods. Since most high-sugar foods are also high-fat foods, desperation eating packs a double caloric whammy. Well-timed and well-balanced meals will boost your metabolism because you won't be hungry as often, and therefore will be less likely to reach for non-nutritious foods.

Avoid Social Eating

We are all at our most vulnerable when eating in social situations. At parties, after one cocktail or in the midst of conversation, we find ourselves accepting hors d'oeuvres one after another, and then eating whatever is put on our plates, including dessert. To spare yourself, eat healthy food, especially protein, before you go to the party, and then stick to nonalcoholic, low-calorie beverages. This will lower your susceptibility to eat or drink more

than you intend. It is possible to avoid social eating, but it takes a lot of discipline and commitment to healthy living. Find what works for you, and go with it.

Don't Shop When Hungry

Grocery shopping when hungry frequently leads to impulse purchases that contain more fat and calories than you would choose if you shopped when satisfied. One of the best ways to boost your metabolism is to plan meals ahead of time, create a shopping list, and adhere to the list when you shop. This way you're far more likely to make healthier food choices.

Avoid the Most Dangerous Aisle in the Supermarket

Avoid the bakery aisle at all cost! In the past, trans fat was commonly used in baked goods because it made them soft and flaky, contributed to a delicious flavor and mouth-feel, was inexpensive, and extended the shelf life of the product. However, due to regulations passed by the Food and Drug Administration (FDA), all packaged goods are now required to list the amount of trans fat per serving and many companies have elected to cut back on the amount of trans fat used in their products as a result of this disclosure.

Be careful though; companies are only required to list the amount of trans fat per serving, and they don't have to list anything under 0.5 grams. That means if you eat more than the recommended serving—a metabolism don't on any day—you could be eating a dangerous amount of trans fat.

Some items in the bakery may not be labeled, but you can ask the bakery manager for nutritional information. If she doesn't have it, then ask to see the ingredient list for your favorite products. If that list includes the words *hydrogenated* or *shortening*, you know that the bread, cookie, or pastry contains artificial trans fat.

Shop the Perimeters

One of the best ways to make the healthiest food selections is to shop the perimeters of your grocery store. Most grocery stores house the produce, dairy products, protein, and fresh food on the perimeter aisles. All those aisles in the middle house processed foods, snacks, cookies, soda, and sugary cereals. Next to making a list and sticking to it, avoiding aisles where temptation might lure you into buying unhealthy foods is the most important thing you can do to boost your metabolism.

Plan Your Meals Ahead of Time

Obviously, planning your meals long before you eat will help you make smarter food choices and balance your diet. Start by planning for one day, then two, and so on until you are planning a week or two ahead. That way you can select the variety of foods needed to provide maximum nutrition and take advantage of all the food tips in this book that will help you boost your metabolism.

The famed Mayo Clinic's website (*www.mayoclinic.com*) provides a calculator for an individualized "Healthy Weight Pyramid." Enter your info for a customized pyramid that will help you plan your meals for optimal nutrition. Then, take their advice, as follows:

- Plan healthy meals and snacks using recommended food servings. Focus on foods at the base of the pyramid—fruits, vegetables, and whole grains.
- Be familiar with the serving sizes in each food group.
- Spread out the food servings throughout the day. Include at least one serving from most food groups at each meal.
- Stay flexible and adjust your food serving goals as necessary. If, for example, you don't reach your fruit goal on Monday, add extra servings of fruit to Tuesday's menu.

Eat Less

The basic methodology behind losing weight is simple—burn more than you consume. To lose a pound of fat in a week, you need to create a deficit of 3,500 calories. You can achieve this by reducing your normal food intake by 500 calories, by burning 500 extra calories each day, or through a combination of the two.

Eat Enough

It's extremely common for people who are dieting to eat too little. You will lose weight to start, but your body won't understand that you have plenty of food available but are choosing to minimize your calorie intake. Instead, your body notices that supply has gone way down, deduces that you don't have enough food on hand to eat, and lowers your metabolism to burn what you do eat more slowly. It also hoards extra fat in case your energy reserves go too low. Instead of depriving your body, keep your metabolism high by eating around 1,200 calories a day. If you do this, your body should continue burning fat and you'll continue to lose weight.

Eat Several Small Meals a Day

The act of eating and digesting burns calories, so every time you eat, your metabolism kicks in. If you eat small meals spaced throughout the day, you'll be firing up the furnace every 2–3 hours. Once lit, your metabolic fires will burn until the fuel runs dry, so making sure your body has a constant supply of fuel is an ideal way to boost your metabolism. That said, it's important that you limit yourself to healthy food in healthy portions. Also, combining protein with a complex carb and a healthy fat is ideal, just make it low-calorie choices and keep those home fires burning.

Stop Eating Before You Feel Full

It takes at least 20 minutes for your stomach to let your brain know that you're full. Slowing down will give your body time to alert you before it's 100 percent full, giving you the option to knowingly and willingly cut back on the amount of food you eat. In simple terms, eat only when you are truly hungry and stop when you're satisfied.

Eating more slowly also ensures proper digestion. To slow down, take sips of your beverage between bites, put your fork down, and enjoy the conversation of others. Sit down to eat instead of eating while standing, driving, or watching television, since eating while doing other things means you are eating unconsciously and can easily consume more.

Stay Hydrated

The liquids you consume have a powerful impact on your metabolism. Some will help it, while others will make it sluggish and may even lead to unhealthy weight gain. We'll discuss the best beverages to boost your metabolism in this appendix. However, the best drink for your body—even if you drink nothing else—is water. This refreshing liquid, which makes up 55–75 percent of your body, regulates body temperature, transports nutrients, carries waste away from cells, protects the organs from damage, and keeps you hydrated. Water is also necessary to keep the metabolic processes functioning and helps you expel waste by keeping you regular (adding fluid to the stool so you don't become constipated). And, in some studies, it's been found that your metabolism revs up and burns 25 calories after you drink a pint of water.

Drink Everything on the Rocks

Whenever feasible, add ice cubes to your drinks. When you drink ice-cold beverages, your body fires up its furnace to warm the water for maximum absorption. Five or six glasses of water, with ice cubes, may burn up an extra 10 calories a day, which could add up to a pound per year.

Have a Few Cups of Java

Caffeine stimulates your central nervous system, digestive tract, and your metabolism. Researchers studied a 145-pound woman who consumed 2 cups of coffee a day. They found that she burned an extra 50 calories in the four hours after drinking the coffee. That said, adding cream and sugar will add calories and fat that will defuse coffee's metabolic benefits, and drinking too much coffee can be detrimental to your overall health. Drinking 1–2 small cups of coffee in the morning, with breakfast, is just enough to get your metabolic furnace burning.

Drink Iced Coffee

Why not kill two birds with one stone and drink your coffee with ice? This way, you get all the metabolic benefits of a normal cup of joe with an icy added boost! To make sure your ice-cold coffee is really boosting your metabolism, drink it black or with skim milk, and avoid adding sugar.

Try Concord Grape Juice

If you're looking for an alternative to red wine, one with similar health benefits, try Concord grape juice. It is high in polyphenols, which have anti-inflammatory and antioxidant properties that help increase your metabolic rate. A Tufts University study found that Concord grape juice helps increase memory and improve cognitive and motor function as we age. Other studies have shown that the juice helps maintain immune function and lowers total cholesterol and blood pressure. Remember to keep portions reasonable (4 ounces) to avoid going overboard on calories.

Have a Cup of Coffee or Tea Before Workouts

Even though energy drink companies tout the benefits of energy drinks before, during, or after exercise, many contain sugar, something you don't need to boost energy for a workout of an hour or less. Many athletes have found that drinking a cup of coffee or tea, with additional water, stimulates their metabolic rate. Try enjoying a cup of coffee or tea (about 200 mg of caffeine) prior to your exercise, and

avoid high-potency caffeinated "turbo" drinks or pills. Of course, check with your doctor if you are sensitive to caffeine. By the way, this does not mean drinking a latte or mocha containing milk and sugar. We're talking about black coffee and tea here. And embrace water as your beverage of choice before, during, and after workouts.

Avoid Soda

The normal bloodstream contains a total of 4 teaspoons of blood sugar. When you drink a can of soda, roughly 10 teaspoons of table sugar are absorbed into your bloodstream, causing your blood sugar to rocket to an excessive level, setting off alarms in the pancreas, and causing a large amount of insulin to come out to deal with the excess blood sugar. Some sugar is quickly ushered into the cells, including brain cells, but the rest is stored in your fat cells. When all this is done, after maybe an hour, your blood sugar may fall dramatically and low blood sugar occurs. A drop in blood sugar causes your body to crave sweets, which are definite metabolism busters. Just say no to soda to avoid rapid swings in blood sugar and the consumption of excess empty calories.

Drink Kombucha

Since the Tsin Chinese Dynasty in 221 B.C., Kombucha tea has been used as a health elixir. Fans claim that it is packed with organic acids that build healthy tissues and normalize blood alkalinity, probiotics that benefit your digestive system, and live enzymes that help fuel the body's cells. It combats free radicals and has been used as a remedy for arthritis, constipation, obesity, arteriosclerosis, impotence, kidney stones, rheumatism, gout, and cancer.

You can find Kombucha at most health food stores.

If you choose to try Kombucha, be sure to limit your intake to 4 ounces daily. If you have pre-existing health problems or drink excessive amounts of the tea, health problems may arise.

Drink Maté Tea

Maté tea is an herbal tea native to South America that is perfect for a midday energy boost. Maté tea has many of the same metabolism-boosting properties of coffee, but contains less caffeine, so it won't make you nervous or jittery. Instead, you'll feel healthy, energetic, and ready to face the rest of your day.

However, be sure to drink maté tea in moderation because, according to the Mayo Clinic, some studies indicate that prolonged use of maté tea may increase the risk of various types of cancer, including cancer of the mouth, esophagus, and lungs. Smoking in combination with maté tea seems to greatly increase the cancer risk.

Know How Many Calories You're Drinking

Beverages can add lots of calories, and you may not realize how many you're actually drinking. Being aware of the number of calories found in common beverages can help you make healthy choices and keep your metabolism running at full speed. Here's a list of drinks that may wake you up to the amount of calories you're taking in from beverages alone. All drinks are labeled for 8-ounce servings unless otherwise noted. Rather than listing all alcoholic beverages separately, please note that most mixed drinks range

from 400–600 calories for 8 ounces, while dessert liquors can jump up to the 800–900 range. Most sodas are around 100 calories for 8 ounces, but most cans contain 12 ounces, or 150 calories.

BEVERAGE	CALORIES
Apple juice	95
Beer (Budweiser)	98
Beer (Bud Light)	72
Club soda	0
Coffee, black	2
Coffee, with cream	48
Coffee, with cream and sugar	91
Cranberry–apple juice drink	152
Diet soda	0
Grape juice	138
Grapefruit juice, canned and sweetened	104
Grapefruit juice, freshly squeezed	88
Hot cocoa	197
Lemonade	100
Milk, skim	79
Milk, 1%	102
Milk 2%	113
Milk, whole	145
Milkshake, chocolate	270
Orange juice, freshly squeezed	102
Prune juice	161
Red Bull	100
Red Bull, sugar-free	10
Tea, sweetened	77
Tea, unsweetened	2
Tomato juice	39
Tonic water	77
Wine, dessert	311
Wine, red	163
Wine, white	154

Drink out of Tall Glasses

We all know that our eyes can trick our minds, so be sure to pour your beverages into tall glasses (and fill them up with ice cubes for an extra metabolism boost) to make it look as though you're drinking more than you are. Don't fill glasses to the rim, and you'll be more likely to view the consumption as a treat rather than a chore. Also, invest in attractive glasses that you love, and even ice cube trays in fancy shapes. Buy fresh lemon to perch on the edge of water glasses—the citrus will help kick your metabolism up a notch as well. Do whatever it takes to make drinking healthy, zero- or low-calorie beverages a lot more fun.

Keep Healthy Snacks in Plain View

Store healthy snacks in attractive glass containers to keep them visible and easily accessible. Store fresh fruit in bowls on the counter and raw vegetables in plastic containers on the top shelf of your refrigerator. If you have unhealthy snacks, push them back in dark corners of cupboards you rarely use—or better yet, don't buy them in the first place. Train yourself to reach for the healthy snacks by making them easy to grab, and you'll soon become so accustomed to this behavior that it will be a natural habit.

Take Healthy Snacks on the Road

When traveling, avoid having your hunger dictate your food choices by planning ahead to ensure you have healthy snacks on hand. Fruit, nut, and seed mixtures or slices of cheese with whole-wheat crackers, whole fruits, raw vegetables, or even low-sugar granola bars, are far preferable to chips, candy bars, milkshakes, or the myriad poor choices that are readily available at every gas station or market. Also, take along bottles of water or fruit juice to quench your thirst.

Eat Smaller Portion Snacks, Not Meal-Size Ones

Snacking is not meant to be an extra meal. A healthy snack should be portion sensitive—a small amount of something nutritious—to keep the metabolic fires burning and tide you over to your next meal. Snacks should be small amounts of nutrient-dense foods, ideally consisting of protein and carbohydrate. A few whole-wheat crackers with a wedge of farmer's cheese; ¼ cup of cottage cheese with half an orange; a hard-boiled egg and half an apple; a slice of whole-wheat toast with thinly spread peanut butter, and so on—just enough to provide a steady source of energy throughout the day or to stave off hunger that would cause you to overeat at your next meal.

Graze Throughout the Day

Rather than downing two or three super-size meals a day, which actually trains your metabolism to slow down, eat smaller meals more frequently. Researchers have long confirmed that eating small (healthy) meals or snacks every 3–4 hours works well to keep your metabolism burning and churning. If you make your snacks and meals healthy, you'll likely reduce your caloric intake at regular meals and lose weight over the long haul. Make sure, however, that you are not choosing high-fat, high-calorie carbohydrates, such as chips or cookies.

Don't Eat Before Going to Bed

Contrary to the popular idea that you shouldn't eat after 7 P.M., the amount of calories you consume throughout the day is actually more important than when you eat them. However, it *is* best to eat more calories earlier in the day and make sure the last meal of the day is light on calories and fat. You can eat after 7 P.M., but keep that snack or small meal closer to 200–300 calories and eat it at least 2 hours before bedtime. If you're convinced that you need something just before bed, limit it to 100 calories and try to eat at least 30 minutes before lying down. It's easier for your stomach to digest food while you're still awake and sitting.

Chew Gum

Gum chewing can help boost your metabolism in a couple of ways. First, just the simple act of chewing gum can help you hold off on grabbing foods that aren't metabolism boosting throughout the day. Second, a Mayo Clinic study concluded that gum chewing actually boosted metabolism by up to 20 percent and could help participants lose up to 10 pounds a year! That's a lot of Double Bubble!

Follow the 90/10 Rule

People who focus on overall fitness know that eating healthy is not an all-or-nothing activity. They know that if they make the majority of their food choices great, they can indulge occasionally. Create a 90/10 rule of your own: if 90 percent of your meals are full of lean protein, produce, lean dairy, and whole grains, indulging in less-than-nutritious choices 10 percent of the time won't slow down your metabolism.

Create and Adhere to Restaurant Rules

Eating in restaurants often leads to a downfall. Because it's so tempting to let down your guard and eat all the things you'd normally avoid when eating in, set some ground rules to minimize caloric or fat overload. For example, never order meat that has been fried or sautéed and always request that it be cooked without oil or butter. Do the same for your veggies, although it's great to eat them raw. Keep baskets of bread off the table; you don't need that! Request all sauces and dressings on the side, and drizzle very small amounts on the dish. Stick with water for your beverage or the occasional glass of red wine. Make it a golden rule never to order dessert for one and, when sharing, take three small bites and put down your fork or spoon. End your meal with coffee or tea for a treat.

Use Visualization

Imagination is a wonderful thing—it allows us to visualize ourselves stronger, thinner, healthier, or whatever else we desire. Many believe that visualization leads to manifestation, particularly if you practice daily. When you wake up, spend 5–10 minutes visualizing yourself as leaner and sexier: the picture of health. If you have trouble visualizing yourself that way, find a picture of someone in a magazine who has the body you desire, paste your head on it, and place it on your bathroom mirror or the refrigerator. What you focus on is what you manifest, so focus on being the healthiest you that you can be. Go for it!

Index

Note: Page numbers in **bold** indicate recipe category lists. Letters in parentheses following recipe names refer to the following recipe icons: (A) Antioxidants; (C) Calcium; (F) High Fiber; (P) Protein; (S) Spicy; (SF) Superfood.

ABOUT THE AUTHORS

Chef **Susan Irby** (Orange County, CA) is the author of *The $7 a Meal Healthy Cookbook* and *Substitute Yourself Skinny*. Known as the Bikini Chef and specializing in "figure-flattering flavors," Chef Susan has made appearances on BBC radio, *The Patti Gribow Show*, and hosts *The Bikini Lifestyle with Susan Irby, The Bikini Chef* on KFWB News Talk 980, Los Angeles.

Rachel Laferriere, MS, RD is a Licensed Dietitian/Nutritionist in Rhode Island and a Certified Nutrition Support Dietitian. She currently works with adult patients as a clinical dietitian. Her work has been published in the *Tufts Daily* newspaper and *Nutrition in Clinical Care*.